PERKS AND PARACHUTES

PERKS AND PARACHUTES

Negotiating Your Best Possible Employment Deal,
from Salary and Bonus to Benefits and Protection

John Tarrant

with Paul Fargis

A Stonesong Press Book

TIMES BUSINESS

RANDOM HOUSE

To All Those Who Helped

An earlier edition of this work was published in 1985.

Tarrant, John J.
    Perks and parachutes : negotiating your best possible employment
deal, from salary and bonus to benefits and protection / John Tarrant.
        p.   cm.
    Rev. ed. of: Perks and parachutes. 1985.
    Includes index.
    ISBN 0-8129-2677-3
    1. Executives—Legal status, laws, etc.—United States.   2. Labor
contract—United States.   3. Executives—Employment—United States.
I. Tarrant, John J.   Perks and parachutes.   II. Title.
KF1423.T37   1997
344.73'01891—dc20
[347.3041891]   96-16081

A Stonesong Press Book

Random House website address: http://www.randomhouse.com/

Manufactured in the United States of America on acid-free paper

9 8 7 6 5 4 3 2 1

Revised Edition

Acknowledgments

Grateful thanks to all who helped in the research and development of this new edition. We would like to especially cite Judith Fischer, Managing Director of *Executive Compensation Reports;* Steven Singer, Compensation Manager of GE Capital; Rhoda G. Edelman, Managing Director of Pearl Meyer and Partners, Inc.; Terisa E. Chaw, Executive Director of National Employment Lawyers Association; Ken Cole, Publisher of *The Recruiting and Search Report;* Betty L. Laurie, American Compensation Association; and Karl Weber, our editor at Times Books.

Contents

PERKS AND PARACHUTES

1

Pay, Perks, Parachutes, Protection

Getting It in Writing

Not long ago, practically all executives of typical American companies held their jobs "at the pleasure" of their employers. Maybe they were paid well, but they could be fired without warning. Some received generous severance pay; for others, the severance was minimal or nonexistent. There were very few guarantees.

All that has changed. An increasing number of executives have employment agreements now. Others are about to negotiate their first contracts. Still others will be offered contracts by their employers, covering various aspects of their jobs.

A lot of people who could enjoy the benefits of an employment agreement don't know how to go about getting one.

And then there are the men and women *who already have what amounts to a contract covering many key areas* but don't realize that they have it.

The use of written agreements between employers and managerial, professional, and technical people is spreading horizontally (many more people are involved) and vertically (the use of contracts extends

3

farther down the organizational ladder, well into the middle management ranks). A 1995 survey by Pearl Meyer & Partners, the prominent executive compensation consultants, found a proliferation in contracts for senior executives. Pearl Meyer also reported that, when changing employers, middle managers were getting pacts at the rate of 20 percent to 25 percent, up from 5 percent or less five years earlier.

As we will see, some interesting variations on the use of contracts have developed. For example, in these days of downsizing, many executives are surprised to be offered an agreement *after* they have been terminated. The agreement would give the laid-off individual more severance money in return for some restrictive pledges: not to go to work for a competitor, not to contact customers and prospects garnered while employed by the company, not to use corporate information, not to lure away other employees, and so on. Terminees in such circumstances must confront an unexpected negotiation, full of difficult trade-offs, at a time when they are ill-prepared for it.

The downsizing trend flows side by side with the merger trend. After the "merger mania" of the 1980s, the merger trend eased somewhat. Now, however, it seems to be in full flood. *The Wall Street Journal* reported, on July 3, 1995, that "mergers and acquisitions continue to grow at a sizzling pace. . . ." The volume of takeovers during the first half of 1995 hit a new record.

The specter of a takeover gives executives yet another urgent reason to get their employment terms in writing. Without a written agreement that contains some form of change-of-control protection, managers who have done a good job, and who have committed themselves to their organizations, are finding themselves thrust out of their jobs summarily.

Outplacement as a Key Benefit

Outplacement has become an essential discipline. If you have to look for another job, you can benefit from the help of a capable outplacement specialist. A growing number of contracts provide for outplacement. Before long, the practice of specifying this service is likely to become standard for most contracts. This book recommends building outplacement into the employment agreement. Some of the exhibited contracts contain specific language designed to do just that.

Contracts for All

An individual employment contract (as opposed to a collective bargaining agreement negotiated by a union) is not something reserved for entertainers, athletes, coaches, and the chairman of the board.

Not that it's easy to obtain a contract. Leanness and meanness appear to be with us permanently. During the tough times of the 1980s, companies cut back. As things improved in the 1990s, companies—contrary to the rosy expectations of some employees—have continued to hold the line or have cut back even more.

A lot of people are just glad to have jobs at all. But that doesn't mean they need to live from day to day, unprotected, never knowing when the ax may fall. Nor does it mean that they must do without agreements that spell out what they are entitled to in bonuses, perks, options, and other intricate aspects of executive compensation today.

The Pendulum Starts to Swing Back

The pendulum swung very far in the direction of stripping corporate staffs. Now, the pendulum seems to have reached the end of its arc and is starting to swing back. Why? Because businesses are feeling the effects of a disorder that has been called "corporate anorexia." Companies have cut back so drastically and eliminated so many jobs that they have lost the vigor needed to grow.

On July 5, 1995, *The Wall Street Journal* reported on this development: "After nearly a decade of frantic cost-cutting, the down-side of downsizing is beginning to take its toll. . . . 'Survivor syndrome' takes hold, and overburdened staffers just go through the motions of working. New-product ideas languish. Risk-taking dwindles because the culture of cost-cutting emphasizes the certainties of cutting costs over the uncertainties—and expense—of trying something new."

Corporate leaders, worried about losing the capacity to grow, try in various ways to expand without adding to staff. They look around for companies to acquire. Suffering from the loss of talent resulting from sweeping layoffs, they retain fired executives as consultants.

Both of these tactics are limited. The number of takeover candidates that promise a fruitful and growth-promoting match becomes more limited every day. And the replacement of on-staff talent with consultants has its limits as well. In some cases, the strategy is merely a subterfuge. More often, it fails to provide corporate planners with the ability to figure out who is going to run key parts of the growing concern.

As firms try to cure or prevent corporate anorexia, managers and professionals have greater scope to make better deals and to protect themselves with employment agreements.

How Can They Get Deals Like THIS?

You'll be reading the verbatim provisions of actual executive contracts—complete with names and numbers—in this book. The general public doesn't usually see documents like this. When the provisions of high-level employment agreements hit the headlines, people are often shocked at the amounts, at the kinds of bonuses and perks executives receive, and at the whole idea that managers have contracts, just like entertainers and athletes.

In mid-1995, Time Warner fired Doug Morris, chairman of Warner Music U.S. A storm of controversy had hit the record division as politicians jostled each other to denounce the record company's promotion of "gangsta" rap.

Before firing Morris, Time Warner had terminated another top executive, Robert Morgado. Morgado had a contract; Time Warner settled with him. The amount? $40 to $50 million.

Doug Morris had a contract too. But Time Warner did not settle with him; they fired him "for cause." Morris sued for breach of contract. Among other things, Morris claimed the company had sent him a letter promising to name him CEO of Warner Music; the failure to honor that pledge, the suit alleged, was a "material breach" of Morris's employment agreement.

Time Warner struck back, accusing Doug Morris of failing to tell his bosses about "improper sales practices" at Warner Music. The company declared that it would seek the return of more than $10 million already paid to Morris in salary and bonuses.

The swirl of charges and countercharges was eclipsed by other headline news about Time Warner. But the lawsuit continued on its way toward verdict or settlement.

Meantime, as some of the details of Doug Morris's contract emerged in court papers, the media took note. On July 10, 1995, *The New York Times* offered readers a "rare public glimpse into the fine print of perquisites" for a high-ranking executive.[1] The story disclosed that Morris's "base salary was relatively modest. It was the signing bonus and the annual bonus that put him in the stratosphere." Then there was the stock: Doug Morris held options on 631,248 shares. If he exercised all his options, he would make $11.7 million.

And the story did not neglect Morris's perks—including cars, jets, a home audio system, and financial advice.

You may be interested in the following relevant excerpts from Doug Morris's contract:

SALARY—Company shall pay to you salary at the annual rates specified below:

PERIOD OF TERM	ANNUAL SALARY
8/1/94–12/31/95	$750,000
1/1/96–12/31/97	$800,000
1/1/98–12/31/99	$850,000

SIGNING BONUS—In consideration of your entering into this Agreement . . . Company will pay you a one-time signing bonus of $5,500,000. . . .

ANNUAL BONUS—Company shall pay to you an annual bonus . . . based on your performance and the performance of the Division and taking into account the profitability of Company . . . the amount of annual bonus shall be determined in the sole and complete discretion of the Chairman of the Board but shall not be less than $4,000,000.

LONG-TERM INCENTIVE BONUS—You shall participate in the Warner Music U.S. Long-Term Bonus Plan to be established for senior executives of the Division and its record music labels. . . . Your long-term incentive bonus shall constitute up to a 60% share of each pool.

---

[1] *The New York Times*, July 10, 1995, "The Perks of a Music Man (Annotated)," by Mark Landler.

STOCK OPTION GRANT—Promptly following execution of this Agreement, you shall receive options to purchase 150,000 shares of Common Stock of TWI [Time Warner International] at fair market value as of the date of grant. You shall be considered for additional grants of options to purchase . . . stock during the Term.

ADDITIONAL BENEFITS—Company . . . shall provide you with a car and driver . . . shall pay directly to you or reimburse you for receipt of financial advisory services not to exceed $75,000 per year. . . . Company shall also make the corporate aircraft available to you . . . and shall refurbish your home with audio and video equipment from time to time.

This book uses actual contracts as its case material. You'll be reading real employment agreements. Some of them sport well-known names: Eisner, Gerstner, Welch, Agee, and others.

The point is: Don't just find out what they make and how they make it. *Become literate about executive compensation today.* Without a thorough grasp of what goes into a good contract and how to obtain one, you will be losing out on things that you have worked hard for, things that are very important to you.

As you read, you'll gain greater familiarity with the strategies, the ploys, the implications, and the reasons behind everything that goes into (or is left out of) a contract. Do you know why most salaries, even for the topmost business leaders, remain under $1 million? Because if the salary goes over a million, the company has to answer to Uncle Sam. You'll see why stock options have gotten so big. You'll come upon the argument that it's unwise to include perks like cars and country club memberships in the employment agreement.

You will acquire *compensation literacy*—the rock on which you will build your strategy as you negotiate for money, power, and protection.

The Spread of the Contract Concept

Two decades ago, those pursuing management careers signed contracts only in special circumstances. The accepted view of a manager's career was that it held the potential for power, status, and money. The downside was the manager's total vulnerability to firing without recourse, often for reasons having little or nothing to do with performance. The executive could be terminated because the economy had turned down, because a superior's son-in-law had received his MBA, because of a reorganization, because the "chemistry" was bad—or just for no reason at all. And the amount of severance bestowed on those headed out the door often depended on how much the employer felt like giving them.

Today, if anything, there is more pressure on executives than there used to be. Events happen faster; decisions are more momentous; the competition for jobs and promotions is fiercer; and those who survive corporate cutbacks find themselves laboring long hours under terrific stress. All the more reason to get as many arrangements and assurances in writing as you can.

Unfortunately, because competition is intense and jobs are precious, many people don't even think about contracts. Yet, if they approached matters the right way, they could indeed *get it in writing*.

Contracts Are a Two-Way Street

It may be easier to obtain a contract than you—and many other people—think. One reason is that contracts have substantial benefits for the company as well as for the employee.

Nowadays, employment agreements are a standard tool for savvy human resource specialists and the companies that employ them. One catalyst, curiously enough, has been downsizing. Downsizing thins out the ranks and makes many survivors gun-shy about asking for more. But downsizing also makes it more important for companies to be able to keep their key people. With less built-in redundancy, the corporation needs to know that good executives are going to be around a while. Otherwise, long-range planning may take on aspects of a crapshoot.

Employers snap on "golden handcuffs" by offering rich helpings of "pie-in-the-sky" via deferred compensation, stock appreciation rights, stock options, and other favorites. These future goodies are spelled out in contracts.

Golden handcuffs can be negotiated. Employees who understand the issues can work out agreements that do not enslave them to the organization, and that provide substantial present-day rewards to go along with those that are deferred.

More People—at Lower Organizational Levels—Are Getting Contracts

Each year, millions of middle- to upper-level executives sign all sorts of agreements relating to the employment situation. White-collar workers are now commonly involved in agreements covering bonus arrangements, performance yardsticks, incentive stock plans, commissions, benefits, and the like. A particular agreement may not be called a contract. (The company is certainly going to try *not* to call it a contract.) It may not look as formal as a full-blown contract. But it performs the same function—and, if necessary, has the same force.

Too frequently, middle managers don't realize that they may be able to negotiate some of the terms of these agreements. They may not even realize that the agreements exist and that they carry guarantees as well as obligations. Just about anyone whose compensation/benefit arrangement is in some way variable is in a contract situation.

As we will see, employers want managers to own plenty of company stock. Companies are instituting programs using stock as the principal carrot in incentive plans. In some corporations, stock ownership is mandatory; depending on their salary level, managers are required to own specified levels of stock. Where they used to get a cash bonus, they now get stock.

As stock plans and bonus arrangements get more complicated, they generate more "paperwork" (when we use the term, we include electronic data-keeping). Health plans, insurance plans, retirement plans—all require written explication. But these pieces of paper are more than explications. They are incremental employment agreements.

So, without the word "contract" ever being spoken, employer and employee can, between them, build a structure of agreements that covers most of the areas that are detailed in a formal contract.

Trends That Are Shaping What You'll Be Paid

The amount you get paid in the years ahead—and the form in which it is paid—will be shaped by a number of trends that have changed the nature of executive compensation.

1. *Compensation keyed to performance.* Michael Reiff, Vice President, Compensation and Benefits, CitiCorp, observes a dominant tendency of

the 1990s: a "much stronger tie of senior executive pay to corporate performance." Tim Haigh, Managing Director of W.T. Haigh & Company, Inc., a firm of compensation specialists headquartered in Boston, concurs: "We are seeing a strong performance orientation in compensation and benefits."

At the topmost levels of larger companies, the move toward performance linkage is expedited by federal tax legislation limiting the deductibility of executive compensation in excess of $1 million, unless that compensation can be shown to have grown out of company performance.

2. *Performance measured by stock price.* Performance can be measured in a number of ways—net sales, bottom-line profit, and so on. However, the yardstick of choice today is a measurement keyed to the return reaped by those who invest in (and thus own) the company. In many of the compensation plans analyzed in this book, the principal measure is the price of the company's common stock. Executives' bonuses, deferred compensation, and stock plans wax or wane depending on what the stock does.

3. *Emphasis on executives' owning stock.* More and more, a company (as represented by the board of directors) will demand that its executives hold substantial amounts of company stock. Some firms establish guidelines as to the amount of stock that should be held by the CEO, executive vice presidents, and on down the line. At RR Donnelley (according to Pearl Meyer & Partners, specialists in this type of research), the guidelines for the CEO range from one times salary up to five times salary. Union Carbide recommends that corporate officers own one times their salary; the COO, three times; and the CEO, four times. At Fluor, CEO stock ownership is pegged at 700 percent of salary. Warner-Lambert requires that key managers hold a specified, though undisclosed, amount of the company's stock.

Stock ownership requirements are reaching down into the organization. In 1993, Kodak established stockholding requirements for its top forty officers. American Express expects 175 executives to own shares in amounts from two times to five times their base salary.

In this kind of arrangement, the required value of stock owned is expressed as a function of base salary. For example, a manager might be expected to attain stock ownership amounting to four times base salary in five years. (Five years is the usual period.) The guidelines may have teeth in the form of penalties—for example, deferral of bonuses. PPG, Mellon Bank, Allegheny Ludlum, Bell South, RJR Nabisco, and Dresser are among the companies that tie achievement of stock ownership to equity rewards such as options, grants, restricted stock, or stock purchase programs. At First Chicago, future long-term incentive awards may be affected by noncompliance with the stock ownership policy.

Judy Fischer, Publisher of *Executive Compensation Reports* (the authoritative source for information about corporate compensation programs and trends), observes: "More companies are requiring executives to own specified levels of stock, usually based on a multiple of salary. They are adopting programs to facilitate compliance with mandatory stock ownership guidelines, e.g., stock in lieu of cash, stock matching, and piggyback grants."

Big Option Deal for Bronfman

Seagram gave President/COO Edgar J. Bronfman, Jr. a total of 1.5 million option shares. The option has a life of ten years. In August 1995, the year of the deal, Seagram stock was around the mid-30s.

In 1995, Pearl Meyer conducted a study of large service and industrial companies, where the trend toward formal stock ownership policies is accelerating sharply. The survey found that 37 percent of the firms studied now have publicly disclosed stock ownership policies. In 1994, the figure was 22 percent, up from a mere handful prior to that. "We estimate that an additional 10 to 15 percent of the companies we studied have not disclosed their guidelines, bringing the number with ownership policies to approximately half the survey group," said Steven Hall, Managing Director of Pearl Meyer. "More and more companies are moving toward mandated 'at risk' executive ownership. This is a strong alignment of management and shareholder interests and an increasingly bold endorsement of effective corporate governance," Hall added.

Nor is the push for stock ownership restricted to the very top managers. Companies are turning toward plans that call for executives and professionals well down the organizational ladder to be stockholders. For example, in 1995, General Electric had more than 17,000 employees below the executive officer level who had been awarded stock option grants.

4. *Deferred compensation.* Tax law changes make deferred compensation a more desirable option. In addition, companies are using deferred compensation as golden handcuffs to keep key managers from leaving.

How Some Corporate Stars Are Paid

We can begin to demonstrate some of these trends by examining the recent compensation history of two high-profile executives: Louis Gerstner of IBM and John F. Welch, Jr. of GE.

Louis Gerstner

On March 26, 1993, Louis Gerstner signed an employment agreement with IBM containing the following provisions:

- Annual salary of at least $2,000,000.
- Annual incentive target opportunity of at least $1,500,000 (minimum 1993 award of $1,125,000).
- Long-term performance incentive with a target opportunity of at least $500,000.
- Up-front bonus consisting of a special one-time payment of $4,287,096 to cover benefits Gerstner forfeited when he resigned from RJR Nabisco.
- $160,130 for reimbursement of certain taxes.
- A ten-year option for 500,000 shares of IBM stock at $47.88 (the market price on April 23, 1993).
- Annual pension at age 60 of approximately $1,140,000.

The agreement guaranteed Gerstner a per-share yield of $8.125 on 3,211,320 shares of RJR Nabisco stock on which Gerstner held options. Gerstner was also guaranteed $8.125 per share for 300,000 RJR Nabisco shares that RJR Nabisco held as collateral for a loan taken by Gerstner to buy those shares. (In 1993 and 1994, IBM paid Gerstner $7,752,854 and $637,500, respectively, to satisfy these provisions.)

In the event of termination without cause, or a change in control, the pact assures Gerstner 36 months' salary, prorated incentive payments, the right to exercise all options, and other benefits.

In March 1993, when IBM made this agreement with Gerstner, it had no employment agreements or change-in-control deals with any other top executives.

In working out his arrangement with IBM, Gerstner enjoyed the able collaboration of New York attorney Joseph Bachelder. As compensation deals become more complex, expert help becomes more desirable. Bachelder, founder of the law firm bearing his name, has represented such people as John Sculley (in his negotiations with Apple) and Lawrence Bossidy, Chairman of AlliedSignal.

Usually, Bachelder is paid by the executives he represents. Sometimes, he is hired by the executives he represents. And sometimes he comes as part of the package. A company is trying to hire a desirable recruit. The company hires Bachelder to work on behalf of the recruit, as did IBM in Gerstner's case. (Executives involved in negotiations with a prospective employer might consider asking that the company pay for a qualified negotiating partner who is chosen by the employee.)

For 1994, IBM's Executive Compensation and Management Committee awarded Gerstner (in addition to his base salary of $2,000,000) an incentive payment of $2,600,000. In June 1994, the committee approved a stock option grant to Gerstner covering 225,000 shares of IBM stock. IBM said that, in approving this grant, several factors were considered: option grants given to CEOs of other leading companies; IBM's size and complexity; the challenges that Louis Gerstner faced as head of IBM; and improvement in business results. The option grant carried an exercise price of $60.94, the average market price on June 27, 1994.

John F. Welch, Jr.

In 1992, John F. ("Jack") Welch, GE's high-profile chieftain, received a salary of $1,600,000 along with a bonus of $1,900,000—a total of $3,500,000 in annual cash compensation, maintaining his position among the highest-paid CEOs in the world. That cash compensation, high as it was, was dwarfed by two contingent long-term incentive awards. One award bestowed on Welch 100,000 restricted units of GE stock having a value of $7,800,000 when granted.

This scheme amounts to a massive, luxurious pair of golden handcuffs. The provision attached to the stock grant is that "Mr. Welch remains CEO throughout the vesting period, which begins three years after the grant date and extends to retirement." That grant brought Welch's aggregate holdings of restricted stock to $20,520,000.

Besides the restricted stock, 1992 brought Welch an award of 150,000 units of stock appreciation rights (SARs) exercisable in four equal installments beginning one year after the grant. Because these SARs would have no value whatever if GE's stock price was below $80 per share, the CEO has a strong motivation to stay with the company and do everything within his power to boost stock prices. The closing price for GE stock on December 31, 1992, was $85.50 per share.

In 1990 and 1991, Welch had been granted 100,000 SARs and 140,000 SARs, respectively. The conversion threshold was set at appropriate levels in each case. In 1992, Welch exercised 155,000 SARs, with a value of $6,670,000.

The year 1993 brought Welch $1,750,000 in salary and $2,200,000 in bonus, totaling $3,950,000. The board's compensation committee decided not to award any restricted stock units (RSUs) to the company's top executives. However, Welch was granted 200,000 SARs. The incubation period was stretched out: half of these SARs would become exercisable in 1996, and half in 1998. These SARs would have no value at all if GE's stock price were below $96.625 per share. (The December 31, 1993, closing price for GE stock was $104.875 per share.)

On December 31, 1994, the closing price for the company's stock was $51 per share. This reflected a 2-for-1 stock split, but, even so, the options did not fare all that well in 1994. Many people saw their options struggle during that year.

In 1994, Welch received total cash payments of $4,350,000— $1,850,000 in salary, $2,500,000 in bonus. He was given no additional RSUs. However, he was granted 320,000 SARs, half to become exercisable in 1997 and half in 1999. These rights have no value at all if GE's stock price is below the $51 per share at which it closed when 1994 ended. These awards are also forfeited if Welch leaves the company for reasons other than retirement before they can be exercised.

GE's determination to grant such SARs to its leader "was to provide a strong incentive for him to continue to serve the share owners by remaining CEO of the company and to increase the value of the company during the remainder of his employment."

As GE stock hovered at around $57 per share in mid-1995, Welch's prospects for cashing in the 100,000 SARs exercisable in 1996 (with a minimum of $96.625) did not look promising. However, he would have had reasonable expectations of better luck with the 320,000 SARs granted to him in 1994, because the target per-share price was $51.

Ted Turner

Mergers and acquisitions create strange situations. When Time Warner took over Turner Broadcasting, Ted Turner became the number-two person in the new colossus. Turner's contract—including around $5 million annually in salary and bonus, $10 million a year in long-term incentive compensation, and lucrative stock options—gave Turner a deal that seems to far exceed that of his nominal boss, Gerald M. Levin.

The Global Marketplace

It's One World in business—and that's another reason contracts are important.

Business today is international . . . multinational . . . global in scope.

That reality affects our politics, our economies, and our culture. It also affects the relationships between employer and employee. Consider this situation. A senior manager is approached by a headhunter. The job looks exciting, the status is high, the money looks good. The company that the manager would be running is American, but it is owned by a consortium comprising Japanese and Mid-Eastern interests. Although the cash the manager receives will be in U.S. dollars, there are questions about the stock, the parachute, and the laws that will govern disputes. This relationship calls for a sound, detailed agreement covering all the points that would be spelled out by a conventional agreement with a domestic firm, plus a host of other considerations.

Employment contracts were in common use abroad, particularly in Europe, before they began to appear in U.S. companies. Their use is in keeping with the general philosophy in many foreign countries, where the manager is regarded as a true professional and is accorded considerably more respect and deference than in the United States. In Germany and France, as well as in Japan, it has been practically unheard-of to fire executives because the chemistry is wrong, or because a new broom is sweeping clean, or to "straighten out" glitches in the organization chart. In the rest of the world, managers are far less likely to survive from one day's combat to the next. True, as business becomes global, a blending of business cultures occurs. American business culture influences that of, say, Germany, and vice versa; but there are still significant differences.

Curiously, managers in foreign countries, who have less need of the protection afforded by written contracts, are much more likely than their American counterparts to have them. In some countries, government regulations make a contract necessary, or the contract is simply a normal stage in the employment process. In the United States, plenty of employers still say, "Contract? Why do you want a contract? We never give contracts." Abroad, there will be hard bargaining about what goes into the contract, but far less questioning of the need for a contract at all.

As business has become increasingly international, management as a profession has become an international vocation. Executives from other countries routinely work in the United States, either for branches of their own companies or for American firms, and countless American managers are assigned to offices abroad. Americans who go to work for foreign companies may confront the question of an employment contract for the first time. When they go to work in overseas subsidiaries of American companies, they may have to do so under contract to satisfy local law and custom. American managers who do not have full-fledged contracts will inevitably be in frequent contact with those who do. They become familiar with the concept and its advantages to both parties.

When an American manager who has been exposed to the contract concept abroad is transferred back, or is recruited by another company, he or she is likely to think of a written contract as an important structural component of the deal, not just for protection, but for facilitation. The contract, if it is done right, spells out the complex aspects of the arrangement and anticipates areas of possible misinterpretation or disagreement.

Americans who become familiar with the notion of full-scale employment agreements during involvements abroad tend to push aggressively for contracts at their next jobs. As they move to more senior positions in their companies, they carry a greater understanding of, and tolerance for, the signing of written contracts.

As movement of managers between countries accelerates, the use of contracts grows. Companies that have resisted the notion of written contracts are coming to accept them because they help to give uniformity to relationships between people and organizations of different countries and cultures. The *process* of forging a written agreement between people or entities from different countries is beneficial. The author of this book finds that, when a top American manager sits down with a potential recruit from, say, South Africa, to work out an agreement, they discover differences in viewpoints, assumptions, and semantics that would, if left unattended, cause big problems later on, not just in the employment arrangement but in the effectiveness with which the recruit does his or her job. The contract negotiation uncovers these potential problems at an early stage, when they can be cleared up without detrimental effect.

All in the Family

When the bonds of kinship fail, a binding contract helps.

In 1994, a jury decided that Herbert Haft had wrongfully dismissed his son, Robert Haft, from the family business, including Robert's chairmanship of Crown Books. The elder Haft had claimed that Robert breached his contract. The jury ordered that Robert Haft be paid $34 million in cash and stock.

Protecting the Parachute

Another factor in the spread of employment contracts toward the ranks of middle managers is top management's desire to protect the "golden parachute." As takeover mania seized American business, the parachute emerged. At first, it was a device to provide a soft landing for top executives who would be swept out in a change of ownership. Then the golden parachute was translated into a strategic tool to resist takeovers—to make it so prohibitively expensive for one company to acquire another that the effort was abandoned. In themselves, steep parachute deals were not equal to the task. No matter how much money the acquiring company was forced to pay the outgoing CEO, that sum did not constitute a sufficient deterrent. However, as part of a general "poison pill" defense (which sometimes takes on more of the look of a Doomsday Machine), tactical golden parachutes carry a big price tag.

The takeover tide ebbed for a while, then began to flood again. Many stockholders got sticker shock when they looked at the barricades erected by their managements against changes in control. The enormous amounts of money involved in these payouts, combined with the absence of stockholder approval, generated a lot of unfavorable publicity for golden parachutes and put enormous pressure on senior executives privileged to have them. The cost of golden parachutes, combined with stockholders' perception that antitakeover defenses were being used to protect management jobs rather than to enhance return on investment, made it essential that something be done.

The instinct for self-preservation has not been expunged from human genes, and senior managers are not likely to lose their desire for takeover protection. Instead, they are increasingly impelled to share the wealth by issuing golden parachutes to people at lower levels of the organization.

This at least removes one of the most egregious features of the golden parachute (as seen by its detractors): its former availability only to an exclusive club at the top.

Keeping Secrets, Controlling Competition

Another factor that is spurring the use of contracts is the growth in company secrets that must be kept and in the number of people who, of necessity, become privy to those secrets. Written agreements with provisions designed to protect those secrets are increasing. The primary purpose of some agreements is to limit or prevent the revelation of confidential material. Originally commonplace in hi-tech industries, such contracts are now used in other industries where a company may be damaged if a competitor obtains certain inside information. Confidentiality clauses are now written into all kinds of contracts.

Another self-protective measure is the "noncompete" agreement, in which an executive agrees not to go to work for a competitor (or to start a competitive enterprise) for a specified period. As we shall discuss, such contracts, although not necessarily enforceable in court, can cast a blight on the employment prospects of departing executives, besides eating up their money, time, and energy.

Typically, the noncompete clause is written into a contract with someone who is currently on or is being added to the payroll; it comes into effect when the person leaves the company, and it may be enforced, to a degree, by a threat to withhold deferred compensation. Lately, firms are using a different approach. They have found that they don't necessarily have to sign a noncompete provision with a current employee. Rather, they wait until the employee is terminated and *then* offer more severance money (perhaps in a lump sum) if the individual agrees to a noncompete arrangement. Downsizing firms are using this approach with entire classes of employees who might be in a position to do damage.

From the company's point of view, this approach has solid advantages. In negotiations with an employee who has just been laid off, the company can concentrate on the desired restrictions, without giving the employee anything beyond a boosted severance sum. Moreover, if the dismissed employee is hurting for money and is in a depleted emotional state, winning the desired agreement may be fairly easy. (Later in this book, you'll see such an offer in its entirety, along with recommendations on how to handle it.)

The Compensation Jungle

Companies currently make all sorts of written employment agreements with executives. The desire to motivate and the need to provide tax shelters have stimulated a jungle-like proliferation of exotic compensation methods: restricted stock units, stock appreciation rights, deferred compensation, complex bonus tie-ins, and so on. Some agreements must make up for what an executive is losing in compensation from his or her previous company. Perks—for example, club memberships, automobiles, houses—are still important, although they do not offer the shelter from the tax authorities that they once did. All of these things must be set down in orderly fashion. When they are—and when both parties sign off on their status—a contract is created.

Above all, business must find ways to attract and keep executive talent. With corporations stripped down to leaner and meaner cadres, the loss of a key manager can be a great blow. When a company comes bearing golden handcuffs, an obvious way to lock in top talent, the astute manager wants to go further and work out a full-scale employment agreement. If the company wants to be able to plan on the manager's being around for a while, it will look more favorably on the option of a contract.

And, because the middle managers of today are the policy-level leaders of tomorrow, the contracts are likely to be given to those below the top echelon.

Stocking It Away at Infinity

President/CEO Mel Karmazin's employment agreement with Infinity Broadcasting exemplifies emphatically the ownership-as-compensation trend. The contract allows Infinity to pay portions of Karmazin's base salary in stock or stock warrants. His entire 1991 salary—$750,000—was paid in warrants.

What's in the Contract

For all the above reasons, written contracts are being offered to ever-increasing numbers of white-collar employees. The most highly publicized deals are given to CEOs, but countless middle managers are under contract today, or will be negotiating contracts soon. If you have a management or professional job, and you have hopes of moving up, you may—sooner than you think—be confronting questions like these:

- Is a contract to my advantage?
- What should it cover?

- How long should it run?
- What are the dangers?
- How much bonus can I realistically expect to get?
- How much stock in the company do I want?
- What happens if I want to leave before the term runs out?
- *How can I negotiate the best possible agreement?*

Let's first examine the pros and cons of a contract from the employer's point of view.

Employers' Goal: A Limited Giveaway

Employers, by and large, dislike the idea of making employment agreements with executives. Contracts limit top management's authority. The idea that executives should be dismissible at will has taken some hard blows, but it is by no means dead. A company can fire a manager with, say, four years to go on a five-year contract, but the severance pay will be pretty steep.

Another reason that employers resist the broader use of contracts for managers is that it establishes precedents. When a certain number of managers win contracts that provide them with extremely attractive stock option arrangements, the pot will almost inevitably have to be sweetened for everybody else.

Many employers are highly reluctant to lose "the ultimate motivator," the right to fire. They fear that managers who are protected by contracts will no longer show the desired amount of drive. Although industrial psychologists have insisted for years that motivation must lie in positive things, not in the threat of dismissal, somehow that idea has never really caught on with some bosses.

However, contracts do have distinct advantages for employers (and more employers are realizing this and acting on it).

The most obvious advantage for the employer is that the employee is locked in for the life of the agreement. Downsizing has not been accompanied by lowered emphasis on signing up the best management talent. A world-renowned soft-drink giant used to recruit shoals of promising MBAs and dump them in the shark pool, to sink or swim in a highly competitive atmosphere. The firm did not worry about training managers or retaining talent. There were always plenty more in the pipeline. But changing realities have forced the company to take a new approach. The crest of the post-World War II baby boom has passed. There are fewer gifted young managers to choose from. The emphasis now has to be placed on identifying good managers, developing them, and keeping them as long as possible.

To keep the talent, a company may need golden handcuffs; and golden handcuffs, in turn, lead to the use of full-scale contracts.

A second advantage to the employer is that a contractual relationship eliminates or at least reduces the friction and divisiveness caused by annual bargaining between employee and employer. When the issue of compensation has been minimized for, say, a five-year term, it's easier to concentrate on meeting corporate objectives.

Some firms still cling to the approach that welcomes the annual bargaining sessions, tying them in with performance evaluation. These days, human resource executives are, in growing numbers, rejecting conventional performance evaluation programs as being more trouble than they are worth.

Contracts make it easier to do human resource planning: to try to project what the organization chart will look like five years hence, plot the courses of managers who are earmarked to fill certain jobs, and identify the strengths and weaknesses of the executive corps of the company. If the firm is considering important new steps—production of a new line, penetration of a new market, expansion overseas—it needs to be sure the right people are running things. The existence of an employment contract is no guarantee that a particular person will still be on board five years in the future, but the likelihood of that person's remaining is enhanced. Employment agreements let planners build their future scenarios with greater assurance.

As mentioned earlier, the need to keep company secrets and stay ahead of the competition—as, for example, in Silicon Valley—makes contracts with noncompete and nondisclosure clauses valuable tools for management.

The bottom line: Contracts have plenty of significant advantages for employers. However, employers are not, on the whole, jubilant about the growing trend toward putting terms in writing, nor are they eager to offer contracts to their managers.

Their attitude is realistic because a *well-negotiated employment contract favors the employee more than the employer.*

How the Contract Pays Off for the Employee

The biggest advantage a contract has for the employee is that the company is *committed in writing* to the provisions of the working arrangement. It would be naive to think that every provision of every contract is going to be carried out to the letter. But an employee is a lot more certain of getting what has been promised when the provisions are spelled out in writing.

When you have a contract, you have assurance of a job and a minimum income for a stated period of time. If the employer breaks the contract by firing you, you're entitled to collect the severance money called for in the agreement. If the employer has established a complex compensation plan, you're able to review its provisions to make sure you're getting all you're entitled to. If the company suffers reverses, those without the protection of a contract are (all other things being equal) more vulnerable than you. If you have a contract, the company is obligated to honor it unless it goes bankrupt. If you have a well-drawn contract, you are protected in case of a merger or takeover; the successor firm assumes the obligation of making good on the agreement.

Your contract can protect you from being transferred to duties or locations you don't want. It can assure you of a piece of the action if the company makes a profit, while limiting your downside risk when times are hard. A contract can enhance the value of your estate. It can ensure that you enjoy certain status-enhancing perks.

But what about the negatives? A contract ties you down. You're locked into a situation that you may want to get out of before the agreement runs its course. Younger, fast-track executives in particular may resist locking themselves in because they want the freedom to consider other career opportunities that they fully expect to receive.

The fact is, however, a well-negotiated contract ties the employer down more than it does the employee.

Both parties have ways to try to break contracts. As we will see, some companies have tried to avoid paying the full severance by threatening to allege that the employee was fired "for cause," leading to a long, drawn-out lawsuit that the company can afford better than the individual. Employers may try to make life miserable for the employee (while staying within the letter of the contract) by such ploys as making the person report to someone lower down in the organization, pulling away perks, or creating unpleasant assignments and working conditions.

Such ploys—and others—can be anticipated and forestalled in the written agreement. (We will show you specific language designed to give you that protection.)

But what about the manager who has signed a five-year contract and wants to leave after three years for a better job? The company is entitled to insist that the terms of the pact be honored. But is it a good idea to force a key employee to stay unwillingly? Won't the individual's talent be outweighed by anger and resentment?

No; trying to use threats and muscle against an executive in such a case is a losing proposition.

A much better strategy is to try to lock in the valuable employee through positive means—as strong a set of golden handcuffs as can be forged, in the form of deferred compensation, stock options, and pension benefits. The idea is: Make it so costly for employees to leave that the decision to remain looks attractive, no matter how good an offer another company has made.

The loophole is that if a company wants an executive badly enough, it will offer compensation for the loss the recruit suffers in leaving the former employer prematurely. IBM paid Louis Gerstner more than $12 million to "make him whole" for the bonuses and stock he had to abandon when he left RJR Nabisco.

If the employment agreement has a noncompete clause, then the company, if it wishes, has more leverage in making life tough for the departing individual. "Noncompetes"—which basically forbid the manager to go to work for a competitor for a specified length of time after leaving the original firm—are not always easy for the company to enforce. Laws vary from state to state. Many courts look askance at this kind of limitation of freedom. Nevertheless, the existence of a noncompete clause makes it potentially possible for the company to go after the departing manager with a full battery of legal armament. This naturally deters the would-be contract-breaker. It also may deter a would-be employer who is willing to pay but not to get into legal hassles.

On the whole, contracts favor employees more than employers. That's why experts advise companies to go slow in this area. Robert

Half, the well-known commentator on employment issues and author of *Finding, Hiring, and Keeping the Best Employees* (John Wiley & Sons, Inc., 1993), comments: "While no one can fault anyone for asking for an agreement with a new employer, the tendency to award them to a wider variety of employees strikes me as problematic . . . this movement in employment is at odds with an employer–employee 'marriage' in which mutual growth and respect should be the goal."

Half infers that a contract means employees are more concerned with their security than with their contribution to the team. This author disagrees strongly. There is no reason to think that people covered by contracts—especially contracts spelling out a plethora of incentives—are tempted to "coast." On the contrary, a well-drawn-up "prenuptial agreement" is likely to enhance an employee's performance.

Robert Half goes on to say that employment contracts "must be the result of prudent corporate thought, aided by enlightened and expert legal counsel." And here is a key point. The contract is likely to work in the employee's favor—*if* the employee negotiates the right kind of contract. If the employer gets the employee to sign an agreement skewed in the company's favor in one or more important ways, then the employee has lost the advantage. For example, a pact may contain a fabulously lucrative severance provision, but if the language defining termination "for cause" is loosely drawn, then the employer may be able to get out of the obligation without paying a penny.

The employer's strategic thrust in negotiation will be for ironclad rigidity in provisions favorable to the company (for example, protection of secrets, and noncompete provisions), while keeping the language as vague as possible in areas like termination and, perhaps, bonus criteria. The employee will want to optimize those sections offering the greatest payoff and protection while whittling down the scope of the employer's discretion and control.

This book covers the issues you will be negotiating when you bargain for your first or next employment contract. It will help you to shape your negotiating strategy and sharpen the tactics you need to win a favorable agreement.

You will find comment and recommendations on every aspect of working out the optimum deal with your employer. The book supports its points with a variety of excerpts from actual contracts existing today between companies and managers. In some cases, we have reproduced the entire document, punctuated by observations, comments, and recommendations. Legal documents do not make for spicy or lively reading, but, to strengthen your hand, look this material over. The deals worked out by Gerstner or Welch or Agee may someday have relevance for your own situation.

The more familiar you become with the various provisions available in a contract and the subtle ways in which the wording can give the edge to one side or the other, the better equipped you will be to avoid traps and to secure a contract that gives you what you want.

The Buyout Bugaboo

In November 1995, AT&T shook up the business world by offering buyouts to 77,800 managers, half the company's supervisory force.

Managers—already buffeted by the chill winds of downsizing—now must cast a watchful eye toward another dark cloud forming in the sky, a threat embodied by the question: "What should I do if they offer *me* a buyout?"

The word "buyout" in this context is somewhat misleading. The company is not offering to buy out the remaining term of an acknowledged contract. The offer is, rather, an incentive to accept an immediate severance deal.

Buyouts are typically offered to groups of employees; lump-sum payments are based on such factors as base salary and length of time with the company. It's take-it-or-leave-it time; the company won't negotiate the monetary terms of the deal. (If it negotiated in one case, it would face the possibility of having to negotiate in every case.)

According to a rule of thumb suggested by human resource people, most buyout offers provide for around two weeks' pay for every year of service. Any higher ratio is generous; anything lower is cheap. The deal may also include health benefits for a specified period, retirement credit, and outplacement.

The offer carries a message that the next deal (if there is one) will be lower in value. If a company sweetened its successive buyout offers, nobody would be motivated to accept the first one.

The big question you face if you receive a buyout offer is: "What happens if I turn it down?" Your age, your family situation, your job prospects, your value to the firm—these factors, along with others, bear on the decision. If you think a buyout may be in the offing, it's wise to assess your chances as objectively as possible, considering questions like:

- What's my greatest strength? Is it unique? Who else can do what I do?

- Can the company get for less money what I provide?

- What's the job picture in my industry? In my discipline? Are people with my specialty getting offers? When was the last time a headhunter called?

- Am I identified with the company's future, or its past?

If ever you were capable of cold-blooded objectivity about yourself, this is the time for it. Put yourself in the company's shoes and look at yourself in the context of: your competition within the organization, your age, your pay, and the ways in which you fit (or don't fit) into company plans.

Wiggle-Room

The basic terms of a buyout are fixed, but certain aspects of the deal may be negotiable—the exit date, the extension period for health benefits, the bonus payouts, and the vesting of stock options. Employees who have contracts possess an advantage in dealing with the buyout specifics.

Even if you don't have a formal contract, your negotiating position may be strengthened if you're able to produce documents that *have the force* of a formal employment agreement. (We'll discuss these in Chapter 6, "The *De Facto* Contract: You May Already Have It in Writing.")

2

What the Typical Contract Covers

The basic elements of a full-scale employment agreement are:

- Term—how long the contract runs.
- Duties—description of the job and status.
- Compensation—salary, bonuses, stock options, and other monetary perks.
- Benefits—life and health insurance, retirement qualification, and other nonmonetary perks.
- Severance—what amount is to be paid to the fired employee.

Beyond these basics, contracts may cover a variety of items—perks like limousine transportation, a company car, or club memberships; consulting provisions; hiring bonuses; or conflict resolution mechanisms, such as arbitration. Two important ingredients are added to many contracts:

1. Golden parachutes, including a "trigger" clause spelling out just how the provision comes into effect if there is a change of ownership.

2. Noncompete and nondisclosure restrictions.

With or without a more formal employment agreement, all jobs involve documents that explain elements of the relationship between employee and employer. Some of these documents may be "generic" material given to groups of people—bulletins describing benefits, explanations of stock option plans, company policy statements, orientation brochures. Some will apply specifically to individuals, for example, memos clarifying just how and when bonuses will be paid to eligible personnel, specifications for office furniture, reporting relationships, restrictions on outsiders' visits, and so on.

You can best get a feel for the structure of a contract by looking at some actual employment agreements. In this chapter, we'll begin to examine some actual contracts, adorned with the thickets of verbiage that lawyers so love. If your eyes start to glaze over, it's all right to skim as long as you have an idea of what's in the particular provision and can refer to it later. At salient points, you'll come upon explanatory comments to guide you toward the significance of what you're reading.

Some of the contracts we'll examine typify the kinds of employment agreements held by midlevel managers. (Many people have cooperated; where appropriate, we have preserved their anonymity.) We also present, for your edification and inspiration, examples of contracts and deals enjoyed by high-profile executives: Eisner (Disney), Welch (GE), Gerstner (IBM), and others. (Occasionally, we quote from Michael Eisner's pact with Disney. The full text is reproduced in Appendix 2.)

Analyzing a Managerial Employment Agreement

On the following pages are some employment contracts that exemplify the points we'll be covering in this book. Later, as we focus on each element of a desirable contract, we'll use other examples. By reading these complete-text documents, you can get a feel for what you may be facing or negotiating. Let's start with an agreement between a manager and a soft-drink company. The manager has moved to the soft-drink company from a consumer goods multinational. Our interspersed comments appear in italics.

THE STATE OF TEXAS
COUNTY OF DALLAS

This Agreement made this [date] between [company] and [manager].

WITNESSETH

Whereas, the Company desires to employ [manager] as an executive officer of the Company and [he/she] is willing to accept such employment and thereafter to perform the services hereafter described, upon the terms and conditions hereinafter set forth.

Now, therefore, it is agreed between the Company and [manager] that:

1. *Employment.* The Company hereby employs [manager] for the period beginning on the date that [he/she] reports to work at the Company's offices in Dallas and ending three (3) years after such date; provided that this agreement shall terminate and be of no force or effect unless [manager] reports for work to begin [his/her] employment prior to [date].

> *This contract runs for three years. Most employment contracts run for three to five years, but there are exceptions. Michael Eisner and Disney tied the knot for ten years. There can even be lifetime contracts; later, we include an example.*

2. *Duties.* During the period that [manager] shall be an employee of the Company, [he/she] shall have and exercise such duties, powers, and authority as may be assigned to [him/her] by the Board of Directors of the Company. [He/she] shall report and be responsible to the Board of Directors, the Chairman of the Board, and the President. [Manager] agrees to perform the duties enumerated in this paragraph and to serve as an employee for three years from the date of the commencement of [his/her] employment.

> *This fairly general description of duties allows for the manager to be shifted to another job. Some duties clauses are "job-specific," laying out a title and a menu of responsibilities. The duties clause, as we'll see, can establish the basis for an employer's claim that the terms of the agreement have not been met by the manager.*

Conversely, the clause can protect the manager from being as-
signed to inappropriate duties.
   This contract also specifies the positions within the com-
pany to whom the manager must report. This detail can come in
handy if, say, the firm tries to subordinate the manager to an indi-
vidual lower down on the corporate totem pole.

3. *Compensation.* In consideration of [manager] entering into and executing this agreement and serving as an employee for said three-year period, the Company shall pay to [him/her] during the period of employment a salary at the rate of $ _____ per year, plus such additional or increased salary, compensation, or benefits as the Board of Directors may direct, payable in substantially equal semimonthly amounts on the fifteenth and the last day of each month. Shall [manager] die or become disabled after the commencement of [his/her] employment and prior to three years thereafter, the amount of the then unpaid compensation, including all bonus payments to which [he/she] is entitled, shall be paid in equal monthly installments to [him/her] or [his/her] estate.

Compensation is the centerpiece of most contracts. This agree-
ment does not establish specific amounts or a range; instead, it
sets a minimum.
   When you negotiate a contract, it should be standard pro-
cedure that a minimum level is set as a floor, with no limit on the
upside.

4. *Moving Expenses.* [Manager's] expenses reasonably incurred in moving [him/her] and family from [location] to Dallas will be reimbursed to [him/her] by the Company in full in accordance with the Company's policy in connection with executive transfers, and [manager] shall also be paid an additional amount in cash equivalent to [his/her] income tax liability attributable to receipt of moving expenses.

Contracts signed when an executive joins a firm often cover one-
shot relocation expenses. Because the IRS considers a wide
range of bonus and expense payments to be taxable income, com-
panies "make whole" their employees through the practice known
as "grossing-up": the firm foots the tax bill. Such reimbursement,
in a kind of tortoise-and-hare race, may lead to additional

tax liability, whereupon the company may be grossing-up the gross-up.

5. a. *Purchase of [previous] Residence.* Concurrently with [manager] entering upon employment with the Company, the Company will cause [his/her] residence in [previous location] to be appraised by a competent appraisal firm and will purchase the residence from [manager] at the appraised price less the amount of any indebtedness, liens, or encumbrances burdening the property, which mortgages and encumbrances will, however, be assumed by the Company.

   b. *Loan.* To assist [manager] in acquiring a residence in Dallas or its suburbs, the Company will lend to [him/her] the amount of $ _____ for a term of three years, such indebtedness to bear interest at the amount of _____ % per annum and to be secured by a first lien on said Dallas residence purchased by [him/her].

6. *Reimbursement for Expenses.* [Manager] is authorized to incur reasonable expenses for promoting the business of the Company. At the end of each month, the Company shall reimburse [him/her] for all expenses, including entertainment, travel, and miscellaneous other expenses reasonably incurred in promoting the business of the Company and in performing [his/her] duties as an employee hereunder.

> *Reimbursement for expenses is routine. Unless there is something special about the expense arrangement, why put it in the contract? It's best to screen out extraneous verbiage. Sometimes such clauses are simply legal "boilerplate." And, every now and then, the routine expense account can become an issue. We'll see an example in the melancholy fiasco engulfing utility CEO James Smith, who was sued over what seem like relatively low-level expense-account violations, and who was even brought to the dock in a criminal trial. (He was acquitted.)*

7. *Restrictive Covenant.* During the term of this agreement, [manager] shall devote [his/her] best efforts and full time to advance the interests of the Company and to perform [his/her] duties hereunder, and during such time [manager] shall not directly or

indirectly, alone or as a member of a partnership, or as an officer, director, or shareholder of a corporation, be engaged in or concerned with any other commercial duties or pursuits which are in any manner competitive with the Company.

> *This is a relatively general form of the noncompete clause. Noncompete and nondisclosure limitations loom large in many contracts. Severance pay may be linked to noncompete limitations extending well beyond termination. The company's desire for such an agreement may provide the opening for you to negotiate a full-scale contract.*

8. *Employee Benefits.* Nothing in this agreement shall be construed to impair or limit [manager's] right to participate in all employee benefit plans of the Company of every nature and [he/she] shall, in fact, be entitled to participate in and be a member of all such benefit plans in proportion to [his/her] compensation hereunder. "Benefit Plans" shall include, but not be limited to, group life, hospitalization, and major medical insurance coverages; stock options; stock purchase or bonus plans; retirement programs; profit-sharing arrangements; and other incentive compensation plans. [Manager's] eligible dependents shall also be covered under any such plans and benefit programs to the extent that dependents of other employees are similarly provided for. Specifically, [manager] will be made a participant in both the Company's existing incentive compensation plans, the short-term and the long-term, copies of which are appended as exhibits to this agreement. If requested, the Company will enter into agreements with [manager] providing for the deferral of all or part of any bonus payments payable under such plans.

> *We'll be looking at—and analyzing—contracts that describe in great detail the complexities of today's incentive compensation approaches. Here, let's just note in passing that the language of this pact gives the manager the option of deferral. Nowadays, a stock option plan is likely to be structured so that deferred compensation is built in. Corporations don't offer a choice.*

9. *Reorganization.* If the Company shall at any time be merged or consolidated into or with any other corporation or entity, the

provisions of this agreement shall survive any such transaction and shall be binding on and inure to the benefit of the corporation resulting from such merger or consolidation or the corporation to which such assets will be transferred (and this provision shall apply in the event of any subsequent merger, consolidation, or transfer), and the Company, upon the occasion of any of the above-described transactions, shall include in the appropriate agreements the obligation that the payments herein agreed to be paid to or for the benefit of [manager], [his/her] beneficiaries or estate, shall be paid, and that the provisions of this paragraph 9 be performed.

The contract is binding on any successor company following a merger or acquisition. This, of course, is not a golden parachute, which would specify a severance deal to come into force only on change of control of the corporation.

10. *Benefit.* This agreement shall inure to the benefit of and shall bind the parties hereto and their respective legal representatives, successors, heirs, descendants, assigns, and personal representatives.

IN WITNESS WHEREOF, the Company and [manager] have signed this agreement as of the date and year first set forth above.

[COMPANY]

By [CEO]

ATTEST:

[Company secretary]

By [Manager]

Contracts can be amended. One basic amendment is a simple extension. The above agreement was extended by means of the following letter:

[date]

Dear [manager's first name];

In accordance with the action of the Board of Directors at its last meeting, I am pleased to submit this letter agreement amending and extending your employment Agreement of [date] in the following particulars:

The term of the Agreement and of your employment is extended for one year

beyond the original three-year term, with the same effect as if the original

agreement had been for a term of four years terminating in [year], rather than for

three years, terminating in [year].

In all other respects, the [year] Agreement shall continue in full force and effect as originally written.

If this is in accordance with your understanding, please indicate in the place provided below and return one copy to me.

Sincerely

[CEO]

AGREED:

_____

Another Contract, with Different Features

The contract we just examined encompasses the majority of the elements of a standard agreement. However, one element common in most pacts is absent: a section on the possible causes or justifications for termination of the agreement.

The following contract covers essentially the same ground but includes a couple of additional points: language on termination, and the resolution of disputes through arbitration. We'll go into greater detail on both topics later in the book.

EMPLOYMENT AGREEMENT

This Agreement, entered into at [location] as of this [date] by and between [name of the company], with its principal executive offices located at [address] (hereinafter called the "Company"), and [individual's name] (hereinafter called the "Employee").

WITNESSETH

In consideration of the mutual covenants herein contained and other good and valuable considerations, the parties hereto agree as follows:

SECTION I—TERM OF EMPLOYMENT AND DUTIES

1.0 The Company employs the Employee upon an active full-time basis, as [complete job title] subject to the order, supervision, and direction of the Board of Directors of the Company and any officer senior to [him/her], and the Employee has accepted and agrees to remain in the employ of the Company in the aforesaid capacity upon the terms, conditions, and provisions herein stated from the effective date hereof [date] through [a date three years in the future].

1.1 During the term of [his/her] employment, the Employee agrees to devote [his/her] full business time, attention, skill, and efforts to the business conducted by the Company and to continue to act as [job description] as aforesaid, and faithfully to perform such executive, administrative, and supervisory duties and to exercise such powers as specified in the Regulations of the Company from time to time and as the Board of Directors and officers senior to [him/her] may prescribe.

1.2 The Employee's duties shall be performed principally at the Company's headquarters located in [location]. It is intended that the Employee will move [his/her] principal residence to a home to be selected by [him/her] in the general area of [location] by approximately [date], at which place [he/she] and [his/her] family shall reside.

1.3 There is attached hereto, and marked Exhibit A, a copy of Exhibit A to a letter dated [date], executed by the Company and the Employee, setting out the general terms of the Employee's employment, the principal terms of which are incorporated herein. Reference is made to paragraph I.E., titled "Relocation Expenses," which shall apply to the change of location of the Employee's principal residence, required by the preceding paragraph 1.2.

SECTION II—COMPENSATION

2.0 The annual base salary of the Employee shall be the sum of [$ _____] per annum, payable in equal semimonthly installments.

2.1 The Board of Directors of the Company reserves the right to increase the compensation of the Employee, specified in this instrument, at any time or times hereafter and no such increase or adjustment shall operate as a cancellation of this Agreement, but merely as an amendment to this Section II, and all the other terms, provisions, and conditions of this Agreement shall continue in force and effect as herein provided.

2.2 The Employee will be reimbursed for [his/her] reasonable travel and living expenses, incurred when traveling on the Company's business, pursuant to its established policies.

2.3 The Employee shall be a participant in the Company's [year] Incentive Plan, pursuant to which it is possible for [him/her] to earn a bonus not to exceed [_____%] of [his/her] annual base salary, provided the prescribed target profits and objectives set out in the Plan are achieved, as well as in subsequent plans (if any) which may hereafter be adopted.

2.4 The Company will, during the term of this Agreement, maintain at its expense, term insurance upon the life of the Employee in the face amount of [$ _____], payable to such beneficiary as the Employee shall designate from time to time in writing to the Company and, in the absence of such designation, to [his/her] estate. Such insurance shall be in addition to such group term insurance as the Company maintains for the benefit of salaried employees generally of the rank and status of the Employee.

2.5 The Company will grant to the Employee, effective upon [his/her] entering into the Company's employ on [date], an option to purchase [number] Common shares, par $1 per share, of the Company under and pursuant to the Company's [year] Stock Option Plan, the option price to equal 100% of the fair market value of the optioned shares on the effective day of the grant.

SECTION III—NONCOMPETITION AND SECRECY

3.0 So long as this Agreement is in effect, the Employee shall not directly or indirectly become or serve as an officer or employee of an individual, partnership, or corporation, or owner or part owner or shareholder of any business, or member of any partnership, which conducts a business which, in the reasonable judgment of the Board of Directors of this corporation, competes in a material manner with the Company, unless the Employee shall first have obtained the written consent of the Board of Directors of the corporation.

3.1 At all times, both before and after the termination of [his/her] employment, the Employee shall keep and retain in confidence and shall not disclose to any persons, firm, or corporation (except with the written consent of the Company first obtained) any of the proprietary, confidential, or secret information or trade secrets of the Company.

SECTION IV—TERMINATION

4.0 Nothing herein is intended to prohibit the Company from terminating this Agreement for serious misconduct on the part of the Employee or other good cause; provided that, in the event that the Employee's employment is terminated rightfully by the Company, nevertheless the Employee shall be entitled to receive such benefits under the Company's benefit plans, in which [he/she] is a participant, as are provided by the terms thereof applicable to the termination of participants generally.

4.1 If the Employee shall become totally and permanently disabled (as said term is defined in the group long-term disability insurance now being carried by the Company), the Company may not terminate this Agreement on account of such disability unless and until the waiting period (for payment of benefits) prescribed in such (or similar substituted) insurance then in force shall have expired during the continuance of such disability.

4.2 Any dispute or difference of opinion between the Employee and the Company as to the latter's right to terminate this Agreement shall be submitted to and determined by arbitration in accordance with the provisions of Section VI hereof set forth below.

SECTION V—OTHER RIGHTS AND PLANS

5.0 Nothing herein contained shall in any manner modify, imperil, or affect existing or future rights or interests of the Employee to receive any employee benefit to which [he/she] would otherwise be entitled or as a participant in the present or any future incentive, profit-sharing, or bonus plan of the Company providing for [his/her] participation, or in any present or future stock option plan of the Company, to the extent such plans are applicable generally to salaried employees, it being understood and agreed that the rights and interests of the Employee to any employee benefits or as a participant or beneficiary in or under any or all said plans, respectively, shall not be adversely affected hereby.

SECTION VI—ARBITRATION

6.0 In the event of any difference of opinion or dispute between the Employee and the Company with respect to the construction or interpretation of this agreement or the alleged breach thereof which cannot be settled amicably by agreement of the parties, then such dispute shall be submitted to and determined by arbitration by a single arbitrator in [city where headquarters are located], in accordance with the rules, then obtaining, of the AMERICAN ARBITRATION ASSOCIATION, and judgment upon the award rendered shall be final, binding, and conclusive upon the parties and may be entered in the highest court, state or federal, having jurisdiction.

SECTION VII—ASSIGNEES BOUND

7.0 THIS AGREEMENT shall be binding upon and inure to the benefit of any successor of the Company and any such successor shall be deemed substituted for the Company under the terms of this contract. The term "successor" as used herein shall indicate any person, firm, corporation, or other business entity which, at any time, by merger, consolidation, purchase, or otherwise, acquires all or substantially all the assets or business of the Company.

7.1 Neither this Agreement nor any of [his/her] rights or duties hereunder may be assigned by the Employee without the written consent of the Company.

SECTION VIII—MISCELLANEOUS

8.0 This Employment shall become effective [date].

8.1 The headings or captions of sections or paragraphs are used for convenience of reference merely and shall be ignored in the construction or interpretation hereof.

8.2 As used herein, terms such as "herein," "hereof," "hereto," and similar language shall be construed to refer to this entire instrument and not merely to the paragraph or sentence in which they appear, unless so limited by express agreement.

8.3 This is a [state] agreement and the same shall be construed and the rights of the parties determined in accordance with the laws of [state].

IN WITNESS WHEREOF, the Company has caused this Employment Agreement to be executed by its duly authorized officer, and [employee] has affixed [his/her] signature hereto, as of the day and year first above mentioned.

[Company name]

By: [President's signature]

[Employee's signature]

EXHIBIT A

I.   Three-year contract, on following major terms:

   A. Salary [amount per year].

   B. Potential Bonus of up to 50% of salary based on profitability and objectives under Incentive Bonus Plan.

   C. Additional Term Life Insurance Policy for [sum] payable to whomever [he/she] chooses.

   D. Stock Options for [number] Common Shares under the [year] Stock Option Plan. Option prices determined by the mean between high and low sales on [stock exchange] on first day of employment.

   E. Relocation Expenses.

      1. Use of [name of relocation service].

         a. Price set by [relocation service] to be based on average of three appraisals on present value of house. Price to sell in 60 days and close 30 days later.

      2. Closing cost of new home in [location].

      3. Moving Expenses.

         a. Packing and moving of household items.

         b. Up to 30 days' temporary living expenses for family in [location].

         c. Mileage for cars from [location] to [location].

         d. Three trips for spouse to look for new home in [location].

         e. Miscellaneous other costs of actually moving family from [location] to [location].

      4. Interest differential for three years.

         a. [Company] will reimburse you for the difference between the interest on the present balance [approximate sum] on your home in [location] and the interest on a mortgage of equal size on a new home in [location]. This will be paid on a monthly basis for 36 months.

5. To whatever extent the above items are taxable, [company] will "gross up" to provide you with these costs on a tax-free basis.

F. Directors reserve the right to increase salary.

G. Usual noncompetition and secrecy covenants.

H. Arbitration clause.

II.   Executive Medical Plan.

III. Company Car.

IV. Country Club in [location].

[Company]

[Signature of treasurer]

ACCEPTED:

[Employee signature]

[Date]

Michael and Mickey Make a Deal

Typically, the higher you rise in an organization, the more your compensation package comprises bonuses and stock options. The two contracts we've just examined contain provisions for incentive pay under existing company programs. At a certain point, you may find yourself negotiating complex deals that are not part of the organization plan but are tailor-made for you.

Chapter 9, on compensation, offers a guide through the salary/ bonus/stock thicket. To give you an idea of what is possible, here is the relevant section of the ten-year agreement signed in 1989 between the Walt Disney Company and Michael D. Eisner. The full text of the Eisner/Disney pact (Appendix 2) makes instructive reading.

Now let's look at the part of the contract relating to what Michael Eisner gets paid.

3. Salary

Executive shall receive an annual base salary of $750,000. The Board, in its discretion, may increase the base salary upon relevant circumstances.

> *Compensation is the centerpiece of most contracts. Eisner's contract is a good example of the prevalent tendency to make salary subordinate to other sources of remuneration. Although $750,000 is not exactly the tip of the iceberg, it does not begin to suggest what Disney actually pays its CEO. As we're about to see, this is only the beginning.*
>
> *Compensation specialists often advise companies to keep the salary numbers under six figures, because anything over a million dollars makes a particularly tempting target for activist stockholders. (There is no suggestion that this was a consideration with Disney.)*
>
> *More often than not, an executive employment agreement carries a clause entitled "Compensation," which covers all the components of the pay package. As we are about to see, the Eisner–Disney deal document covers bonuses, bonus payments, and stock options separately (and exhaustively).*

4. Bonus

(a) Executive shall, as provided in, and subject to, paragraph (e) below, receive an incentive bonus for Company's fiscal years ending September 30, 1989 and September 30, 1990, in an amount equal to 2% of that portion of the net income of Company for each such fiscal year in excess of the amount determined by multiplying stockholders' equity for each such fiscal year by .09. For purposes of all calculations of stockholders' equity under this Agreement, stockholders' equity for any fiscal year shall be the average of the four quarterly stockholders' equity figures reported by the Company for that fiscal year.

> *Bonuses should be computed in ways that are objective and understandable. At one time, bonuses were subjective; they were decided on the company's Mount Olympus by the top brass, who passed out the cash according to whim. Today's executive looks for understandable and accessible criteria.*

(b) Executive shall, as provided in, and subject to, paragraph (e) below, receive an incentive bonus for each fiscal year of

Company which shall end after September 30, 1990, and on or before the termination of this Agreement and for such additional periods as are provided in paragraph (e) below, in an amount equal to 2% of that portion of the net income of Company for each such fiscal year in excess of the amount determined by multiplying stockholders' equity for each such fiscal year by .11.

Incentive bonuses typically involve a percentage of money above a threshold. Executives negotiating agreements must scrutinize both elements. Many have been seduced by a high percentage, only to find, to their sorrow, that the barrier was impossibly high.

(c) In the event that there shall be a combination of the Company with another company or a capital restructuring of the Company, or any other occurrence similar to any of the foregoing, and as a result thereof the amount or value of the bonuses payable pursuant to either or both of the bonus formulas set forth in paragraphs (a) and (b) above would be, or could reasonably be expected to be, significantly affected, thereby appropriate(s) will, at the request of either party, be negotiated to establish a substitute formula or formulas, or if the parties cannot agree as to whether or not an occurrence which would give rise to the right of either party to request adjustment(s) pursuant to the foregoing has occurred, the parties shall submit such matter to arbitration by a qualified individual investment banker with at least ten years' experience in corporate finance with a major investment banking firm. Neither said firm nor said individual shall have had dealings with either party during the preceding five years. Upon failure to agree upon the selection of the arbitrator, each party shall submit a panel of five qualified arbitrators, the other party may strike three from the other's list, and the arbitrator shall be selected by lot from the remaining four names. The arbitrator shall have the authority only to determine (i) whether the matter is arbitrable under the conditions of this subparagraph (c) and (ii) the substitute formula or formulas that will yield an equitable and comparable result in accordance with the foregoing.

Well! Seems like a lot of huffing and puffing over the question of how disagreements get decided. The elaborate minuet leading to the selection of an arbitrator is reminiscent of the diplomatic arguments about the shape of the negotiation table before the talks to end the Vietnam War even got started.

However, more and more contracts establish machinery to resolve conflicts. Arbitration is an orderly and prompt alternative to a lawsuit, which takes years and costs vast amounts of money. Later in this book, we'll discuss conflict resolution provisions and suggest specific language you may want to consider.

Take another look at the first sentence of the foregoing 4(c) passage. Note the wording: "or any other occurrence similar to any of the foregoing . . . ."

No doubt there is good reason for adding these words. However, anyone who enters into a contract should question the inclusion of such all-encompassing language. It's broad and somewhat vague, and thus it can be used to advantage by one party or the other.

(d) Each incentive bonus shall be payable (i) 30 days following the date Company's audited consolidated statement of income for the applicable fiscal year becomes available or (ii) on the January 2 following the end of that fiscal year, whichever is later (the **"Bonus Payment Date"**).

(e) Executive shall be entitled to receive the bonus provided for in paragraph (a) or paragraph (b) above, as the case may be, for each fiscal year during which he is employed hereunder and, in addition, for the next twenty-four months after termination of his employment, except that said post-termination bonus coverage (i) shall only extend for twelve months after termination if Executive takes employment (other than as an independent producer) with another major entertainment company within twelve months of termination and (ii) shall not apply if Executive has been discharged for good cause. The bonus formula set forth in paragraph (a) above shall be applicable to any part or all of any period prior to September 30, 1990 in respect of which a post-termination bonus is payable, and the formula set forth in paragraph (b) above shall be applicable to any part or all of any period after September 30, 1990 in respect of which a post-termination bonus is payable.

5. Bonus Payments

(a) Bonuses for the fiscal years ending September 30, 1989 and September 30, 1990 shall be payable in cash.

(b) Bonuses for fiscal years ending after September 30, 1990 shall be payable in cash or a combination of cash and Restricted Stock (as hereinafter defined) as follows: that portion of the bonus for each such fiscal year which does not exceed the Cash Limit (as hereinafter defined) shall be paid in cash. To the extent that the amount of the bonus calculated in accordance with Section 4(b) hereof shall exceed the Cash Limit, the remaining unpaid portion of such bonus shall (except as otherwise provided in Section 12(a) (ii) hereof) be payable in Restricted Stock. For purposes of the foregoing, the term **"Cash Limit"** shall mean, with respect to any fiscal year of Company, the amount of the bonus which would be paid to Executive pursuant to Section 4(b) hereof if the net income of Company for such year were equal to the product of stockholders' equity for such year multiplied by .175.

Like many compensation packages these days, this bonus arrangement is driven not by such factors as net income, but by stock price.

(c) For purposes of this Agreement the term **"Restricted Stock"** shall mean shares of Company common stock which are issued to Executive pursuant to Company's 1987 Stock Incentive Plan (the **"Plan"**) in accordance with, and subject to, the following terms, restrictions, and conditions:

  (i) All shares of Restricted Stock shall be subject to forfeiture (i.e., all right, title, and interest of Executive in such shares shall cease and such shares shall be returned to Company with no compensation of any nature being paid therefore to Executive), if Executive's employment with Company is terminated for good cause (as defined in Section 10(a) (iii) hereof prior to the earlier of (x) the expiration of the three-year period commencing on the Bonus Payment Date upon which such shares were required to be delivered to Executive pursuant to Section 4(d) hereof (it being understood that if such shares are for any reason delivered to Executive on a date other than the Bonus Payment Date, such Bonus Payment Date shall nevertheless constitute the date on which such three-year period shall commence) or (y) September 30, 1998 (the **"Restricted Period"**). Any shares of Restricted Stock issued to Executive after September 30, 1998 shall be deemed to have been issued subject to restrictions which shall have expired, and, accordingly, will be free of all restrictions hereunder.

(ii) During the Restricted Period, Executive will have voting rights and will receive dividends and other distributions with respect to shares of Restricted Stock issued to him but will not be permitted to sell, pledge, assign, convey, transfer, or otherwise alienate or hypothecate such shares.

(iii) All restrictions on the shares of Restricted Stock issued to Executive hereunder will immediately lapse in the event of the death of Executive or disability of Executive resulting in a termination of employment by Company pursuant to Section 10(a) (ii) hereof.

(iv) All restrictions on the stock will lapse immediately in the event Company enters into an agreement pursuant to which either the Company or all or substantially all of its assets are to be sold or combined with another entity (regardless of whether or not such sale or combination is subject to the satisfaction of conditions precedent or subsequent) and, as a consequence thereof, the market for public trading of Company common stock would be, or could reasonably be expected to be, eliminated or materially impaired.

Still with us? Good. Yes, it's heavy going, and a lot of this may not apply directly to you (at least not yet). Nevertheless, the Eisner–Disney agreement contains the basic elements of the typical compensation deal. There are complications and elaborations that need not trouble you much; but it's good to be aware of them, and of their function. In the sentences just above, for example, we see a safeguard for the receiver of stock options, in case certain things happen to make the stock value plummet.

(v) Executive shall enter into an escrow agreement providing that the certificate(s) representing

Restricted Stock issued to him will remain in the physical custody of Company (or an escrow holder selected by Company) until all restrictions are removed or expire.

(vi) Each certificate representing Restricted Stock issued to Executive will bear a legend making appropriate reference to the terms, conditions, and restrictions imposed. Any attempt to dispose of Restricted Stock in contravention of such terms, conditions, and restrictions, irrespective of whether the certificate contains such a legend, shall be ineffective and any disposition purported to be effected thereby shall be void.

If you receive stock, read the fine print. You might, for example, be tempted to use it as collateral. If that's a no-no in the agreement, you're in trouble.

(vii) Any shares or other securities received by Executive as a stock dividend on, or as a result of stock splits, combinations, exchanges of shares, reorganizations, mergers, consolidations or otherwise with respect to shares of Restricted Stock shall have the same terms, conditions, and restrictions and bear the same legend as Restricted Stock.

(d) In determining the number of shares of Restricted Stock to be issued in respect of any bonus, the Restricted Stock will be valued on the basis of the average closing price of Company common stock during the period starting on the third business day and ending on the twelfth business day following the release for publication by Company of its annual summary statement of sales and earnings for the applicable fiscal year (as such release is defined by Rule 16-b-3 (e) (1) (ii) promulgated by the Securities and Exchange Commission pursuant to the Securities Exchange Act of 1934, as amended).

(e) Company shall in due course after the execution of this Agreement (and in no event later than the date Restricted Stock is first required to be issued to Executive hereunder) adopt rules pursuant to the Plan regarding restricted stock which shall reflect the foregoing provisions and such other provisions as are in the reasonable opinion of Company's counsel customary with respect to restricted stock. In the event that the Plan should for any reason become unavailable for the issuance of Restricted Stock, Company shall cause the shares of Restricted Stock required to be issued to Executive hereunder to be issued pursuant to another plan of Company on substantially the same terms and conditions as such Restricted Stock would have been issued under the plan.

6. Stock Options

(a) Executive shall be granted options pursuant to the Plan to purchase (i) 1,500,000 shares of Company common stock having an exercise price equal to the per-share fair market value (determined in accordance with the applicable provisions of the Plan) of Company common stock on January 11, 1989 (the **"A Options"**) and (ii) 500,000 shares of Company common stock having an exercise price equal to the per-share fair market value of the Company common stock having an exercise price equal to the per-share fair market value of the Company common stock on such date plus ten dollars ($10) (the **"B Options"**). Seventy-five percent of both the A Options and the B Options will vest in increments as nearly equal as possible on September 30 of each year starting September 30, 1990, and continuing through September 30, 1995. The remaining twenty-five percent of both the A Options and the B Options will vest in increments as nearly equal as possible on September 30th of each year starting on September 30, 1996 and continuing through September 30, 1998. Such options shall be subject to, and governed by, the terms and provisions of the Plan except to the extent of modifications of such options which are permitted by the Plan and which are expressly provided for herein.

> *Stock options are considered great motivators. They can act as golden handcuffs. And they spur recipients to their best efforts, because there's no use exercising the option unless the stock price goes up. A CEO like Michael Eisner can have a considerable effect on stock prices. Executives at more modest levels in the organization must do their utmost while hoping for favorable numbers.*

(b) Executive agrees to enter into a stock option agreement with Company containing the terms and provisions of such options together with such other terms and conditions as counsel for the Company may reasonably require to assure compliance with applicable state or federal law and stock exchange requirements in connection with the issuance of Company stock upon exercise of options to be granted as provided herein, or as may be required to comply with the Plan.

(c) If Company has not already done so, Company shall register Executive's shares pursuant to the appropriate form of registration statement under the Securities Act of 1933 and shall maintain such registration statement's effectiveness at all required times.

(d) Company shall, to the extent permitted by law, make loans to Executive in reasonable amounts on reasonable terms and conditions during his employment by Company to facilitate the exercise of the options granted to him as described above.

The company loan is the collateral perk to the stock option. We'll discuss later in the book the implications of making the company your creditor, and the question of what happens if you leave the company before the loan is fully repaid.

The Eisner–Disney compensation sections show how much ground an employment agreement can cover. Now let's resume our overview of different kinds of contracts. There is a much simpler (though equally binding) format.

Letter of Agreement

The letter of agreement is, in effect, a stripped-down contract. It may be couched in legal language, or it may be more informal. Usually, the biggest differences are:

- Length—the letter of agreement is shorter.

- Format—the letter of agreement is, as the name suggests, framed as a letter.

- Coverage—the letter of agreement may not go into extensive detail about, say, the more complex aspects of bonus or option plans. These are covered in separate documents.

In addition, the letter of agreement, which almost always incorporates issues that have already been discussed, may require the formal approval of the board of directors.

Here is a typical letter of agreement (minus the identifying names).

(Date)

Mr. _____

_____

_____

Dear _____

In view of the fact that you have assumed the responsibility of _____ at _____, Inc., I am pleased to confirm your employment agreement as follows:

Your employment with _____ is to continue for a period of _____ years commencing _____ and ending _____, during which time you are to serve as _____ of _____. You are to be paid, as of _____, $ _____ per year in equal monthly installments. $ _____ of such annual compensation will be includable in the calculation of your pension benefits under the _____ retirement plan.

However:

(a) If you are removed from the position of _____ of _____ but remain as an employee of _____, or an affiliated company of _____, your salary will continue at the rate of $ _____ per year as provided above.

(b) If:

(1) You are discharged from employment for any reason except malfeasance or other willful misconduct, or

(2) are unable to work by reason of disability, or

(3) after discussion and review of the matter with senior management of the company you resign as an employee because of significant changes in management policy unacceptable to you or because of significant changes in management personnel not acceptable to you, you will be paid at the rate of $ (half the designated annual salary) commencing with date of such discharge, instead of $ _____ per annum.

If you die during the term of the agreement your estate will be paid at the rate of $ (half the designated annual salary) per annum commencing with date of death for the balance of the term of the agreement. The management will recommend to the Committee on Stock Options and Stock Bonuses and the Board of Directors of _____while you are _____ that you are awarded pursuant to the _____ Key Employee Stock Bonus Plan in each of the years _____, _____, and _____, _____ shares of stock of _____, but if such award is not made in full or in part in any of those years while you are _____, in lieu of such award you will receive payments at the end of each of the years _____, _____, and _____ in an amount equal to the market value of the shares not awarded (based on their market value averaged for the month of December of each year) (discounted at 12% per annum from the normal vesting date had the shares been awarded on December 1 of each year). Additionally, if you are discharged from employment or resign from employment for any of the reasons set forth above, you will also receive a payment in an amount equal to the market value (discounted at 12% per annum from normal vesting date) on date of discharge of the unvested shares awarded to you pursuant to the _____ Key Employee Stock Bonus Plan which would have vested had you remained as an employee on the fifth anniversary of the last award.

In addition to the salary, stock options, and stock bonuses referred to above, the Board of Directors may award to you such incentive compensation as it deems appropriate.

In the event that you are discharged or resign from employment, in consideration of the payments referred to above, you may not until (day following the expiration date of the agreement) engage in any other employment or business activity competitive with the business of _____ or its present subsidiaries.

You agree that at such time as you leave the employment of _____ either during or subsequent to the term of this agreement you will maintain the confidentiality of all information regarding the company which you have, or will have received as an employee, officer, or director, and that you will not make any disclosure thereof to anyone else except as to matters which have been the subject of public announcement or disclosure or that are generally known in the trade or except as required by law.

This agreement is subject to the approval of the Committee on Compensation and Employee Benefits and the Board of Directors of _____.

Kindly sign and return a copy of this agreement in confirmation of the foregoing.

Very Truly Yours

_____
(CEO)

CONFIRMED

_____

How a Description of the Deal Becomes a Letter of Agreement

We'll be examining negotiating tactics by which you can wind up with what amounts to a letter of agreement—even though that was not the ostensible purpose of the process. As we'll see, the road to a letter of agreement often leads through the tangle of a complicated compensation deal. The compensation arrangement *must* be put down on paper. Once this is done, a few additions turn the document into the equivalent of a full-scale contract.

The following letter of agreement is built around a plan that keys the executive's bonus compensation to the earnings of TV stations. The agreement contains some characteristics typical of deals involving managers who run strategic business units or other types of free-standing divisions within the framework of a larger corporation.

LETTER OF AGREEMENT

AGREEMENT made as of [date] between [company] and [name] residing at [address].

WHEREAS, the Company is desirous of assuring itself of the services of Employee as [job description], for the period and on the terms and conditions hereinafter set forth.

NOW, THEREFORE, in consideration of the premises and their several and mutual covenants herein contained, the parties hereto do hereby agree as follows:

1. The Company shall cause its wholly owned subsidiary [TV station] to employ [name], and [name] agrees to serve [TV station] for a period commencing [date] and ending [date three years in the future] at an annual base salary of [$ _____] per year, payable in equal installments on the 7th and 22nd of each month, and incentive compensation, payable annually as hereinafter provided, equal to 1½% of the net operating income (before federal income tax) in excess of $5,000,000 of [station] for each full fiscal year of the Company during the term hereof, and prorated for any partial fiscal year of the Company during the term hereof, computed in accordance with generally accepted accounting principles and as provided herein. The amount of [station]'s portion of such operating income as calculated for and included in the [company] Annual Report to Shareholders shall be binding and conclusive on the parties hereto: *provided, however*, that [station] shall be charged with interest income and

expense for funds borrowed by and allocable to it, and *provided further* that there shall not be any charge against [station] for Corporate Office expenses, whether or not the Company commences allocating such expenses to [station] for reporting in its Annual Report.

[Employee name] shall receive hereunder as additional incentive compensation, payable annually as hereinafter provided, an amount equal to 1% of the net operating income (before federal income tax) in excess of $1,500,000 of the Company's wholly owned subsidiary [here the letter names a second TV station], for each fiscal year of the Company during the term hereof, and prorated for any partial fiscal year of the Company during the term hereof, such income to be computed in accordance with the provisions hereof applicable to [first station]. Such additional incentive compensation from [station] shall have no effect upon the base salary to be paid to [name] hereunder.

Payment to [name] of amounts earned hereunder as incentive compensation shall be payable on the first working day of January [199–, 199–, and 199–], based upon the net operating income of [station 1] and/or [station 2] for the most recently ended fiscal year of the Company prior to such date. Such salary and compensation shall be in addition to participation in any insurance, bonus, pension, stock option, stock purchase, profit sharing, or other benefit plans of the Company in which [name] may be eligible to participate under the Company's policy with respect to such plans.

The Company, [station 1], and [station 2] shall, by action of their respective board of directors, agree to perform all provisions hereof, on their part to be performed, during the period of this Agreement.

2. [Employee's name] shall exercise all of the executive and administrative responsibilities of President of the Television Broadcasting Division of the Company, subject to its By-Laws and the supervision of the Board of Directors of the Company. [Name] shall devote all of [his/her] time during ordinary business hours to the interest and business of the Company faithfully, diligently, and to the best of [his/her] ability. In connection with

such employment [name] shall (without additional compensation therefore) (i) perform such executive services and duties as may be required of [him/her] during ordinary business hours for any other broadcasting facility now or hereafter owned by the Company and (ii) serve as a director and officer of the Company and any of its subsidiaries if elected by the Board of Directors or stockholders of the Company or any such subsidiary.

3. [Name] shall be entitled to annual vacation time with full pay in accordance with the Company's vacation policies.

4. In the event that [name] is wholly or partially "disabled" (as that term is hereinafter defined) for a period of six consecutive months, the Company shall have the right to terminate this Agreement by written notice thereof to [name]. During such six-month period, the Company shall pay to [name] the base salary payable hereunder, and [name] shall be entitled to the incentive compensation applicable to such six-month period, payable in accordance with Paragraph 1 hereof. In addition, [name], [his/her] executors, heirs, or assigns shall be entitled to the incentive compensation applicable to the balance of the fiscal year of the Company (ending during the term of this Agreement), if any, in which [name] becomes disabled. "Disabled" as used herein shall mean a state of physical or mental incapacity or inability which prevents [name] from rendering fully the services required hereunder.

5. [TV station 1] shall reimburse [name] for all reasonable items of traveling, entertainment, and miscellaneous out-of-pocket expenses incurred on behalf of [both TV stations], payment to be made against vouchers signed by [name] for such expenditures.

6. This Agreement shall inure to the benefit of, and shall be binding upon, the successors and assigns of the Company. None of its provisions may be waived, changed, modified, extended, or discharged except in writing signed by the parties against whom the enforcement of any waiver, change, modification, extension, or discharge is sought.

7. This Agreement shall be governed by the laws of [state].

IN WITNESS WHEREOF, the parties hereto have executed this Agreement as of the date and year first above written.

[COMPANY]

By

_____

Executive Vice President

By

[Employee]

Agreements for Professionals

What if you join a professional organization—a firm of architects, an advertising agency, a consulting group—as a partner or member of the firm? You have an assigned role, but you don't receive a specified salary. Instead, you share the earnings of the firm.

Here is a letter of agreement used by a consulting firm.

(Date)

Mr. _____

_____

_____

Dear _____:

The mission of [company name] is to provide meaningful and lasting assistance to clients in the areas of [areas of the firm's expertise]. To further that mission, _____ is pleased to offer you, effective immediately, the position of Vice President with responsibility for the _____ area.

SCOPE OF RESPONSIBILITIES

It is anticipated that the _____ area will include:

[Here the letter gives a brief outline of the job.]

As head of the _____ area you will be instrumental in developing and providing a valuable service to _____ clients.

COMPENSATION

The compensation program at _____ has been established to reward superior performance while recognizing the limits of _____'s resources. It is designed to encourage the growth of each practice area and maximize the synergy among the areas. There are three components to _____'s compensation program. These are described below.

1. You will receive twenty percent (20%) of net project revenue for professional fees actually collected by _____ for each project which you bring into _____, whether in _____ or any other practice area, as a finder's fee. If a new contract is the result of joint effort with other _____ employees, this fee will be shared appropriately. Net project revenue is defined as project revenue less direct and indirect expenses not otherwise billed.

2. You will receive fifty percent (50%) of your billing rate, to the extent actually collected by _____, for actual project work performed, up to fifty percent (50%) of net project revenue. If part of a project team, compensation will be determined by a formula based on actual hours worked and comparative billing rates. During [year] your daily billing rate is $ _____. It is our practice whenever possible to bill for all direct costs and/or to "pass through" to all clients an additional ten percent (10%) for indirect costs.

3. At [company], employees are eligible to receive a discretionary bonus of up to twenty percent (20%) of their [year] earnings, payable in early [following year]. This bonus plan is funded by fifteen percent (15%) of all [year] net project revenues which will be reserved in a discretionary bonus pool. Bonus allocation will be approved by [company] shareholders.

The remaining fifteen percent (15%) of all net revenue is retained by [company] to cover any additional overhead, provide a return on investment, and fund future growth.

Compensation from finder's fees, advances from clients, interim payments, and final project fees will be distributed, as described above, on the next payday following receipt from client companies.

PROPRIETARY PROPERTY

Any inventions, improvements, work product, or ideas made or conceived by you in connection with or during the performance of work for _____ or its clients shall be the property of _____ or its clients, as the case may be, but shall not be your property, and you will cooperate, at no charge to _____ or its clients, to vest title to such proprietary property in _____ or its clients.

CONFIDENTIAL INFORMATION

No information of a confidential nature relating to, or information not publicly known about _____, its business ventures, or its clients may be used or disclosed during or after employment with _____ without the written consent of _____.

CONFLICTS OF INTEREST

During your employment, you or members of your immediate family may not engage in activities or have personal or financial interests which impair, or appear to impair, independence or judgment or otherwise conflict with your responsibilities at _____.

NONCOMPETITION

For a period of twelve (12) months after the termination of your employment, you will not, directly or indirectly, receive any fee or render any services for or in connection with any entity that was a client of _____ during the twelve (12)-month period preceding the termination of your employment, except for clients that are acquired by _____ as a sole and direct result of your contacts and business development activities.

BENEFITS

In recognition of your ability to obtain benefits elsewhere, you have chosen to decline benefits through _____ .

TERM OF AGREEMENT

This letter, once signed by both parties, will constitute the Employment Agreement. The conditions of this Agreement will last for a period of one year, but may be reopened after the initial six months by either party, or sooner by mutual consent. Employment with _____ can be terminated by either party, with or without cause, upon one month's notice.

Sincerely,

[Signed by Chairman and President of firm]

ACKNOWLEDGMENT

I acknowledge that I have read the Agreement and that in consideration of my employment, any wages paid me and other good and valuable consideration, I do hereby agree to abide by the terms of this Agreement.

I understand that if I have any questions concerning my obligations under this Agreement, I should consult with [company].

[Signature of Employee]

[Date]

A Contract Is a Contract Is a Contract

An employment agreement can be short or long, simple or elaborate. It may even (as we'll see) be a collection of documents that were not originally intended to constitute a contract.

With an employment agreement, the deal between you and the employer is set forth clearly and enforceably.

Now let's examine how to get a contract, and what should be in it.

3

Initiating the Request for a Contract

When do you ask for a contract? The most logical time is at the beginning of your association with a potential new employer.

At that point, you're negotiating with a company that is likely to make you an offer; or, the offer has already been made, and now you're discussing the shape of the deal that will be required to bring you on board. You want a *written* contract. You don't know how the employer feels about written employment agreements, so the best course is to assume that:

1. Few, if any, contracts have been given to managers.

2. The idea of giving one to you will meet resistance.

Your first considerations are:

- When to make your request.
- How to make your request.
- How to respond to the employer's likely first question: "Why?"

Why indeed? Think through your reasons for wanting a written agreement *before* the session at which the subject is likely to come up.

Your principal reason: The arrangement should be spelled out on paper so there can be no ambiguity about any of its aspects. That clarity benefits both parties. You're not impugning anyone's integrity, nor are you trying to pull a fast one. The contract is simply a document that records the agreement in an orderly way.

View it like a purchase order. Buyer and seller trust each other implicitly, but they still want written records of the transaction.

When should you bring up the subject of an employment agreement? It should not be the first request you make. To broach the topic of a written pact within five minutes of shaking hands places far too much emphasis on the *fact* of the contract. Your mission at this stage is to determine whether you want to work for the company. If you conclude that you'd like the job, you set out to establish a good relationship that gives you what you want in money, perks, and power.

The written contract is not an end in itself. It is a very important *means* to an end—or actually, to several ends. It will ensure that you receive what you're entitled to, and it will protect you if things go wrong.

It's probably best to wait until the bargaining is well along before saying you want an agreement in writing. Work out the general guidelines on compensation, authority, job title, and reporting relationship. Then talk contract when it's appropriate. (However, as this book points out, an increasing number of employers are initiating the topic of a contract without waiting to be asked. These employers are likely to be asking for a very narrow agreement that features noncompete and nondisclosure agreements. Fine; you're willing to talk about the kind of pact that protects the employer; but you also want to broaden the discussion, to build a comprehensive agreement covering all salient aspects of the relationship.)

How do you bring up the subject of a contract? It's best not to introduce your desire for a written agreement as if it were of the same importance as your requests in the areas of compensation, authority, and standing. The following, for example, might *not* be an appropriate way to handle it:

> I want a total package amounting to $500,000 per year, with about half in base salary and half in bonuses and stock. My stock option program should be no less than those enjoyed by the other top five officers of the company.
>
> Bonuses would be keyed to the performance of my unit. My title would be President of the Consumer Products Division,

reporting directly to you as CEO. I would want a completely free hand in hiring and firing. *And I want all this in writing, in an employment contract.*

The last sentence may shake up the employer considerably. It changes the whole tenor of the negotiation. Whatever your meaning, the employer may feel that you're implying, "I don't trust you," and "I'm more interested in the job itself than in what I can contribute to the company."

Let's pause at this point and consider these implications. If your wish for a contract is indeed driven by mistrust, or self-interest, or a combination of the two, then you have to ask yourself a more introspective question.

Do I really want this job? A management position should mean more than a favorable deal that is couched in ironclad terms. Pervasive mistrust of the employer is an unhealthy way to begin the relationship. And tactics that engender mistrust by the employer are equally unhealthy.

In the real world, however, practical considerations sometimes make it necessary for a person to go to work for an employer whose integrity—or, at least, whose reputation—is less than that of, say, George Washington. Sometimes the money is so good that you can't turn it down. Sometimes the visibility of the position is a great career-enhancer. Sometimes you just really need the job. In these situations, it is extra-important to negotiate for a contract.

But you can't say that to the employer, so how do you raise the subject?

The "Of Course" Ploy

One approach is the "Of Course" method. This can work especially well if:

- You're pretty sure that the employer has made written agreements with some people.
- You're able to say you had a written agreement (of some sort) on your previous job.
- Contracts are reasonably common in the industry.

Here's how it works. You're discussing some aspect—not necessarily a major one—of the relationship, and you say, "That's no problem. I suggest the agreement should read this way: 'If the Executive's salary is increased during the term of the agreement, the increased amount shall be considered the base salary for other parts of the agreement.'"

You've introduced the idea of a contract without making a big deal of it. The employer can stop and say, "What agreement?" (If you don't get this reaction, you simply proceed on the basis that a written contract will be the outcome.) You respond that you're assuming that there will be a written contract.

And that's *all* you say at this point. You don't explain why that is your assumption. You don't begin to make your arguments for a contract. You don't respond as if the employer had demonstrated any opposition to the idea at all.

The employer may not dispute you in any way. That doesn't mean he or she buys the idea. It may only mean that the issue is not important enough to go into at that time. Whatever the reason for the employer's lack of response, your approach is to proceed with the discussion as if the written employment agreement is a foregone conclusion.

However, the employer may either question the notion of a contract, or object to it. The question can be worded in various ways. Whatever the wording, the real meaning (the "metamessage") is: "*Why* do you want a written contract?"

Make your answer *general*, not *particular*. There is nothing about *this* situation, *this* company, or *this* person that impels you to want to get the agreement in writing. In general, you see a contract as a logical—indeed, an inevitable—way of concluding an agreement: "Because it's useful in clarifying points like the ones we've just been discussing. When you put things in written form, you sometimes catch contradictions and omissions you've overlooked. As we all know, human memory is fallible. You find it useful to keep a written record of *all* the important business arrangements you make, I'm sure."

Don't act as if you're expecting an argument. Your posture is that no reasonable person could contradict what you've just said. Continue to the next point, assuming that the matter of a written "record" is settled. The employer's question about why you want one does not imply that there is any problem in granting one. True, many employers will, at this point, have distinct objections to the concept. Don't make it easy for those objections to be voiced.

The employer may persist: "Oh, there's no need for a written contract. We always work on a handshake basis."

You agree heartily: "Of course. When we shake hands on the deal, I am committed and I know you are too. The part about putting it down in writing has nothing to do with commitment or trust. That's there already. The written agreement is a record, for understanding of the details; there's something to refer to if any questions ever come up in the future. It's procedural—a way of getting the nuts and bolts out of the way so we can concentrate on the important things."

If the employer continues to resist, you are surprised: "Do you have some objection to putting what we've talked about into writing?"

This puts the ball in the other court. Making the employer explain what's *wrong* with a written contract is better than having to explain why you want one.

Very few people are going to say something like, "Because we don't want to be fenced in by a written agreement." The response is likely to be more general, citing precedent or policy or both: "We never have written contracts with executives. Never found that we needed them. We would not want to change our policy on that now."

One way to handle this kind of objection is by *intensifying* it. You restate the objection in a way that makes it *stronger* than the employer's words: "You mean you never put any kind of arrangement into writing? Option plans, pensions—nothing?" Don't overdo your reaction. You are not "Shocked! Shocked!" like the French police officer played by Claude Rains in *Casablanca*. You're surprised, that's all.

Because it would be ridiculous to maintain that the company never puts any parts of employment arrangements in writing, the employer is likely to say something like, "Oh well, yes, we prepare written records and memos covering matters like options, and we keep them on file. What we don't do is make employment contracts with executives. We have a contract with our unionized employees, not with members of management."

This is the prevailing position in many companies. Management views an employment contract as something negotiated with people whom human resource jargon calls the "nonexempt" ranks, the wage-and-hour workers. Because the word "contract" is linked to the collective

bargaining process, the corporate view is that there is something unseemly about a manager's asking for one.

You can't change feelings by logical argument, but you can bypass
feelings as an obstacle unless they are very strong. Just say, "Well, of
course this is nothing like the rank-and-file contract. It's just a memo-
randum, or letter of agreement, that puts our arrangement into writing.
I know you have no objection to that."

Keep pressing for the written agreement. At the same time, maintain your posture that you know the employer has no objection to it,
and that references to precedent and policy are slight pro forma matters. Unless the employer has major reasons for opposition, he or she
may wind up this part of the discussion by saying, "I see no reason not
to cover a few of these points in writing if you wish. But I wouldn't
think we need anything as elaborate as a formal contract."

That's all the assent you need. Once the employer agrees that
"something in writing" is OK, you can proceed to work out the elements of your relationship with the company, with reasonable assurance
that you'll wind up with some written document. You don't have to call
it a contract, and the employer doesn't have to acknowledge that it's a
contract.

Once the negotiation focuses on questions of "formality" or "elab-
orateness," you've won your point. You don't care how formal the document is; you just want it to be accurate and complete. The employer's
attorney will put in plenty of formal jargon anyway.

Handling More Stubborn Opposition

Suppose the employer responds with greater emotional or situational
opposition: "Why do you insist on a contract? Don't you trust us?"

Your posture is total surprise: "That never crossed my mind. I'm
sure if we didn't have full trust in each other we wouldn't be sitting
here. But of course everybody uses written agreements all the time—
sales, suppliers, advertising agencies, all kinds of relationships. Business
runs on them. I want to come to a mutual arrangement that pleases both
of us, get it down on paper so we can both see there's no misunderstanding, then put it away in a drawer and forget about it. Is that OK
with you?"

If the employer is adamant, insisting that there will be no written contract, and will not be budged from that position, you must decide what course you should take.

One course would be to turn down the job unless you do indeed get a contract. That would be very extreme (but an employer's ironclad refusal to put things in writing is pretty extreme too). Consider the relationship in the light of what this impasse tells you about the employer and about your future if you join the firm.

Probably you will want to continue to work out an agreement, even if the employer will not put the terms in writing. The firm's refusal may not mean as much as the employer thinks it does. (See Chapter 6, on the "*De Facto* Contract.") The various elements of your arrangement will, one way or another, find their way into writing. You don't have to call them a contract, but, according to recent court decisions and practice, that is what they are. In Chapter 6, you'll find recommendations on how to see that all the salient aspects of your job are put in writing; how to keep them up to date; and how to build and maintain a file that constitutes your *virtual* or *de facto* contract. (When you are dealing with employers who go ballistic at the idea, you might even call it a "Stealth Contract.")

Don't drop the idea of a written agreement altogether at this point in your negotiation. If you do, it will look as if you cave in quickly or you were not serious about a written agreement in the first place. More importantly, you may be able to use the employer's unwillingness to conclude a formal contract—and your reluctant acceptance of that unwillingness—as a subtle way of winning on other points involving perks, bonuses, or whatever.

Ask again about the reasons for the employer's unwillingness. If the explanation is nonresponsive—a repeated lame story about tradition, for example—try to figure out the real reason.

Many companies feel that giving one individual a contract will open the floodgates to a multitude of similar demands. If the employer views this possibility as a very bad thing, you might do what one senior executive did. He negotiated an agreement, shook hands on the deal, and then made a little pitch: "I'm not reopening the subject of a contract for me. We've settled that. But I'd like you to know that in due course I am going to ask for a review of the company's no-contract policy in general. We have important goals to reach. I intend to recruit the best talent available to achieve those goals. To get that talent, I will sometimes be talking to people who have been working abroad, where contracts are much more usual. So when the time comes, I am going to ask for a review of the policy. I owe it to this corporation to do that."

He got the policy modified after a year or so—and he got a contract for himself.

"Nobody in Our Industry Does It"

In this chapter, we are discussing how to handle employer resistance to the *idea* of a contract. (Later, we will talk about negotiating the *provisions* of the contract.)

So far, we've based our observations and recommendations on the proposition that, although the particular employer resists the idea, contracts are not unheard-of in the industry.

The concept of a written employment agreement for managers and professionals has now made its way into just about all areas of business. But there are still pockets where your request for a contract is a truly pioneering venture. If this is the case, your approach will be somewhat different.

Consider introducing the subject after you have made a substantial concession—on, say, an up-front bonus, a reporting relationship, or a title. (Perhaps you did not really expect to win on that point; like lots of skilled negotiators, you have used it as a gambit.)

Let's say you insist that you would be leaving a secure arrangement in moving to this new job. You'd like the job, but in fairness to your family you want the risk to be reduced by an extremely handsome severance deal. You bargain hard for it. The answer remains "No." Finally, you concede: "All right, then; I can see that you are not willing to move on this, that it means a lot to you. It means a lot to me, too. But there are so many other reasons that I'd like to join you, I am willing to back off. You'll agree to six months' base salary? OK. You're willing to put that in writing, of course . . . ."

Inasmuch as the employer is hardly likely to refuse to put in writing what was just agreed to, build on that foundation. Make the next "put-it-in-writing" point one that favors the employer: "You'll want to add something to the effect that the agreed-on severance will not be paid if I'm caught embezzling, or something like that."

You don't have to continue to refer to a written contract as you negotiate each point. Finish up the bargaining; then say, "How shall we work this? Shall I draw up something and give it to you? Or do you want to have Legal do it?"

For this employer, you will want to prepare an answer to the "Why?" question that is crisp and convincing, and does not arouse suspicion: "You hear and read more about the use of contracts for managers these days. I think it's a good idea. Practically every other relationship is formalized on paper. Why not a relationship important as this one? The provisions of our contract give us a set of reference points in case there is ever any question. No misunderstandings, no ambiguities—and no hidden resentments. I'm enthusiastic about the concept, and I intend to make use of contracts in recruiting the kind of people we need in the part of the operation I'll be running."

When contracts are a rarity in the industry, you can make a point that is both compelling and important: "Up till now, employment agreements have not been used to any extent in this industry. Inevitably, that's changing. But we have a chance to get the jump on our competitors in the race for talent. When our competitors go after top people who are used to written agreements, they will lose them if they keep their heads stuck in the sand. We can lead the way—and really build a strong organization for the future."

Take it for granted that—whatever past practice has been in the industry—this particular employer is open-minded and flexible. If the employer continues to resist, ask for a more detailed explanation: "It can't just be because nobody else in the industry does it. You didn't build this company to its present standing by following what others do." Emphasize the regularity, precision, and peace of mind offered by a contract, without in any way implying a lack of personal trust in the relationship.

Asking for a Contract from Your Present Employer

When you raise the idea of a contract with your present employer, be ready for the "Are you nuts?" stare and the "Don't you trust me?" and "Why rock the boat?" responses.

Contracts for managers are still relatively new in many corporate precincts where the notion arouses an automatically negative reaction. Resistance is couched in objections that are used over and over. The first class of objection centers on the very idea of putting it in writing: "We have never used contracts here!"

There are at least two types of tactics you can use. One is to broaden the definition of "contract": "That may be true in the strict sense of the word. But we're not talking here about the kinds of contracts they give movie stars or athletes, but just about written agreements covering certain areas, like compensation. You have to use written records to cover the ins and outs of stock options, for example." Work along the lines that putting an agreement in writing is nothing new, that well-run companies use it everywhere.

A second approach is what might be called "safety in numbers." Help the employer get over the idea that this is a radically novel departure from the norm. You can cite evidence from this book, for example, the 1995 Pearl Meyer survey showing that not only are overwhelming numbers of top executives getting written agreements, but, in 1995, the rate of middle managers with pacts reached 20 to 25 percent, up from 5 percent just five years before.

At this stage, it's best to avoid the touchy and controversial topic of golden parachutes; OK for the top brass, déclassé for everyone else. If you are not among the very senior officers, the employer may feel that you are being pushy in demanding the same kind of protection given to the upper crust. As we point out elsewhere, more and more companies are feeling compelled to extend the golden parachute concept down through the organization, because stockholders and regulatory agencies have cast a cold eye on reserving this protection to a privileged few. But this is not a club you ought to select from your bag at this point.

Maybe the subject of golden parachutes can't be avoided. The employer may maintain that you will receive, as a matter of course, documentary records of your stock options. But it is out of the question for you to expect a contract that ensures you a certain level of severance pay, or that calls for you to receive special perks, or that gives you protection in case of a change in corporate control. That arrangement is reserved to high-level people because of their vulnerability in takeovers.

You will do best to avoid discussing the ethics of issuing golden parachutes only to the top brass. You might state your case this way:

And those [perks/parachutes] are perfectly justified. Senior executives need to protect themselves against situations that can't be foreseen—situations in which they can get hurt because of circumstances that have nothing to do with their performance. I'm happy that you accept that principle. It's fair and it makes sense. All I'm looking for is an orderly agreement, on paper, that offers the same kind of protection at a different level. There is no foreseeable reason why this agreement would ever have to be taken out of the drawer and looked at again. And since you agree with the idea that things can happen that penalize managers unjustly, then surely there's no objection to putting these thoughts in writing.

Your approach is to move the discussion past the resistance to the *idea* of a contract for a manager and onto the specific provisions of the contract. You want to do this as quickly as possible and with minimal fuss. Once the employer is focused on issues, the general objection to the contract itself is less likely to recur.

You can help to move the negotiation to the next plateau by using a tactic like this:

We seem to agree that the general idea of written agreements for executives is not taboo. So I'm wondering if there is some particular area that you're reluctant to put in writing. For instance, you're not bothered by the idea of a severance paragraph, are you? It seems more businesslike to have this on paper, doesn't it?

If the employer says, "We have no objection to putting this in writing, but the terms you're asking for are out of the question," then you can move on to discussion of the issues.

Making a Contract with a Foreign Employer

Business knows no boundaries today. The company you work for—or the firm that wants to hire you—may be based in Tokyo, Stuttgart, or Bahrain. The American firm you've been with for years may tomorrow become the subsidiary of an organization based in Geneva or London.

At the beginning of the 1980s, more than 1,000 firms operating primarily within the borders of the United States were under the controlling interest of foreign owners. These firms employed more than

1.6 million people. In addition, foreign companies maintained more than 30,000 establishments in the United States. The foreign presence in the United States doubled in a three-year period.

Then the trend really got rolling. In 1985, overseas investors acquired more than 200 American companies. In 1986, 260 American corporations were taken over by foreign interests. By 1987, foreigners owned more than $1.3 trillion of American assets. Companies that were staples of American enterprise came under foreign ownership: Carnation, Celanese, Doubleday, and Goldman, Sachs. Landmarks, from Pebble Beach to Rockefeller Center, were taken over by the Japanese. *U.S. News and World Report* (March 30, 1987) carried an article by Cindy Skrzycki titled "America on the Auction Block." The piece began, "The 'For Sale' sign is up across the United States, and foreign investors have been on a shopping spree from coast to coast. Germans, British, Australians, Japanese, Dutch, Swiss and French, to name just a few, have been loading up on everything from American chemical plants to government securities to factories that produce vinegar."

In the years since, the tide of foreign acquisition has continued to roll. Foreign corporations, including Japanese entities, have endured some high-profile flops—for example, Sony's misadventures in the entertainment arena. However, the reality for executives is that the chances of working for a foreign-owned company increase every day.

People who grow up within a certain culture take for granted a great many things that seem outlandish to people from other parts of the world—business practices as well as social customs. When Americans go to work for foreign firms, they may make certain assumptions based on their American experience and the traditions within which they were raised. At the same time, their employers are making assumptions drawn from *their* backgrounds. These conflicting assumptions can be a prescription for disaster.

For this reason, it is especially important to have an agreement with a foreign employer that covers all salient aspects of the job. The contract should spell out:

- Job title and scope of the job.
- Precise time frames and goals for measuring performance.
- Amounts of all compensation, expressed (preferably) in dollars and with the method of payment spelled out.

- Exact severance arrangements.

- Optimum help if the job is discontinued, including particularly a provision for outplacement services.

- Protection in case of a change in control.

- Lines of authority.

- Location of principal place of work.

- Method for conflict resolution, including designation of the country whose laws will control.

- All other contingency arrangements.

If you take a job that requires you to spend substantial amounts of time abroad, you may want an agreement that provides for bringing a spouse or companion along for a specified amount of time per year, with arrangements for living accommodations. If children will be living at least part of the time in a foreign country, you may want to make provisions for schooling and travel expenses to and from the United States.

All of these issues, and others, get worked out with foreign companies. Trouble arises when a company's understanding about the deal is different from yours. Misunderstandings can arise from barriers of language and culture. Thus, it is exceedingly important to have a workable contract.

4

When the Employer Suggests a Contract

Self-protection is the fundamental reason why employers ask employees to sign contracts. The company wants to be protected against the employee's revealing confidential information or becoming a competitor. The company also wants to be protected against "corporate anorexia," the talent-starvation that can be a side effect of downsizing and intensive cost-cutting.

Executives who are in the process of being hired may be surprised when the idea of a written contract is introduced. Typically, the candidate has had several interviews at which key questions of money and status have been worked out. The process seems to be all over except for the handshake. Then comes the "mere formality." The contract may be offered almost as an afterthought, a custom so meaningless that the employer nearly forgot to mention it.

If you're really sold on the job, your first instinct may be to grab a pen and sign. A swift second thought should caution you that you had better read the document *very* carefully.

But that can be awkward. You're sitting in the employer's office. The two of you have practically had a love feast. You really feel that you're about to join an organization that not only pays well and offers a fine opportunity, but gives you the chance to work with a great bunch of people. You might feel that even to imply you want to scrutinize the document before signing it might send a signal that you really don't trust your new friends.

Resist that feeling. If your new friends really are your friends, they will understand your feelings. Indeed, they will want you to examine the document. The boss ought to say, "You'll want to look this over thoroughly before signing it. Why don't you take it with you. Meanwhile, we can clear up all the other details . . . ."

The new employer might not say that, however. He or she might just sit there—or hand you a pen. You can hastily glance at the agreement and dash off a signature. Or you can settle yourself carefully in your chair and go over the contract carefully, clause by clause, even if the boss begins to indicate impatience through tapping fingers or some other form of body language. You may ask questions, even request changes, right there on the spot.

You *may* do that, but it's pretty awkward. The best thing is to get the hell out of there, give yourself a chance to read the document at leisure, and get advice—including legal advice—if you have the slightest question.

Here's a graceful way to do that. *Assume* the final interview is over and you've been hired. Assume also that *of course* the employer would never expect you to sign a contract before reading it carefully; after all, you'll be expected to be careful in reading what you sign on the job.

Take it for granted that you will take the contract with you now. Say something like, "Thank you. I'm delighted that we're all set. I know I'm joining a great company. I look forward to getting started. How about three weeks from Monday, September twenty-fourth? That will give me time to wrap up everything with my present company. There are a couple of important matters pending, but by really pushing I can settle everything by then. Meanwhile, of course, I'll look this over and bring it in with me on the twenty-fourth. Or would you prefer that I mail it or drop it off before then? Whatever's most convenient."

If there is no problem about the contract, the employer is likely to agree—having no particular reason not to. If the employer insists that you sign right away, ask yourself, "Why?" And ask the employer, too: "I'm always careful about signing off on anything. You'll find I work that way. That's what I'd like to do with this. That's OK, isn't it? What would be the reason to get it signed right away?"

Listen carefully to any reasons for signing the contract in a hurry. Does the employer seem to be trying to hustle you along so that you don't have time to reflect on the contents of the agreement? Ask yourself why your would-be bosses are so anxious to have you sign a contract that they spring it on you when you're least likely to take the time to consider it.

If there's too much of a rush, slow the process down. One way to do this is by using the approach that many *employers* use: "A contract? Somewhat unusual, isn't it? I haven't heard much about contracts in our industry. I guess one of the big reasons they're used is to keep executives from going to work for competitors after they leave. Is that why they're used here?"

Give the employer a chance to explain why the written contract is so important. Ask, "Am I right in assuming that everybody around my level has a written contract? Not everybody? Do you use them with people in particular divisions of the company?" Your posture is that of a person who is eager to learn about your new employer's way of doing business.

Meanwhile, glance over the document you've been handed. Does it contain the standard sections set forth in Chapter 2: term, duties, compensation, benefits, severance? Don't try to scrutinize these sections in detail. Look for the part(s) of the agreement that explain the company's eagerness to get your signature. Having read this book, you will be familiar with what noncompete and nondisclosure clauses look like. You will also know that the section covering reasons why you can be fired "for cause"—if the wording is overly broad—can give the employer a way of dismissing you at any time, without paying you the agreed-on severance.

Keep asking questions: "I guess what I'm most curious about is your philosophy about written employment agreements. How do you find them useful? Since I will be hiring people, I'll be using them as well, won't I?"

Express your pleasure in the company's acceptance of the principle: "I knew you were a forward-looking organization anyway, but this is particularly great to hear. A lot of companies still resist the idea of a contract, don't they?" You're positioning yourself to take the offer of a contract as a starting point, and to shape it in a way that is more favorable to you.

If the employer insists that the written agreement is a mere formality, of modest importance, he or she cannot very well resist your casually taking it with you. Employers who insist on a quick signature have to give you a good reason. Whatever the reason, you owe it to yourself to check the document over with special care. There may be a joker hidden somewhere, a negative aspect of the job that you haven't considered. Never agree to a murky, unfavorable, or dubious clause because you are seduced by all the other aspects of the job. A rush for agreement to a contract signals that there may be something you don't know; and that unknown factor may render all the positive aspects of the deal worthless.

In one case, a trade book editor accepted a seemingly magnificent deal from a small publishing firm. He was to set up and run a new division. In a hurry to get going, and pleased with everything about the situation, he signed a contract that looked innocuous. When the crunch came, he found that the employer had just wanted to skim the cream of his expertise. Once the new division was set up and running, it was turned over to the son of the chairman/CEO. The editor found to his horror that one clause in the contract nullified the safeguards he thought he had. He was out on the street.

"Do You Mind If My Lawyer Looks It Over?"

Under ordinary circumstances, no sane person would pledge himself or herself in writing to a huge commitment—say, buying a house—without consulting a lawyer. Yet, a surprising number of employment contracts are signed by persons who lack the savvy to understand what they are signing but do not seek the advice of someone who *does* possess the required know-how. There are a number of reasons for these quick and uninformed signings.

"What are you accusing us of?" The employer reacts with shock when the employee intimates that there might be some reason to get a legal opinion on the agreement. Does this mean a lack of trust? The surprise and indignation may be real or simulated; the employee can't tell. But it's an uncomfortable moment. Nobody wants to accuse others of evil intentions on insufficient evidence. Besides, it will be necessary to retain the goodwill of the bosses. Who wants to start a job under the shadow of having implied the top brass are dishonest? Much as the employee wants to have the contract looked over, it seems too touchy an issue.

"Don't look a gift horse in the mouth!" The company offers a really attractive package—salary, bonuses, perks. The employee has been taken up to the top of the mountain and shown a breathtaking view of

money, status, power, and the path to advancement. When the question of a contract is raised, it seems foolish and ungrateful even to read the fine print, let alone have a lawyer look it over.

"*It's just a formality.*" If the contract is a standard form, what's the big deal? A job candidate who has been talking about vision and scope and seeing the big picture does not want to look like a nitpicker.

"*If I make waves, they might change their minds.*" Often, a person who has set what seems like a very high goal in negotiation feels that its attainment will be resisted to the death, and that the objective can be reached only by a combination of luck, timing, and maximum effort. When the employer says "Yes" to the candidate's major demands, the candidate thinks, "God, I'd better nail this down before they realize what they're doing!"

The employee is only too glad to get the whole thing wrapped up by signing a contract. (This same dynamic works in favor of hawkers who sell merchandise off the backs of trucks: "Get it while it's hot!")

"*I'll worry about that later.*" The mind has a remarkable ability to resolve the "cognitive dissonance" that springs up when we really want to do something but are confronted with substantial reasons why we should *not* do it. Here's how it happens when you're talking about taking a new job. You want the job. You're eager to start. Being a self-confident, positive person, you know you will make the most of the opportunity, and you're in a hurry to get the talking over with and get started.

But they want you to sign a piece of paper. You've spotted a clause that looks as if it might cause problems down the road. You could say, "Hold everything!" and thrash the matter out until you're satisfied. But that would get in the way of what you really want to do, so the drive to accomplish the immediate objective takes precedence. You tell yourself that there is nothing in the agreement that can't be handled in due course. After all, the employers don't think it's a big deal, so you think, "What's the matter with me? Why am I nitpicking?"

Having decided that negotiations can be reopened later (everybody says, "Sure, we can sit down and talk about these things any time you want") and the offending language stricken, you go ahead and sign. Probably, you reason, the clause is actually harmless. If it's not, the offending language can be changed any time I want. And anyhow, even if push comes to shove, they'd never try to enforce the provision; maybe it's not even enforceable. Besides, they seem to have other bigwigs sign similar agreements, and you haven't heard of any trouble.

And on and on; you focus on the reasons why it's OK to sign the deal, even though one part of your logic circuitry is blinking a red alarm.

People who are not lawyers tend to moderate the implications of contract provisions, putting them in the most favorable possible light. (Lawyers look at the worst-case scenario.)

When They Hand You a Contract Along with a Promotion

All of these pressures bear on the person who is being recruited for a new job. However, the manager (who has not yet taken the job) has a choice of ways of giving himself or herself the time to examine the agreement properly.

But what if your present employer has just told you you're being upped to a bigger job? The pressure against getting legal advice can be even heavier when an employee is being given a promotion and the employer tenders a contract as part of the arrangement. The entire proceeding has been a celebration. Your boss talks about the great job you're doing. You respond in kind: you appreciate the chance to do even more for the firm.

You spot something you don't like in the written agreement. But you don't want to introduce a sour note. And, because you're to take up your new duties right away, you can't resort to the same delaying tactics available to somebody who is being recruited.

Your approach is to show yourself so eager to plunge ahead and meet the new challenges that you want to put *all* the merely procedural aspects of the promotion aside. Start talking about the big picture, how the company sees your new role, what resources you will be given to achieve your goals, and so on. Brush aside all the stuff about paperwork as mere clerical activities that can be done in due course. After all, the employer hasn't indicated that there is any great urgency about signing the contract. If it is pro forma, you'll get around to it later. Meanwhile, the important thing is to get on with the major aspects of the new job.

If the employer insists on the signature right away, you're a little surprised: "Oh, I didn't realize it was so important. All right; I'd better get on this right away. As soon as we're finished here, I'll give it my full attention and get back to you with it as fast as possible. Of course [with a smile] you wouldn't want me, as my first act in my new assignment, to sign off on something I hadn't read."

Negotiate—But Get Expert Advice

When the employer offers a ready-made employment contract, you can be sure it has been crafted by lawyers and/or specialists in this area. Examples in this book show the meticulous detail that some of these specialists weave into contracts, making them all-encompassing, long, complicated, and hard to understand.

The employer has already enjoyed the fruits of legal advice. The company's lawyer doesn't have to be sitting in on the negotiation. The attorney's invisible hand rests on the discussion and on the pact that the firm wants the employee to sign.

Employees rarely have lawyers sitting with them during hiring discussions. After all, the major reason for the meeting is to talk about job responsibilities, compensation, relationships, and so on. These are not matters to be resolved through third parties. You don't need a lawyer to work out the goals you are supposed to meet in your new position.

So, in most circumstances, the only way a lawyer gets into the act on the side of the employee is by commenting on the language of the contract *after* the negotiation but *before* the signing.

There would be little or no hesitation about signing employment contracts right away if they were always couched in crystal-clear language, were short, and covered only the salient points that had just been agreed on.

But contracts tend to be longer, more obscure, and wider-ranging than the negotiations they are supposed to formalize. And here is where the trouble comes in. The employer's attorneys, if they are any good, have already anticipated and eliminated aspects that are apt to be troublesome for the company. This doesn't mean they have stuck in traps to catch the unwary employee. But it is likely that they have not been zealous in championing the employee's rights.

Even if you have the most implicit trust in the boss and the company, and that trust is well-justified, you still should give yourself the opportunity to make a methodical review of the contract. This book is designed to help you get a better understanding of the language you'll confront, and the implications of that language. However, you may need advice, perhaps legal advice, and you should not hesitate to get it.

Don't feel awkward about withholding your signature. As we have been discussing, the employer should not be rushing you into signing something you haven't read thoroughly. If you feel pressure—and if it is not self-imposed pressure—then you have all the more reason to check everything out.

But you still feel under an obligation to forgo that step, or to make your inspection of the contract cursory.

Resist that feeling of obligation.

None of the reasons outlined above for doing without a thorough review (including a lawyer's advice) is logical. Is the employer really going to have second thoughts and snatch a legitimate offer off the table? If there is any likelihood of this happening, then the employee should have second thoughts, contract or no contract. If you think your bosses might do something like that, sit down and go over the reasons for your suspicion. If you cannot resolve your mistrust, you are not apt to be in a happy situation.

Suggesting that you want an attorney to look it over is not an insult. Rational employers do not hold grudges against people who are careful enough to get legal advice before signing an important document. Deferring potentially troublesome questions instead of resolving them when they should be resolved is no better a tactic in a job negotiation than it is in any other situation. When you buy or lease a car, you read the paperwork; why not for a new long-term work relationship?

Right now, you may not even dream that you're going to be asked to sign an employment agreement. However, if you're unprepared, you will make mistakes when and if you do have to face the document.

There may be reasons for being troubled by some aspects of a written employment agreement, but there is no excuse for being surprised. Anticipate the possibility that your present employer may present you with a contract to sign. Figure out, first of all, the ways in which you are going to give yourself time for examination.

Sometimes, when an employee has asked for a contract, the company digs in its heels, resisting the request fiercely. Then, suddenly, the employer produces a contract, saying, "OK. You asked for it. Everything you wanted is in here. Sign it and we'll get this show on the road." It's like hurling your weight against a closed door, only to find that the door swings open upon impact. You stagger through, off balance. When you've been insisting on a contract, you feel uncomfortable about saying, "Thanks. I'll sign it after I've shown it to my lawyer."

But, uncomfortable or not, that's what you should do. Let's look a little further into the ways in which you can do it.

Getting Time to Check with Your Lawyer

The first and most important thing about obtaining legal advice is determining to do so—and sticking to that determination. Frequently, executives who have nerved themselves to say, "May I have my lawyer look at this?" are surprised to find no resistance at all. The employer responds, "Of course. Take your time."

Suppose the employer asks, "Why a lawyer?" The answer is, "I make it a point to always have a lawyer look over any legal document." This should take care of it.

But the employer may reply, "It's all right. Our counsel has looked at it." This may be said in all sincerity; to the employer, one lawyer is the equivalent of any other lawyer. The fact that it is the *company* lawyer makes no difference. The boss, innocent of any hidden agenda, figures that the document is fair and reasonable.

From the employee's point of view, this is *not* all right. The company lawyer has not only looked at it, he or she has *prepared* it. And what seems neutral and fair to the company's legal talent may be a little slanted in the company's favor. That's only natural. If you're on the receiving end of this rejoinder, you still want your own attorney to see it.

But you have to be tactful. The employer might be startled, hurt, and angered by an implication that you think there might be something fishy in the document. A boss who is trying to pull a fast one might feign outrage. An honest and sincere boss may *really* be outraged. And, although that reaction might not be apparent at the moment, it might fester, slowly poisoning your interpersonal relationship on the job.

Your tactic is to answer something like this: "Of course your counsel has looked it over. And I could waste a lot of his time asking dumb questions. But that doesn't seem fair. Let me take this along. I'll get back to you with it tomorrow."

Go on immediately to another topic, without dwelling on the unimportant detail of the employment agreement: "It might be worthwhile to talk a little about how my new job is going to be announced. Since that might be a little tricky, I'd like to make some suggestions. . . ." Continue talking about noncontractual matters. Suppose the employer then says, "Can't we get this settled? Why don't you sign this thing?" Ask in reply, "Is it that urgent? After all, it's pretty much a formality. Your handshake is good enough for me . . . ."

Continued pressure by the employer should be a warning. What's the big hurry?

A Few Minutes to Look It Over

If this were a perfect world—or at least somewhat more perfect than it actually is—you would always be able to look over a contract at your leisure. And if an employer exerted heavy pressure for an immediate signature, you'd always be able to sift the employer's motives and pull out of the deal if necessary.

But we don't always enjoy such luxuries of choice. Let's say, for example, that you know you are in hot competition for a job (or a promotion) with at least one other candidate. You also know that there are legitimate reasons for the company to want to get the whole thing wrapped up immediately, including the inking of the agreement. Maybe it's a matter of management style: the person who wants to hire you is the kind of person who is frustrated by hesitation, even momentary hesitation. Or it's corporate culture: fast decision making is prized as a positive executive attribute. Maybe it shouldn't be, but it is. If you get the job, you may be able to modify that aspect of the culture.

But first you have to get the job. And they are sitting there waiting for you to sign.

You are not going to be able to take the agreement away to study it and, perhaps, consult with someone else about it. You have to make up your mind *now*.

Maneuver to give yourself a few moments alone to examine the document. Raise some procedural question that does not seriously affect the job offer but will provide a brief recess. In fact, be ready to do this before going into the meeting. The question may involve communications (will there be public or corporate announcement of your hiring? and when?); secretarial help; equipment (the kind of computer you like to use). Your "play for time" should not be a demand for something extra. If anything, it should be the contrary: "I know it's the practice for people at this level to travel first class. For a number of reasons, I'm more comfortable going the most economical way . . . ."

Having raised a minor point that requires your counterpart(s) in the discussion to talk it over, or to make a phone call, you have a moment to scan the contract.

Or maybe you don't have to play for time. Just say, "I guess we have everything settled. I am very pleased, and I will do everything I can to justify your confidence in me. Now all I need to do is sign this. I'll just run my eye over it. I can do that right here, but maybe it makes more sense for me to sit in that empty office over there for a few minutes . . . ."

You have a short time to scan the agreement. If you have briefed yourself by reading this book, you will be prepared to look for the potential trouble spots, for example:

- Crippling noncompete provisions.
- Sweeping nondisclosure prohibitions.
- An overly broad termination clause.
- Bonuses dependent on "pie-in-the-sky" performance or subjective top management discretion.

What if you spot a problem? For example, the termination section includes under "Cause" any action that is "detrimental to the image of the company." That is a dangerous provision to sign. It gives the company latitude to break the contract for almost any reason, depriving the employee of promised benefits, severance pay, and stock options. This does not mean the company *intends* to do this. The company's lawyers may have stuck that wording in there simply because they are paid to protect their client in any and every way they can. (Lawyers have a tendency to do this.)

You are *not* (at this point) objecting to anything. You are just curious, seeking information. As you've been reading the contract, you've been holding a pen in your hand. You make a small check next to the sentence and say, "Why would you think that I might do something detrimental to the image of the company?"

By framing your question this way, you are *particularizing* the provision as being applied to you.

When you *particularize* in this way, the employer is almost sure to respond that there's "nothing personal" about this provision; the company inserts it in any such contract.

You nod your head: "That's interesting. Has there been some experience with this? For example, what would constitute 'action detrimental to the image of the company?' Did somebody go around badmouthing the firm?"

Maybe the employer has an example: "Well, it might be making a speech at an industry forum and ridiculing company products . . . ."

You: "Really? Sometimes I like to start a talk with a couple of jokes. I find it works well when you tell self-deprecating stories about yourself, the company, maybe a product. Everybody knows it's a joke. But once I sign this, I guess I'd better stop doing that . . . ."

Your posture is that of a person who takes the language of the contract very seriously. The employer may say there's no need to change your approach, that this just happens to be general language, routinely inserted. In that case, you might say, "Well, then, why don't we just get rid of this?" You then strike a line through the questionable language.

The employer may not be happy. You've struck out a provision of the contract. At the least, it will have to be retyped (which is, of course, not hard on a word processor). But, moments after a statement that the clause was simply routine and of no particular significance, no effort can reasonably be mounted to reinstate it.

Fraud Narrows Options

Board members at Dr Pepper/Seven-Up receive annual option grants. When a director leaves the board, he or she can still exercise vested options, but if the director is terminated because of "an act of fraud or intentional misrepresentation or embezzlement, misappropriation or conversion of assets or opportunities of the Company," all outstanding options immediately terminate.

Another approach to a problem clause is to try to *expand* it rather than eliminate it: "Then we agree that the way it's written here, this could cover just about anything. Let's give it some more meaning by defining it . . . ." The more definition you're able to get in, the more you protect yourself against an overly broad provision.

Make notes on the contract as you go along. Treat it like a draft, not something that has been engraved in stone.

Once you have established a "working session" atmosphere, at which you *join* the employer in going over the agreement, you can continue to suggest additions, modifications, or deletions. Don't overdo it; just eliminate or at least question the "red-flag" items.

As we will discuss, the biggest reason the company may want you to sign a pact is to keep you from aiding the competition at some future time. Deferred compensation and severance pay are increasingly geared to agreements not to have anything to do with a competitor in any way, shape, or form. In the actual contract excerpts in this book, you'll see that some of these noncompete and nondisclosure clauses can be so general that they seem to forbid you from talking to *anyone* who has ever been contacted by anybody from your firm—whether your firm did business with those persons or not, and even though you have no way of knowing who talked to whom.

In discussing such matters, don't get too serious. Keep it light, but focus on the worst-case scenario to point up the ridiculously extreme nature of the provision: "Now, here's another example of lawyer's language. Since I know my future is with this company, I don't see this as ever being applicable. But is it realistic to expect a person who leaves the firm to never, knowingly or unknowingly, come in contact with anybody who might have been a prospect at some time?"

Employers can, of course, have varying reasons for insisting that clauses stay in. For example, the employer may say (with a greater or lesser degree of sincerity), "I don't know much about these things either. That's why I have to stick with what our attorney drew up."

As a response to this ploy, the employee might say, "OK. I know a quick way to resolve the uncertainties both of us might have. The problem with this vague language has to do with who makes the decision about certain kinds of things—for example, who decides what constitutes an action 'detrimental to the image of the company.' Things like that come up in many kinds of agreements. If we have to leave the ambiguity in the contract, at least for now, then, as I understand it, the standard way of settling the ambiguity is to provide that any difference of opinion can be decided by arbitration, say, by the American Arbitration Association. Since we can't seem to do anything about the vagueness, let's put that in. You can check it with *your* lawyer at your convenience . . . ."

By introducing reasons to change or review any of the contract's provisions, you are giving yourself breathing room to check out the entire pact.

Preparing for On-the-Spot Consultation

Some executives, headed into critical negotiations, make arrangements beforehand to have lawyers or experts (or just people whose opinions they trust) on standby for a telephone conversation. Attorneys are not necessarily thrilled at handling matters this way, but a quick call is better than no consultation at all. If you've made such an arrangement, you don't have to fight a skirmish over each provision as it comes up. Ask questions, make notes, and then—during a casual break for comfort or coffee or whatever—call your waiting confidante. There's no reason to tell the employer exactly what you are doing.

Your lawyer/expert may make suggestions for wording changes, provide definitions of various provisions, and, if necessary, raise the red flag: "Do *not* sign the contract with that paragraph in it. Here's why, and here's what to say . . . ."

Review any contract that is offered to you as completely as possible, and with as much help as you need and can get. Use your basic knowledge of employment agreements, plus your negotiating skills, to overcome any resistance to change.

And, think about building an opportunity for legal review into the *next* contract you negotiate, on either side of the desk.

5

How to Negotiate a
Favorable Contract

I n the previous chapter, we talked about giving yourself time to
review an offered contract when you are in a pressured situation.

Now let's talk about how to negotiate a contract that gives you the
pay, perks, and protection you want and deserve.

A negotiation is an adversarial proceeding. No matter how nice
the other party may be over lunch or a drink, or during the ordinary
course of business, his or her role is changed when the two of you meet
face to face. A friendly or cordial relationship with the other party can,
in certain cases, be a deterrent to effective bargaining. You may not
press as hard on crucial points as you might if the relationship were
more impersonal. The other party may (if only inadvertently) use the
friendship to get you to go easy.

Your first step, therefore, in setting up the psychological environ-
ment within which the negotiation will take place is to view the other
person as an *adversary.* You are not deadly enemies. You are not going to
cut each other's throats. But you are definitely in conflict. Professional
tennis players or high-stakes poker players may be the best of friends
away from the court or the table, but when the game starts they give no
quarter. Purge your mind of any tendency to "go easy" because of an existing friendship or because you don't enjoy being firm with nice people
or because you don't want to "rock the boat." A solid, mature friendship
is not damaged by a negotiation that is conducted toughly but fairly. If
anything, respect is enhanced and you are valued more highly.

It's wise to assume that your opponent has had considerably more experience in negotiation than you. This experience will come into play at critical stages; the adversary's instinct, shaped by experience, will enable him or her to spot your weaknesses and exploit them. Patience is another advantage possessed by experienced negotiators. Success in negotiating sometimes comes down to outlasting the opponent.

You can't tell only from a person's demeanor that you're up against an ace negotiator. Some tough bargainers look and act the part; they are hard-boiled and aggressive right from the start. Others, however, come on as easygoing "just plain folks" who don't know much about negotiating. These adversaries can be the most dangerous. They are especially effective when they confront employees who have known them for a while, and who have come to view them as relatively guileless, "what-you-see-is-what-you-get" people. There is a saying: "Never eat at a place called Mom's, never play cards with a man called Doc." Simple, unsophisticated facades sometimes hide sharp, calculating minds.

You can compensate for the other party's edge in experience by doing a good prenegotiation analysis. You need not probe to the innermost reaches of the opponent's psyche, or build an exhaustive company history, but you have to think about the questions we'll be discussing in this chapter.

What Are the Pressures on Your Adversary?

The other party in the negotiation wants, in general, the same things you do: money, success, recognition, security, pride, the satisfaction of a job well done. Because those who face you in the job negotiation are usually senior to you, they have more to lose.

Another consideration: You are concerned primarily with your own deal. The company, through its bargaining representative, has to think about precedent. Whatever is given to you may have to be given to others.

Your opponent is apt to have two agendas. One is official, one is private. The official agenda covers such priorities as controlling costs, getting and keeping the best available talent for the firm, protecting the firm's confidential information, maintaining an edge against competition, and locking you into the company on terms that are advantageous to the employer and keep you happy and motivated at the same time.

The private agenda involves *image:* self-image and public image. Consider the individuals with whom you are likely to be talking about a contract. Do they like to think of themselves as good people? Fair, understanding, empathetic? Are they careful about how they look to others? How would each prefer to be perceived—as a great person or as a rough, tough S.O.B.? Do they get a kick out of doing battle in a hard bargaining session, or do they prefer that everything always be calm and friendly? Do they buy the Vince Lombardi maxim that winning is the *only* thing?

Some people are so competitive that they go all-out for victory in everything, big and small. (If you are this way, it can be a definite drawback; successful negotiation for a great employment deal calls for willingness to concede on some points.) Win-at-all-costs adversaries will fight you even when it is not to their advantage to do so, or when the prize to be gained is trivial.

Such negotiators try to intimidate opponents. But, if you're not intimidated, they are vulnerable. Their need for constant victory is a weakness that can be turned to an advantage by adroit tactics, just as the lunges of a powerful but unpolished slugger can be exploited by a wily boxer.

Who is looking over your adversary's shoulder? Just about everyone is accountable to other people higher up in the corporate chain of command.

How long has your adversary been in the job? Who is his or her boss? If your counterpart is a CEO who reports to a board of directors, how active is the board? Does the board question the CEO's actions, or is it complacently quiescent?

To the extent you can judge it, how secure is your opponent's position? You can't take an X ray of the organization, but you can, through research, get a sense of the rate of turnover at your opponent's level, the length of time people typically stay with the firm, and other relevant data.

How big a factor is precedent? How much will your counterpart's position be stiffened by the fear of having to make similar concessions to others? This can be a key element in the negotiation. As we shall discuss, it is a standard ploy for companies to say: "It is not our policy to sign such contracts with employees." Sometimes, this is merely a screening objection that conceals the real reason for resistance: The employer does not want to give you what you're asking for. But, in some companies, the "policy" objection is real; the stumbling block is not so much your particular demands as the establishment of a precedent that the company feels will have it handing out contracts like chewing gum samples. (Your opponents will assume that whatever concessions they give you will become known to others in the company—*and they will be right*. It's neither effective nor perceptive to try to obtain special consideration on the grounds that you won't tell anybody, and thus the consideration will remain a secret.)

The negotiation does not take place in a vacuum. It is shaped by the culture of the organization—its traditions, its taboos, its image of itself. Does the company have salary ranges? Does it have a hard-and-fast rule against contracts?

Talk to people who know about the company. Talk to people *in* the company. Individuals well below the top executive ranks—people, say, who handle the nuts-and-bolts human resource work—can tell you a lot in a casual conversation.

The present condition of the company and of its industry can have considerable weight in shaping the climate within which the negotiation is conducted. Your adversary may cite tough times even if they are not particularly tough. Or, even if business in the industry is not good, it may not necessarily have an impact on your bargaining position. (Under certain circumstances, you can make a favorable argument for yourself out of the fact that a company has been struggling. The firm needs to assure itself that its key people are going to stay on board and be strongly motivated. If it fails to offer a good deal, its executives—present and potential—may think about going to work for a competitor, which would just make matters worse.)

When the adversary says, "Things are tight, we can't afford it," you should have done enough homework to be in a position to judge whether the argument is real or bogus, or is somewhere in between. That doesn't mean you should respond to the assertion head-on; often—especially when the plea of poverty is basically fiction—the better tactic is to ignore it.

Have other people gotten contracts similar to the one you're looking for? It's useful to know how comparable deals have worked out. Are those executives still with the firm? Has the company reason to feel that it made good deals with these other persons? If the company made a contract with Smith and got burned, it may not be logical to think that the same thing will happen with Jones, but logic often takes a backseat in negotiation.

Is the person you are negotiating with under an employment contract? Has he or she ever been in your negotiating position? What kind of salary, bonuses, options, and perks are enjoyed by the individuals who will be your bosses and/or counterparts? Elsewhere in this book we show where and how you can get a wealth of information about what people are paid in particular companies and industries, and what kinds of deals their companies give them.

You can't know everything about the persons and the organization with which you're negotiating, but you can arm yourself with a lot of useful information. Scouting your opponent is vital in any contest, and the negotiation of a compensation package, including an employment contract, is one of the most important contests you'll ever engage in.

What Are Your Adversary's Official and Unofficial Positions?

Your opposite number in the negotiation has an official position and an unofficial position. The probable official position is senior executive (maybe CEO), representing the corporation. While wearing this hat, your adversary expresses the company's point of view. The company, through this representative, wants to secure your services at the lowest cost that is concomitant with your best efforts on the job. The company is likely to want certain specific things from you—for example, fulfillment of productivity goals while you are employed there, and a pledge that you will not engage in competition for a certain amount of time after you leave.

Through research and experience, you should know about the prevalence of noncompete and nondisclosure agreements in the industry, and the extent to which this particular company uses them. Let's say that such clauses are common. If the adversary does *not* mention these provisions fairly early in the proceedings, you should ask yourself why. Is the company trying to sneak them in? If so, your response may be to narrow the scope of the provisions themselves and exact concessions on other aspects of the package.

In his or her official *persona*, the company representative pursues the policy line in dealing with you. But that individual across the table or desk has another side—an unofficial position, a personal side. The unofficial position of the company's negotiator—whether that person is a CEO, a senior line manager, a human resource executive, a lawyer, or a member of the board of directors—often affects the bargaining in ways that are not easy to detect. Whatever the adversary's standing, he or she has something riding on the outcome. Executives want to look good to their bosses. CEOs want to look good to their boards of directors. And if you are at a level where you bargain with a member of the board, your opponent wants to look good to other board members. Everyone you confront in negotiation needs money, self-approval, prestige, protection, and security. (And that includes board members. When dealing with the board, find out, for starters, the pay and perks they receive. Get a sense of how seriously they take their responsibilities and how much stockholder and regulatory pressure they experience.)

How much does it mean to your adversary to sign you up? How badly will he or she be hurt if you turn down the deal? You're unlikely to be able to answer these questions completely, but you can get some leads that bear on the answers. At a minimum, pose these questions to yourself before going into the negotiation. Think about the most likely answers. Then, during the bargaining, look for signs that show whether your assumptions are holding up or whether you should change your estimate of your counterpart's stake in successfully hiring you.

Finding Basic Information

Where and how can you learn the things you need to know in order to carry out an optimum negotiation?

Ask the Headhunter

If you have been contacted first by a search consultant, use that expert to find out all you can about the company. Even after you're talking to company people and the search consultant has withdrawn from the picture, don't hesitate to go back to that source when you have questions. Headhunters (the ethical ones, anyway) are paid by the hiring company. They are professionals. They don't look good if their searches produce people who fail, or are unhappy in the job, or leave within a short time.

Because your search consultant wants the negotiation to go as smoothly as possible, you can reasonably expect your questions to be answered truthfully. Why is the company recruiting? How many people have held the job in the past five years? What is the pay range for people of comparable rank? Does the company give contracts? Are stock options used as golden handcuffs? You'll think of other questions too.

Another reason for the headhunter to be straightforward and helpful is that, in due course, you may well be the person who decides which executive search firm to retain.

Read the Business Press

Find out what industry observers are saying about the company. Learn how the money markets view the company's securities. If the firm is booming, its managers may feel they are enjoying a buyer's market and can be less flexible in negotiating. Counter with your own belief that a company that is currently successful is more able to afford to meet the demands of the people it really wants.

If there have been hints that the management ranks are shaky, the employer may be eager to bring in somebody with a good track record.

Pay special attention to hints that the company might be a takeover target. Think about moving parachute protection closer to the top of your priority list.

Listen to What People Are Saying

A lot of what pulses along the grapevine is exaggerated or untrue, but that doesn't make it unusable. The financial markets react to gossip. So may the person you're negotiating with. Is there any hint that the company is in difficulty, or that your adversary's position may be in jeopardy? If negative gossip is circulating, the person you are dealing with may have additional reasons to conclude a successful negotiation and fill an important position.

Seek Information from Within the Company

You're not a CIA agent. You can't penetrate the innermost secrets of a firm that you may be joining. Even so, you can tap some sources on the inside.

The company's annual report is a starting point. The company's public relations operation can yield further information. Call them up. (If for any reason you personally don't want to do this, get a friend—one who might have a passable reason for needing the information—to make the request.) Most public relations people are glad to furnish information packages. What they put out is all positive; they don't get paid to show you the seamy side. But a careful reading of the material can provide interesting insights, and can suggest questions for you to ask.

If possible, talk informally to one or more people who work for the company. Where do they have lunch or hang out after work? The persons you talk with don't have to be members of the top brass. People lower down on the totem pole often know a lot about what is really going on and are willing to talk about it. An executive assistant in Human Resources, for instance, could be an excellent source.

You're not pumping people for information. Talking unofficially with people who work for the company does several things. It gives you a feel for the culture of the place. It's a preview of the attitudes that will be of concern to you when and if you join the firm. And it will give you useful information for your negotiations.

Don't push for the information. That turns people off. Let it come to you. And don't sail under false colors. You can be clear about where you're coming from without being too specific: "I've heard this can be a good place to work."

Develop Sources Within Your Own Company

People can work for a company for years and yet be surprisingly ignorant about the larger entity of the firm. Make it a point—without being obvious—to tap the information available from various sources in your present organization. You can mine glistening nuggets from the official information that any company hands out (and a lot of people throw away without reading). As this book points out, even something as seemingly innocuous as the manual handed out to all new employees at all levels can be very important. Courts have found that the statements in such manuals may, in certain situations, constitute a binding contract.

Your workplace is a community. People are talking with each other all the time—over coffee, in the corridors, in the johns. *Listen* to what they're saying (and sometimes to what they're not saying). Don't assume that you are listening when you're chatting. In a way, listening is becoming a lost art. Rather than hearing and comprehending what others are saying, people simply await their chance to speak. By really listening to the words and what they mean, you give yourself an advantage.

Get to know people from all around the organization, not just your own bailiwick. This is a good idea in general. It is also an excellent way of adding to your store of knowledge about the company's approach to compensation matters. What an acquaintance from a staff department tells you about her job may not be of immediate relevance, but it may come in handy when your boss, or a boss at another company, offers you a package deal.

Use the Computer

With a computer and a modem, you can do extensive and valuable research on persons, companies, and industries. Online services offer archival research facilities.

- *CompuServe* includes ZiffNet's Business Database Plus and Magazine Database Plus. Business Database Plus lets you retrieve full-text articles from more than 750 business and trade journals and 500 specialized newsletters, going back two to five years. You enter a search topic, and the computer finds the relevant articles. Magazine Database Plus accesses full-text articles from more than 200 general-interest and niche publications. (The time span for back issues varies.) Remember that a popular magazine may carry useful information not found in the business press. If you're dealing with a non-U.S. company, foreign ZiffNet sources are available.

- *America Online* provides a variety of informative business databases. Starting with a Standard & Poor's report, you can use the America Online sources to put together an up-to-date and pertinent file on your target company.

- *Dow Jones News/Retrieval* is a one-stop source for timely and authoritative business information pulled from more than 70 databases. This service includes the vast resources of Dun & Bradstreet, which reports on "7.2 million private and public business establishments in the U.S. and the more than 10 million executives who run them." Sales and employee figures, lines of business, net worth, and key executive names and titles are all there. You can get business and financial news, national and international news, government news, and so on. The comprehensive Dow Jones archival databases allow users to retrieve articles from *The Wall Street Journal, Barron's, Washington Post, Los Angeles Times,* and a huge store of newsletters, press releases, and magazines like *Forbes* and *Fortune*. This source also has information on industries and companies all over the world.

- *The New York Times* and other major sources of backdated information are now accessible to online researchers.

Use a computer and modem to build your arsenal of facts. If you don't yet own this hi-tech capability, maybe this is the time to get it. Or, ask a friend—perhaps someone who uses online technology for investment guidance—to collect information on the company you're interested in.

As online services compete ferociously for subscribers' business, they will be offering a wider array of services, better graphics, and easier access to the Internet.

Make the Public Library Your Research Arm

A lot of the information you need may be available in your public library.

These days, people get help from the library for a variety of tasks—solving business problems, refining new ideas, finding better jobs. A good library can give you valuable information that you can use effectively in negotiation.

One *caveat:* Not all libraries boast equal resources. Some are online, some are not. Some have extensive CD-ROM resources, others don't. If you can't find what you want at a small local library, seek another one, perhaps in a bigger town.

You may know the library well enough to find everything you need without help. Or, you may *think* you know everything there is to know about using the facilities, and then miss out on some of the modern capabilities the facility has to offer. Even if you're an experienced library user, it makes sense to talk to a professional librarian about what you want and why you want it. He or she may show you additional sources of data and shortcuts in reaching them.

Be smart about using this valuable resource. Research librarian Carol Weidemeier functions as an information consultant for persons in all kinds of businesses. She can accomplish amazing things—if she has enough time. "Sometimes people rush in, saying, 'I have an interview in two hours!' We can help—but we can do a lot more if you give us two or three days."

The library can provide nuts-and-bolts information about a company—names, titles, numbers—from basic sources such as Moody's, Standard & Poor's, D&B. But you can get a lot more. "We deal with key questions," says Weidemeier. "How sound is the company? What is its philosophy? What is the state of the industry? There are services—Value Line, for example—which go well beyond the basics in drawing a working profile of an organization." Experienced librarians like Carol Weidemeier, in well-equipped libraries, can call on CD-ROM and on-line sources, as well as hard copy, to provide useful and reliable data to their "clients."

"We help solve a range of problems. For example, you're switching companies. You have a 401(k). You assume at first that it makes sense to roll it over to your new employer. But further investigation, using library sources, shows you it's better to keep the 401(k) where it is."

Maintain Your Own Data Bank

Build files on your own company, on companies in your industry, and on companies you would like to work for some day. Run your eye over the index on page B2 of *The Wall Street Journal*. Clip stuff that might be of interest. You need not spend a lot of time looking at it now; file it away for possible future use.

How Can You Find Out What Your Peers Are Making?

Do you ever wonder about the deals that executives in other companies are getting—the top managers and those down through the ranks? What are companies offering their talent in salaries, stock options, bonuses, deferred compensation, and perks? How are executives being protected against takeovers? What are the latest trends in pensions, "tin parachutes," hiring bonuses, "underwater options," and a host of other elements of the complex, fast-changing executive compensation field?

Today, *the* source for authoritative information on executive compensation is *Executive Compensation Reports* (ECR).

ECR publishes a newsletter twenty-four times a year. The letter provides up-to-the-minute facts and informed commentary on all aspects of executive compensation. Readers find out about megabuck deals enjoyed by the world-famous stars of business, along with information, explanation, and projection of trends on a multitude of compensation topics—severance, stock options, life insurance, bonuses, deferred compensation plans—all of them relating immediately to the concerns of managers well down into the midlevel ranks.

Executive compensation has become a very complicated area in recent years, with gross-ups, rabbi trusts, golden boots, and other arcane offshoots. ECR sheds a bright beam of light into this large and densely overgrown jungle. And yet the newsletter is concise, clear, and enjoyable, written with great knowledge, journalistic style, and occasional gleams of wit. Often, a brief story will indicate that additional information, including hard copy of actual documents, is available on request.

ECR collects, summarizes, categorizes, and databases more than 1,200 companies' compensation plans. In addition to the newsletter, ECR issues comprehensive in-depth studies of particular areas: golden parachutes, long-term stock and performance plans, and others. And ECR Research Services conducts customized research to fulfill requests from companies.

Executive Compensation Reports is published by dp Publications, Box 7188, Fairfax Station, VA 22039; phone: (703) 425-1322; fax: (703) 425-7911. The newsletter costs (as of the latter part of 1995) $395 per year.

Corporate libraries and/or human resource departments—at least in larger companies—are likely to be getting this newsletter. No true compensation specialist would be without it. However, although the information is essential to the specialists, the stories are meaty and free of jargon, and they contain material that can be of enormous benefit to all executives, especially when they are going into a negotiation over compensation or are looking for a new job.

Think about getting your own subscription to ECR. It tells you things about business—and businesspeople—you won't find anywhere else. Besides, it's easy and enjoyable reading.

Or, find out whether ECR is available in your own company, or somewhere else. It will help you grasp the ins and outs of compensation. You'll know what to ask for, citing chapter and verse in support of your position. And, beyond ECR's value as a tool to make you a more effective negotiator, its background information makes you a generally better-informed executive.

Ted Turner Hands Out a Fifty Percent Raise

In 1994, Scott M. Sassa, VP–Entertainment, Turner Broadcasting, saw his salary jump to $805,000 from $513,942—up 57%. VP–News W. Thomas Johnson received a 53% raise to $700,000. Executive VP Terence F. McGuirk settled for an 11% raise, to $855,000. These are among the tidbits to be found in *Executive Compensation Reports*.

Make Your Opponent Look Good

Having prepared yourself with facts and a feel for the subject, you sit down to talk about compensation.

Right at the outset, let's emphasize a cardinal point:

Your objective is not to defeat, embarrass, or destroy your adversary. You want to make your adversary *look good*.

A successful negotiation about compensation allows both parties to come away feeling like winners. In addition, your opposite number should be able to *look* like a winner. Otherwise, even if you obtain most of what you want, it may be a Pyrrhic victory. It's different from, say, negotiating with a car salesman or an antiques dealer; you don't give a damn how the other person looks and feels, as long as you get the price down. In a compensation negotiation, always remember that you are going to have to live with the people you're dealing with.

"Absentee" Negotiation

There will be times when your negotiating adversary does things that don't seem logical. For example, let's say you have answered all the opponent's objections to a particular request you've made. It's not the centerpiece of your position, but it's important to you. The other party has no more reasonable objections to raise. Nevertheless, he or she continues to hold out stubbornly—not because you have failed to make your point, but because your adversary doesn't know how to explain the concession to those higher up.

You try to find out the reason for the continued resistance. Is there a hidden objection? You work hard to bring it to the surface. But the standoff continues. The other person is not going to admit the reason for continued resistance.

In this kind of situation—an apparently illogical opposition that survives your reasoned arguments (which are, by and large, accepted)—it's reasonable to assume that your adversary fears his or her inability to justify the move to those further up in the hierarchy.

Assume that your opponent is going to have to explain the concession to a higher-up whose antagonism to the proposition is not based in logic. You are no longer carrying on a debate with the person in front of you. For the moment, you are conducting a third-party negotiation with an absentee negotiator. Furthermore, that absent party may have objections that are not realistic—may even be ridiculous—but will nevertheless keep you from getting what you want unless the bargainer in front of you can see a way to justify it.

Here is where your homework comes in especially handy. You should know something about the culture of the organization, and about the person who is looking over your adversary's shoulder.

Using your knowledge, provide your opposite number with ammunition that can be used in justification. Do it indirectly, without indicating why you're doing it. (It is not tactful to say, "I know you're scared of this guy, so I'm going to tell you what to say to him.") If, for example, the sticking point is a richer-than-usual stock option arrangement, you might remark, "From the company's point of view, this seems like the best kind of incentive compensation. You've done well in getting me to back off my original idea that I wanted a bigger base salary. After all, if I do a good job, the stock goes up, and vice versa. So I'm working toward the company's goals at the same time I'm working toward my own."

When you provide ammunition for selling the agreement, never label it as ammunition. Nor expect your adversary to acknowledge it as such. But he or she will see how the arguments can be used. If the possible objection of a third party is the hang-up on this particular point, you will have gone a long way toward overcoming the obstacle.

Emotional Traps

Executives negotiating for favorable provisions sometimes lose, not on the merits of the issue, but because they lock the employer into a fixed position. Often, the difficulty is primarily emotional rather than procedural or financial.

Here's how it happened in one negotiation. The bone of contention was the "cause" provision, which stated, after the usual references to fraud and embezzlement, that the contract could be terminated for cause if the employee were to "violate company policy." This, of course, is a provision that you should eliminate if at all possible. Ambiguity in the "cause" paragraph is a land mine. It lies there, buried, for years, harmless, because there's no need to activate it; but if things get nasty, the employer can use it to explode your rights to severance pay.

There are right ways and wrong ways to attack an overly comprehensive "cause" provision. In the negotiation we are describing, the manager's approach was head-on: "This will have to come out."

The CEO glanced at the offending language. He seemed surprised at the objection: "You mean the part that says you can be dismissed for violating company policy? What's wrong with it?"

"It's too broad."

"Broad? I don't get it. Why would you want an arrangement that condones the violation of company policy?"

"That's not the point, Jeff. The point is that the agreement just makes this broad reference to company policy without defining it."

"But any senior manager knows what company policy is. My God, he ought to. He helps to formulate it!"

"Company policy can change overnight."

"Well, Andy, I don't know about 'overnight,' but, sure, it can change. I hope we never get so rigid that we're not willing to modify our approach. But so what? When it changes, managers know about it. They should be in agreement with it. And anyway, new or old, it's now the policy and has to be observed."

"It's not really a matter of knowing about company policies, or objectives, or plans, or broad strategies. The term 'policy' can be made to apply to very small points."

"Like what?"

"Well, lots of things. Like, say, *when* a guy decides to eat lunch, or *where*, or *whom* he takes to lunch, or how much detail he puts on his expense chit, or whether he just takes some money out of petty cash."

"Our guidelines on entertainment are pretty broad, Andy. Are you suggesting they be changed? I don't get into that end of it much. What is there about it that bothers you? Do you do that much business at lunch that this should be a big thing?"

"No, Jeff. You asked for an example, and that's just an example. The thing is that if a problem ever came up, the clause could be interpreted to mean that some minor thing was really a violation of policy and therefore it voided the contract. It could be interpreted retroactively, going back years."

"Interpreted by whom?"

And now Andy realizes that he has gone too far. "Well, by anybody. There could be difficulties . . . ."

"What kind of difficulties?"

"Differences of opinion. There are all kinds of issues that could conceivably come up. You know that. Even though a guy is doing a good job, the company for some reason or other wants to get rid of him, and so they terminate the contract . . . ."

"And the fellow receives a good severance deal. That's what we just spent twenty minutes working out. But what you're saying is that we, the company, could welsh on our agreement by citing this clause. Andy, I'll tell you frankly, that's an imputation I don't like. I'm bothered by the fact that you would think of it. I'm bothered by your focus on some dispute between us in the future. And I'm bothered by your objection to language that, to me, is reasonable!"

Now what? Andy can back down, which makes him look like a guy who was angling for every advantage he could get, and then wimped out when he ran into opposition. He can continue to fight, and jeopardize his chances of getting the contract—and even put his future with the company at risk. Or, if the CEO and the company need him badly enough, Andy can bull through and get the clause changed, leaving a negative impression that will substantially affect his relationship with Jeff.

In this case, the manager polarized the situation by backing the CEO into a corner. Jeff was confronted with what seemed to be a slur on his integrity and that of the firm. He could not back down without losing face.

Situations can become polarized for factual reasons, but it's the emotional element that really causes trouble. An employer can compromise on money, conditions of work, or job title, but it's tough to compromise when, by doing so, you seem to admit that you are a liar or a scoundrel.

Here, the wording of the "for cause" provision was probably not a very big deal. It escalated into a big deal because Andy made three mistakes:

1. He didn't plan how he would tackle the problem of the "for cause" provision.

2. He was not looking at and listening to the reaction of the CEO when he brought the objection up. Jeff, the CEO, really did not know what was bothering Andy about these words. The notion that anybody would balk at being asked not to "violate company policy" was outlandish to him.

3. He stumbled into the posture of implying that the employer would use dirty tricks to break a contract. That sort of thing

does happen. The idea of a contract is to keep it from happening to you. And many of the provisions of the contract need never come into play as long as mutual respect and confidence exist between the parties.

Provisions like an overly ambiguous "for cause" paragraph pose a danger to the employee *only* if the employer tries to pull an underhanded trick to avoid paying severance.

When the question is handled in the right way, most employers can see its reasonableness without taking offense.

Some negotiators use "I'm insulted!" as a ploy. They pretend to take the other party's arguments as a personal affront. This is an unworthy tactic, but that doesn't make it ineffective. The other person, who would not dream of issuing a personal insult or of imputing bad faith, is flustered, and may back off.

The pretended insult is a tactical negotiating problem. But the emotional situation that arises when the employer really *does* feel insulted is tougher to deal with.

You can't predict how an employer's representative is going to react to discussion of a potentially touchy issue like the "for cause" language. If the person bristles, you may not be able to judge whether the resentment is real or faked. It's best to frame your approach in a way that avoids personalities.

In the example cited, Andy might have said:

Now, here's a point that is fairly trivial, but I'd like to clear it up. This section says the agreement can be terminated without severance pay if the employee is guilty of embezzlement or a felony, and so forth. That's fine. If I ever did anything like that I'd expect not only to be fired but to be prosecuted. But let's take out everything after that. You probably haven't even looked at it. It's the kind of stuff that lawyers like to sneak into contracts. Look at this. Let's face it. You don't need to get people to sign something like this to make sure they follow company policy. If you thought there was a chance of that, you wouldn't give such people responsible jobs. The only other possible reason for this kind of wording in any contract is to let the company get out of its obligations. Obviously, that's not where you're coming from. The contingency is not likely to come up, and, even if it did, you would never use this language as a loophole. So the only way this could get used is if, God forbid, I found myself dealing with somebody else about the nuts and bolts of termination. So, what do you say? Can we do without this part?

Scapegoating the lawyers who drew up the contract is a useful tactic. Even if the employer supports the wording, he or she can abandon the position gracefully. You have said that these particular words are merely boilerplate stuck in by attorneys, who do this kind of thing instinctively, and that two people who trust each other are not hogtied by the mores of the legal profession. (If you happen to *be* an attorney, you can't use this ploy in quite this way; but you can use a modification: "We both know that lawyers play games with language sometimes . . . .")

Blaming unwelcome provisions on "the lawyers" is sometimes an easy, joking way to bridge any awkwardness arising from objection to part of the agreement.

Avoid the Personal

The basic rule in avoiding emotional polarization is to keep everything objective. Instead of saying, "Under this clause, *you* could demote me without changing my title," say, "Under this clause, an employee might be demoted even while retaining the title. I know that would never cross your mind. That's why you didn't spot it. Look at the language again, though, and you'll see what I mean. We don't want anything like that in there . . . ."

Look and Listen

Body language can tell you when your opponent is getting angry—the white knuckles, the rigid posture, the clenched jaw muscles, and other signs. And even though the person continues to speak in a fairly level way, the strain in the voice tells you this person is "ready to explode."

At times, in certain kinds of negotiations, you *want* to make the other person blow a fuse. This is not one of those times. When you sense growing annoyance or anger, back off. You are here to negotiate a favorable agreement, not to win an argument or score points or make somebody mad.

If the discussion is heating up, change direction and move back into the calm zone: "I seem to have said something dumb here. I didn't mean to. There's no personal implication in anything I say. What I'm talking about is my feeling about the actual language of the clause. And maybe that's the point. It means different things to different people. When I read it, it seems to say . . . ." And you bridge back into a discussion of the language rather than the motives or the actions of the person with whom you're bargaining.

When you appear to criticize the other party, you're courting trouble. But who can take offense at criticism of a piece of paper?

When a negotiation polarizes, it may be best to break it off and resume talking a few days hence. Otherwise, anger may drive your opposite number to say something that he or she will have to stick with (and that *you* are stuck with). When you get together again, resume the discussion as if the polarization had never happened. Your adversary may be glad to go along with your terms. The issue that would have involved embarrassment or loss of face is forgotten; both parties concentrate on objective facts.

The essence of "no lose" negotiation is to see that both parties come out feeling that something has been gained without anything vital being lost. Sometimes, people win objectively and yet feel like losers emotionally. The skillful negotiator does not back the other party into an emotional corner.

Occasionally, you will come across an employer who views the negotiating table as a gladiatorial arena within which personal strengths are to be flaunted and personal hang-ups worked off. This person bullies and cheats for the pleasure of bullying and cheating. You'll be reminded of those Little League coaches who shame the whole concept by yelling at kids, umpires, and other parents. The negotiator cares more about making the other person crawl than about negotiating favorable terms.

Such an individual is irritating as a person, but, if you can stand the irritation, he or she is vulnerable as a bargainer. The first rule is: Never let this person get under your skin. Even if abuse seems to be directed at you personally, overlook it; it is irrelevant to the process and to the achievement of your goals. (If this executive is always like this, and you have to work for him or her, you may want to think twice about the job.)

The abuse is not aimed at you. The other party acts this way toward lots of people, including "friends and loved ones." And he or she probably doesn't always act this way. Most of the time—in dealing with others on the job, for example—he or she may be a perfectly nice person. Hard bargaining just offers unique kicks.

Misdirection is a useful tactic at times. You give the adversary the impression that you are most fearful of loss in an area which is actually of little concern to you. Uncle Remus's Brer Rabbit implored the fox not to throw him into the briar patch. So the malevolent fox proceeded to do just that, enabling the wily rabbit to escape.

The emotional type of negotiator may be particularly susceptible to misdirection. For instance, the employer who likes to come on strong, show who's boss, embarrass "the other guy," and so on, gets the idea that a manager hates the idea of receiving a substantial proportion of the compensation package in stock appreciation rights (SARs). The employer gets this idea because the manager has sold it to him—indirectly, by shying away from the topic of SARs when it comes up; and directly, by saying, "I don't feel SARs are appropriate as a major factor in what I get paid."

So the show-who's-boss employer thinks, "Don't like 'em, huh? Well, I'll show you!" The employer then proceeds to fight to demolish the manager's (sham) defenses against SARs. While concentrating on this victory, the employer does not bargain hard on other terms of the agreement—for example, severance and term of the contract. Getting what he wants in these areas, the employee "gives in" on the stock plan. Everybody is happy.

Trade-Offs You Can Make

You are in a favorable negotiating position when:

- The employer gives the highest priority to one element of the deal.

- You are not as interested in that element as in some others.
- The employer is not aware of your priorities.

Sometimes, a manager is placed in a favorable position because the employer feels that precedent dictates the inclusion of a certain provision. Take, for example, the noncompete clause. The employer insists on a broad noncompete agreement. It's standard. The company requires that it be included in all agreements. A single exception, the company feels, would open the floodgates to a torrent of exceptions.

Whenever the employer insists unduly on a provision because it must be maintained as a norm, rather than because it has particular relevance to you, you have a potential advantage. In most cases, you should try to narrow the scope of the noncompete clause, along with any other provision that places limits on your freedom.

But let's say you don't feel that strongly about it. Your next career move may well be to go into business on your own in a different industry.

Your first tactic is to insist forcefully that the noncompete clause be stricken altogether. You intend to make a career with this firm; but if, for any reason, you were to leave, your only option would be to get a job with another firm in the industry. After all, this is where your expertise lies, and this is where your skills are best known. (Don't refer to the dubious enforceability of such clauses. You will not enhance rapport and trust by stating that the noncompete provision is not worth the paper it is written on. And it will only provoke an argument that gets nowhere.)

The employer insists that the clause must stay in. At last, you give a little ground, saying that if it stays in, it has to be drastically modified. The employer fights this as well.

At the appropriate moment, hint that you may be willing to capitulate—for a quid pro quo. One benefit you might bargain for is a sweetened severance arrangement. If you have to leave the company—and if the company insists on limiting your ability to make a living—then you need more protection.

Beefed-up severance is a logical step from the noncompete. But perhaps you'd prefer to use your capitulation as a trade-off for a higher salary or a bigger bonus. Here, the connection is less solid. Logically, there is not much of a relationship between your on-the-job compensation and a noncompete agreement.

You can ask for the improved compensation in exchange for leaving in the clause the employer insists on. The negotiation—and perhaps the subsequent relationship—will go more smoothly if you can make a plausible connection between the quid pro quo and what you're giving up. Think this contingency out beforehand. After all, you *know* they're going to push the noncompete.

You might say, "Frankly, right at the moment, the idea of what I am free to do if I leave the company is not a big consideration. I intend to succeed here, not somewhere else. You brought the subject up; that's why we're talking about it. Do you know something that I don't know? Maybe you don't plan to keep me around very long . . . ."

The employer will respond that, no, this is just a pro forma thing; they require it of everybody, but they do insist on it for their protection, and so forth.

"Well," your response might be, "nevertheless, it does worry me a little. Maybe I ought to insist on a bigger severance package. But that's negative thinking. Instead, let's talk about these salary numbers. If I'm so valuable that you're going to keep me from working for anyone else, then I'm worth more in salary. Let's up the base thirty thousand. What do you say?"

The employer may answer that the clause is standard; it has no special significance in your case. So you say, "If it's not a big deal, then let's eliminate it. Strike it out and get on to more important things."

The employer won't strike it, and is adamant about an increase in base salary. You then "settle" for what you wanted all along: "OK. But I'll have to ask that the percentages be a little more favorable on the bonus arrangement. After all, you can't really have any objection to that . . . ."

You may not get all you want. But you have a fighting chance of getting something.

Employers, of course, tend to think that because there are standard clauses in contracts, employees should accept them without question. Many employees do; they don't want to rock the boat, and they don't care about the provision anyway.

They are missing a bet. One of the principles of good negotiating is that you do not give up any potential advantage without trying to use it. You achieve a favorable outcome by adroit manipulation of trade-offs. And one of the prime opportunities for advantageous trading occurs when the employer is forced to insist on a provision that you don't care much about.

If You Tune In, He Makes Out

Peter F. Tortorici, President of CBS Entertainment, has a contract that provides for a bonus of $500,000 if CBS's prime-time ratings hit 9.0 on the Nielsen in the first year of the pact. The payouts go up by $100,000 in each succeeding 9.0 year.

Can Resistance Be Met with Questions?

Questions have a number of uses in helping to overcome resistance. The most obvious purpose of a question, of course, is to obtain information. In a negotiation, information is received in a number of ways.

The *content* of the answer constitutes information. Beyond the content lies what semanticist S. I. Hayakawa has called the *metamessage*—the meaning *behind* the words. For example, the employer says, "Rather than tie a large proportion of executive compensation to annual earnings, we are now moving in the direction of keying the pay plans to accomplishment of overall corporate goals." The meaning behind the words is, "When we reward people on an annual bottom-line basis, they find ways to come up with short-term profits that pay off big for them but push the corporation toward obsolescence. From now on, corporate is going to set the goals and enforce desirable behavior by controlling the purse strings. You do what corporate wants or you lose money."

The method of delivery of an answer can give you further information. Is the other person faintly uneasy? Reluctant? Self-confident? Matter-of-fact? By observing the adversary, by listening to the tone of voice, by getting the *feel* of the atmosphere, you can sometimes learn more than you do from the actual words. People are always sending signals. But to be able to interpret these signals, you must first receive them. Practice two-way communication in negotiation. Formulate and ask the right questions—and then switch on all your receivers to monitor and decode the response.

When the employer says "No" to a request, it's almost automatic to ask, "Why?" You not only want to know about the stated reasons for the resistance, you want to gauge its strength and depth.

Courtroom lawyers and experienced interviewers use certain techniques to keep the other person talking and to draw out further responses. One is the *reflection* technique. You "reflect" back what the other person has said. For example, the employer says, "A five-year term is out of the question. Three years is as long as we'll go for." The employee says, "You won't consider five years?" The employer answers, "Well, no, I don't see how we could. Not in the fast-moving circumstances of this industry. We'd be tying ourselves down . . . ."

The employee has simply restated the answer. The employer, feeling the urge to elaborate, indicates that the refusal is not necessarily as firm as it first appeared.

A variation of reflection is *magnification*. You reflect the objection, but with a twist that gives it more force than the original.

"Our policy is to restrict all severance deals to one year's salary, tops. Most are far less than that."

"I see. You have *never* given anybody more than a year's severance?" The *never* is inaccurate and the employer knows that the employee knows it.

"Well, there have been certain exceptions. But those were for very good reasons."

"Very good reasons. . . . What, for example?"

Once the exceptions are out in the open, the "policy" of no-more-than-one-year may not be broken, but it is severely bent.

Sometimes, a person can be prodded to elaborate by *echoing*—repeating the last two or more words with a questioning inflection.

"You will have total control over staffing. Corporate will only get into the act on very rare occasions."

"Very rare occasions?"

"Well, of course, if you were to want to discharge someone who's been with the company for thirty years, is well-liked, and so forth, we would want to . . . ."

In handling resistance, the "Why" question can sometimes be effectively followed by "What?"

"So you do make exceptions. Under what circumstances would you make an exception in this case?"

The answer may not provide total satisfaction, but it may indicate the kind of trade-off the employer is looking for: "I don't know. The thing is, if we buy your approach, we seem to be taking all the risks. If you hit your market-share target, you clean up even if the corporation shows negative earnings . . . ." A revised formula—one that would key more compensation to overall performance—is what the employer wants.

At a certain point, it is frequently useful to ask, in effect, "What would *you* do?" You seem to be heading toward an impasse. You've suggested several formulas, all of which got turned down. But the employer keeps talking. So you put the ball into your opponent's court.

"How would you handle this?"

"You mean if I were calling the shots myself? Obviously, I would want it to be done the way the company has proposed."

"But," you say, "as we've discussed, that doesn't quite work for me. So let's make it hypothetical. If you were in my shoes, and you were absolutely compelled to get a better deal than the present language suggests, how would you go about it? What would you figure to be the best compromise you could expect?"

Your adversary may be surprised by being asked to help you with your case by suggesting tactics. But such a challenge makes him or her think, and the resulting answer can be helpful. An adversary who personally wants to make a deal with you, but is hampered by policy or orders from above, may suggest a trade-off: "I'd forget about the up-front bonus and the performance bonus plan." That's a negative reply, but at the same time it suggests an avenue of attack: the elements of the package *apart* from those mentioned earlier.

Finally, a well-timed question can be used to bring a phase of the negotiation—or the whole negotiation—to a conclusion. You feel a point has been discussed enough. You ask, "Is there any reason why we have to talk about this any more? Let's see if we can find some common ground . . . ."

A problem that has been debated for twenty minutes can be settled in thirty seconds if this question is asked at the right moment.

When Should You Keep Quiet?

Mark Twain said, "The right word may be effective, but no word was ever as effective as a rightly timed pause." And historian Will Durant observed, "Nothing is often a good thing to say, and always a clever thing to say."

Whatever the reasons, silence is not prized by the American culture. American businesspeople negotiating with counterparts in the Pacific Rim often remark on the tendency of Japanese, Chinese, and Korean businesspeople to endure long, frustrating pauses in the bargaining. Silence is a vacuum into which we Westerners tend to rush. When nobody is talking in a negotiation, we have a feeling that nothing is going on.

Patient silence is a useful negotiating tool because it exerts pressure. The negotiator who uses it wisely gains a tactical advantage.

At several points, you are better off keeping quiet rather than talking.

Handling Surprises

Silence is golden when your adversary has just thrown you a curve by introducing an unexpected and perhaps disturbing element. Many inexperienced negotiators think it's important to pretend *never* to be surprised. (They feel that their lack of anticipation makes them lose face.) Confronted with the unexpected, they respond with a rush of words, pouring out faster than their brains can produce them. Results? They say something foolish . . . take an untenable position . . . deny the undeniable . . . provide the other party with an opening . . . disclose information that should be withheld . . . give up a point too easily.

When your adversary introduces a factor you hadn't thought of, the first logical thing to do is *think about it*. Don't play games; say, "I want to think about that for a moment." (There's no need to say you're surprised, or you hadn't thought of it before; another quirk of inexperience is to overexplain.) What's the harm in thinking things over, even in the middle of a discussion?

Hold your silence, withstanding the impulse to fill the vacuum. Then respond—if you have thought of a good response. But what if you haven't thought of a good response? Say, "That's an interesting angle. I'd like to come back to that later." The key tactic is: Don't shoot from the lip.

You may come back to it later, or you may not. If it's a point of real substance, then you will have to deal with it, minimizing the damage to your position, offering a concession, and so on. If, however, the surprising element is a debater's ploy, used by your adversary to throw you off balance, then you have blunted the effectiveness of the ploy. The subject may not arise again.

Dealing with the Incredible

Another opportune moment for silence comes when your opponent has made an unrealistic, doubtful, or patently untrue statement. For example, he or she says, "We have never made more than a two-year agreement." You know perfectly well that's not true. But meeting the assertion head-on might cause the other party to dig in. You don't want to utter the L-word, so you sit there staring, a little startled. The silence places the burden on the other person, who, uncomfortable with the flat statement and the nonresponse, finally modifies it: "Of course, that doesn't include the special arrangements we've sometimes made with certain technical people," and so on. You both know this footnote negates the previous claim. You go on as if nothing had happened.

Closing the Deal

Well-timed silence when you are at the point of closing can help clinch an important point or the entire agreement. You've made your pitch, and the employer is thinking it over. Let the thinking continue. Don't talk. It's anticlimactic and distracting; it makes you sound insecure. Just sit there. At this moment, the weight of silence is doing more for you than any additional argument.

Slowing Down the Pace

Some negotiators try to speed up the exchanges, hustling their adversaries along. If you are confronted with such a bargainer, you may want to slow the pace. Use silence to regulate the pace of the proceedings.

Effective negotiation goes beyond the objective strengths of the opposing positions, just as winning a poker game depends on more than being dealt good cards. Winning negotiators are always in control of the process. They dictate the pace of the bargaining. They never seem surprised or unprepared. By using the right tactics at the right time, they win even when their positions are not especially strong.

Cultivate the art of keeping still. Serene silence is a solid negotiating tool.

Can You Trust Body Language?

The polite and unacknowledged struggle for control starts the moment you walk into the arena. You shake hands and choose a seat without being asked, perhaps moving the chair into a position you like better. You sit upright but relaxed, legs crossed, hands folded loosely in your lap, eyes meeting the other party's eyes.

A lot of nonsense has been written and spoken about "body language." Some enthusiasts claim the body can be used like a radio transmitter. You decide the precise message you want to send. By orchestrating your gestures, you plant subliminal ideas in the other party's mind.

The reverse of this extreme interpretation of the body language doctrine is that certain gestures and postures invariably mean the same thing, beaming messages that can be decoded by those in the know. A person fingers the lobe of the right ear, meaning a guilty conscience! An attractive person sits facing you with legs slightly apart, meaning that anything goes! And so forth.

Treating gestures as if they were the equivalent of exact speech carries the idea to absurdity. You cannot make precise, fine-tuned interpretations of physical movements any more than you can receive brain waves. The title of the old song "Every Little Movement Has a Meaning All Its Own" may someday come true, if we find a Rosetta Stone that enables us to read each twitch and tic. A negotiator who tries to read too much into an opponent's expression or posture is making a mistake. The folding of the arms may indicate a slight gas pain, not a closed mind.

However, there *is* some body language in bargaining. Don't go overboard on trying to read every move the other party makes, but do be aware of movement and posture. For example, if you are expounding at length and the other person swivels away to look out the window, he or she may be pondering deeply what you say; but there is also a good chance that you are losing your audience. Common sense says: Keep your eyes open and register the *possible* significance of what the adversary is doing.

You can *send* signals through posture and gesture better than you can receive them. After all, you have control over your own movements. You know what you want the other person to think; so it doesn't hurt (and it may help a lot) to send a visual message. (Maybe the other party is a devout believer in all the doctrines of body language!)

This observation may be most important at the first moment of the negotiation, before anything is said. Your adversary sees you before hearing you. Your comportment and posture do send a message at the outset; they are the only message until your spoken words start to take over.

Start off relaxed and confident, and stay that way. Move around. Gesture with your hands rather than sitting rigidly. Lean forward to emphasize your seriousness about particular points. Don't move around when you're listening.

Without worrying too much about beaming visual messages, keep your movements in harmony with the points you're making.

Getting Down to Business

Your relaxed, confident posture at the outset is the first of a number of steps toward a successful negotiating outcome.

Take the Lead

In our corporate culture, the person who seems most pressed for time also seems to be the most important. Someone who has six other things to do before lunch is seen as a bigger bigshot than someone who has all day to chat.

That's why it can be a good move for the employee to reverse the usual order and take the lead in moving the conversation from the opening chitchat stage into the actual business. Ordinarily, the boss does that. The person who is behind the desk (literally or figuratively) is assumed to be calling the shots, deciding when the small talk ends and the brass-tack bargaining begins.

Anticipate. Say, "I'm sure time is as important to you as it is to me. Maybe we'd better get started."

The employer will agree, of course, though he or she may be faintly surprised.

Ask a General Question

Adroit questioning is the key to retaining control of the bargaining process. The manner in which the bargaining actually begins is important in setting a tone.

One conventional procedure would be for the employee or job candidate to assume a reactive role from the start, responding to the employer's questions. Another familiar opening is for the employee to make a statement of requirements and then try to defend it.

You don't have to get locked into either of these conventional openings. It's better to establish, up front, that the discussion is not so much an exchange between superior and subordinate as an exchange between equals. You have not come, hat in hand, to make some kind of outlandish request. In fact, the employer should be trying to sell *you*. Some people who are particularly skilled at employment interviews are so good at turning the situation around that an observer would not know who was hiring whom.

One way to get the employer talking is to refer to a major development that has occurred recently. If there is no such news item, comb the annual report and/or other research materials for possibilities: "I note that practically all of the earnings growth you showed last year was in the home electronics area, in one company you acquired two years ago. Do you expect the other areas of the business to show greater growth?"

The employer can tell you to go to hell, that the two of you are not there to discuss the annual report. But he or she will probably not do that. Instead, you will get an answer that is apt to be the party line. The wording of the answer is not as important as the fact that the employer is giving it and you are receiving it. The faint implication is that you are still trying to decide, knowledgeably, whether this corporation is where you want to make your future.

There's another reason to use the annual report as a bridge into the actual bargaining. The chronically upbeat nature of annual reports puts the company in a favorable light. The employer is less likely to plead poverty when you make your demands.

Bridge into Your Negotiating Position

"I appreciate your being frank with me about your outlook. [You say this whether the employer has been frank or not.] It helps establish the context for our meeting."

And now you begin your pitch. If you're new to the company, you recap your track record. If you've been with the company for a while, you recap what you've done for it. You don't dwell on the past long. You move quickly to focus on the future, outlining what you are going to do for the firm.

"I want to be able to take on this job with a totally clear mind. As few outside considerations as possible. That's why I think you'll agree that it's important to get all the details squared away right now, so that there's no misunderstanding."

Then you start putting your bargaining position forward.

As a Negotiator, Be a Salesperson

The bane of a sales manager's existence is a salesperson who will not ask for the order. Companies lose out when their salespeople understand the product, present its features intelligently, establish rapport, listen to the customer's concerns, inspire trust—and then, when the time comes to close the sale, they *don't*. They are Annie Oakleys who don't pull the trigger.

Reluctance to close may stem from fear of rejection or from a feeling that to "put pressure" on the other party is somehow not nice. Often, however, the individual *does not know how to close the sale*.

When you negotiate an employment agreement, you are involved in a sale. Because the product is you, it's tougher to press for agreement. Society tends to condition us against blowing our own horns too much.

In this chapter, we have selected techniques from the sales world and applied them to helping you deploy your strengths advantageously, establish rapport, discover the customer's real motivations, overcome resistance, and close the sale.

In some ways, you have a considerable edge over the typical sales representative. The employer is interested in you as a "product," or else you would not be talking. But you have problems in common with sales reps. Your price may be too high; your conditions may not enable you to fit into the customer's plans; you may not agree on the terms of the deal.

No sale is 100 percent trouble-free. There is always resistance. And even when you've done a good job of presenting yourself, it's always tough to close the sale.

Whew! That Threshold Is High!

In 1994, Maxxam Inc. put in a plan for any executive with a base salary of $600,000 or more. However (according to *Executive Compensation Reports*), only the president's salary ($590,000) could even come close. The other top five managers made between $325,000 and $165,000.

How to Close a Successful Negotiation

During most negotiations, you have to make concessions. The principle is to buy as much with your concessions as you can. Trade-offs are the essence of the process, so use a trade-off to close the sale.

Early in the negotiation, you may have located a no-give point—a position on which your opponent is adamant. Although not of vital importance to you, the no-give point is of considerable importance to the employer, who is concerned with the demands and expectations of a number of people, not just you.

Often, the underlying factor in a no-give position is *precedent*. Let's say you are asking for a base salary that exceeds the range. An employer negotiating with just you in mind might compromise or altogether meet your demand. Employers worried about tearing the fabric of the company's compensation structure cannot give.

Early in the bargaining, you realize this. Don't concede at that point. Without settling your salary demand, proceed to another point.

By not giving in too easily early in the negotiation, even on issues that are not terribly important to you, you give yourself time to spot the exploitable elements in the employer's position. And you store up ammunition to use at the culmination of the bargaining.

You reach the point at which you've achieved the optimum deal. The employer still resists. You need one more push, a closing tool that will nudge the discussion into agreement.

Return to the point on which the employer cannot give in. Harden your stand. Imply that this is a major issue on which you can't compromise either. The employer—who, on the whole, is ready to go along with most of your requests—is on the spot. The negotiator may tell you why there is no give on this point. Or he or she may be unwilling to admit a lack of authority to compromise.

Don't give in. Suggest reopening other aspects of the agreement—points that seemed to have been settled. Your posture is that if you can't get the salary figure you want, you will have to get a bigger concession elsewhere.

Bargain on the points you've reintroduced. You may get marginally better terms on some points; but you're not going to get a major trade-off, and that's not your objective here anyway. You may even "throw away" some winning cards. Let's say the employer has, with great reluctance, agreed to reopen the question of certain perks. Instead of extracting a small concession here, you say, "I'm having second thoughts about this. We agreed before. I'm going to stick to that agreement."

Now all that's left is the sticking point of base salary.

The employer is in no position to say "Yes" to your demands. Nor is he or she free to allow you to get the money through some other means. And besides, several of your demands are objectionable, including your request for a large up-front bonus.

You're ready to close. The employer is reluctant to close.

Now you use a concession on a major point to close the sale. Don't "give in" too readily; you don't want to make it obvious that your hard-nosed stand has been a ploy. Continue to push for your position.

Then, at last, you say, "Are we at an impasse here? *I want to work for you.* But I need a certain salary in order to make the move. I was willing to make sacrifices, including taking just enough up-front money to cover living expenses. The fact is that coming to work for you—which

I'd still like to do, if we could somehow work it out—will cost me a great deal, directly and indirectly. It's not just a question of schools for the kids, getting a house, the cost-of-living differential.

"I was willing to put those considerations aside and take a hit up front. But that was when I assumed the salary package would make me whole. So I guess I have to rethink the whole thing . . . ."

You're giving the employer a chance to suggest that your up-front bonus be substantially increased. The employer's problem with the salary was that it would trash the company's established range. The one-shot bonus offers a way to meet your needs (at least in part) without setting a precedent.

The employer suggests an increase in the signing bonus, expecting you to reject it and bargain for more. Instead, you think it over for a long moment, and then you say, "It's not what I feel I need. But the chance to work for this firm makes up for a lot in my book. OK, I'll agree to that figure, if you'll give me what I'm asking in these other two areas."

"And we'll have a deal!"

You've made what looks like a major concession. Unless there remains some other fundamental problem (and if there is, now's the time to smoke it out), the employer will be inclined to go along.

Wrap up the deal. Agree on a contract. Say, "Great! We won't have any trouble getting all this into a written agreement. I'll write up my notes on what we've agreed on, and leave it to you to put it into proper language."

And you have a contract!

What Happens When It's Impossible to Get a Formal Contract?

But suppose there does not seem to be any way to persuade the employer to sign an employment agreement. They want you. You've hammered out the details of the deal. There is, between you, a general air of comity; they have the right person, you like the looks of your future with the company. Both of you want to get on with the job.

But not with a written contract.

What can you do?

Consider the Reasons

The reasons for an employer's refusal to put an agreement (formally) in writing can be sorted out under four headings:

1. Personal.
2. Particular.
3. Precedent.
4. Policy.

During the negotiations leading up to this point, you will have been alert to the signals—overt and subliminal—indicating the main reasons for resistance. Now consider the possibilities—and the implications.

1. *Personal*. The firm has no ironclad rule against written employment agreements. There are no obvious reasons for resistance in your case. Nevertheless, the company is adamant: No Written Deal.

Potentially, this adamancy is the most troublesome reason. Why would the employer be so reluctant to commit the arrangement to writing? Might the company be less than committed to some parts of the deal? Could it be that the company wants you to accomplish a specific task—reorganization, innovation, redirection—and then might not be all that eager to keep you around? Are there unexpressed doubts about you?

If the principal objection to a written agreement seems to be *personalized*, satisfy yourself regarding the potential problems before you move ahead.

2. *Particular*. By questioning ("What's your big objection to a contract?"), you deduce that the sticking point lies not in the idea of making a commitment to you, but rather in one or more of the *particulars* of the deal that will be captured by the language of that contract. During the negotiation, you have perhaps glided over a difficult area of disagreement, thinking, "We'll get to that later." But you never got to it later. There is still an unresolved issue.

Return to the issue. Link it with the idea of a contract: "OK. We never really resolved that point, and that's why we shy away from wrapping it up in an agreement. Do you buy that? All right. Then it's a healthy thing. Let's settle that point—and get it wrapped up."

Resolve the unresolved issue(s). Be willing to compromise. Then close on the assurance that both parties will sign an employment agreement.

3. *Precedent.* The company will not sign a contract with you because they don't want to establish a precedent. Others, the employer thinks, will demand contracts. The floodgates will open.

This can be a powerful objection, one that you may not be able to overcome. But, as we'll note, it may not be all-important to try to overcome it.

4. *Policy.* The person who is dealing with you cannot agree to a contract (whatever he or she may think personally) because of "policy." Sometimes this is merely "policy in absentia"; there is a perception (valid or not) that the firm "never" gives anyone a contract.

When this is the hang-up, you can take comfort that it is not directed at you. But now you have to make a decision: Should you initiate an all-out fight for a contract at this time? As we will discuss in a moment, that may not be the best tactic.

What Can You Get in a Trade-Off?

You've worked out a deal, but you can't get a contract. All right. You are willing to give up your legitimate desire for a written agreement (at this time); in exchange, you will bargain for a better deal in one or more aspects of the arrangement.

Should you ask for more money? That's probably not a good idea. It looks like a crass willingness to sell out a principle for bigger bucks.

Instead, renegotiate an issue that is central to the idea of a contract. Severance is a good example. You say, "Your handshake is good enough for me on compensation, title, and all the rest of it. The big reason for a written contract is to cover eventualities *that neither of us wants or expects to come about.* Like a situation in which the nature of the company changes, and people like me are left unprotected. That's why we have severance deals. So let's spell out what that severance arrangement would be—even though it is not likely to happen."

Bargain on the terms of a severance deal. Try for the maximum, with as much as possible available in a lump sum. Negotiate for the earliest vesting of the largest number of shares. Try to provide for extension of health benefits, real outplacement help, and similar perks.

You may find that the employer is quite willing to bargain with you on elements of the arrangement. This may be particularly true if the resistance to a full-blown contract grows out of notions of precedent or policy.

Don't shy away from discussing complex details of severance or incentive compensation, or whatever other issues you choose to renegotiate. In a way, the more detail the better: *Complexity makes it necessary to describe the arrangement in writing.*

Cheer Up—You May Have a Contract Anyway!

Spell out the key parts of your employment deal. *Assume* that they will be put in writing: "Maybe it will save time if I draw up a memo of my understanding of what we just worked out. We can talk over any details that don't seem to jibe, and then sign off on it."

Generate Documents

Save all the pages related to the agreement. Documents signed and acknowledged by both parties can have the same force as a contract. And, indeed, when you amass documentary material that covers your employment deal, you may have the advantage of enjoying contractual status on issues favorable to you, without having to sign a provision such as a noncompete clause.

If you can't get a formal contract, get the agreement in writing anyway, piece by piece. Arrange and preserve the written material. You may have a *de facto* contract. More about this in the next chapter.

6

The *De Facto* Contract

You May Already Have It in Writing

hink back to your first day in your present job. No doubt a lot of things were going through your mind. If it was a step up, you felt good about getting the job. You were thinking about the challenges immediately ahead of you. You were reminding yourself to be careful not to screw up (but you were confident that you were fully capable of handling the job, and that you would *not* screw up). You might have had a passing thought about the money you'd be making, and what it would mean in security and pleasure. You probably felt pretty good about your enhanced status; the title, the office, the perks. You were proud of having vindicated the faith that people had placed in you. You were sizing up the people who'd be working for you. At the same time, you were starting to think about your next step up the ladder—the criteria, the competition, the rewards.

The one thing you were *not* thinking about was getting fired.

That mind-set was especially common in the early 1980s, when business was booming along to the tune of "Let the Good Times Roll." For many managers, there did not seem to be any downside. The one potential hang-up was a merger or takeover—but, as protection against that, you had your golden parachute. Apart from that contingency, you were free to enjoy your work and its rewards—the bonuses, the stock options, the amenities, the club memberships, the sweet smell of general corporate success and unbounded optimism.

Then things went sour. "Leaner and meaner" became the watchword. Executives and professionals who endorsed the proposition that it was good to "cut out the fat" found to their dismay that they were deemed to be the fat.

As the 1990s began, the economy picked up again. Say good-bye to "leaner and meaner," right? Wrong. Typically, *The Wall Street Journal* reported, on May 4, 1995:

"Last week, Mobil Corp. posted soaring first-quarter earnings. This week, it announced plans to eliminate 4,700 jobs." Other big corporations that combined high profits with massive layoffs included Procter & Gamble (P&G), American Home Products, Sara Lee, and Banc One. P&G Chairman Edwin L. Artzt spoke for many of his counterparts when he said, "We must slim down to stay competitive. The consumer wants better value. Our competitors are getting leaner and quicker, and we are simply going to have to run faster to stay ahead."

Jobs are still being cut across the board. Whole layers of management have been eliminated from some companies. In others, the layoffs are more selective; the Grim Reaper stalks silently through the corridors, passing by the offices of some fortunate people and marking others for the Black Spot. People are angry and hurt. *The Wall Street Journal* quotes the lament of a 41-year-old marketing coordinator recently fired by Westinghouse. In the 1980s, when the company was staggered by huge losses, she slaved away for as many as eighty hours a week. "I thought they wanted people like me, who would give up their lives and do anything to keep their jobs," she said. Although things picked up for Westinghouse, the marketing coordinator, who had spent twenty-two years with the company, was laid off in October 1994.

Things can get just as tough for those who stay as for those who are fired. The survivors toil away under increasing stress, often obliged to handle more work because of the departure of their colleagues. The pressure multiplies because they feel totally vulnerable; any given day might be their last. The constant fear of job loss casts a shadow over their lives. They cut out the small luxuries that used to make life pleasant. They shy away from major commitments; that dream house, which once seemed almost in reach, now must remain a dream. Some will not allow themselves to become involved in serious personal relationships.

"You Can't Fire Me—I'm a Procrastinator!"

Northwestern University fired Olan Rand, an art history instructor, because, after Rand's mother died, he neglected to let the federal government know about it and collected $33,000 illegally in social security payments.

Fortune (March 22, 1993) reported that Rand then accused the university of wrongful dismissal. His grounds? His procrastination stemmed from depression, which is a disability.

Possible Fireproofing in Old Pieces of Paper

These are the times when your drive toward perks and parachutes is conjoined with anxious yearning for another desirable commodity: *protection.*

You *need* protection. You would have liked a contract. But when you got hired, you were glad to just get the job. And when you tentatively raised the idea of an employment agreement, your employer's frowning disapproval shot that trial balloon down. Besides, the company assured you that you had a permanent place in its plans, but, if anything unforeseen were to happen, you would be taken care of generously.

Those assurances were oral. Now, it's crunch time, and you're afraid those reassuring words won't translate into action.

The bad news is that you wish you had it in writing. *The good news is that you may ALREADY have it in writing.*

In recent years, the courts have supported the idea of the *de facto* contract. This is not a single formal document written in legalese, but rather a collection of documents relating to key aspects of employment: compensation, benefits, incentive pay, severance, status, and so on. A memo about bonuses can be, in effect, a contract. A companywide communication about broad corporate policy may be interpreted as providing specific rights and protections to employees who are alert enough to claim them.

Even the innocuous, often simplistic, orientation booklet for new hires can be made to serve as a binding agreement.

Don't Throw Away Those Old Handouts

The employee policy manual has been a staple of human resource policy for decades, even before there was a separate personnel department. Employees tended to scorn and ignore the manual. It was full of empty pronouncements, platitudes, and vague statements about the company's aims and ideals. Who paid attention to it? Nobody; not even the top executives whose names appeared in it. The manual was ground out by some person in the catacombs of Human Resources. It was given to everybody who joined the firm, from the highest ranking executive vice president to the newest keypunch operator. It contained general information about vacations and other companywide benefits. Usually, it was accompanied with a sheaf of papers about mundane matters like office hours, fire drills, holidays, and job postings. Anything that was likely to change was printed on a separate piece of paper. The employee manual was part of a package—usually the most ignored part.

Then, in the early 1990s, employers got a big shock. Employees who felt they had been treated unfairly went to court claiming that the words in the employee handbook should be taken seriously. *And the courts started to agree with them!*

Today, a majority of states hold that the language in employee manuals can be construed as specific promises that are binding on the employer.

The Ineffectual Warning Label

Human resource people and company lawyers were shocked. However, they regained their composure when many courts suggested that the binding quality of such a document could be nullified by a disclaimer, prominently displayed, sort of like the warning on a package of cigarettes. A lot of employers just added a box saying something like, "Nothing in this booklet can be construed to constitute an agreement or contract," or "Employment by the Company is at the will of the employer, and nothing herein can be taken as contravening that fact."

These employers figured they were now protected from lawsuits that claimed breach of contract on the basis of the policy manual.

The euphoria was rudely shattered in 1994, when the U.S. Court of Appeals decided in favor of Claudine Robinson in Robinson's dispute with Ada S. McKinley Community Services.[1]

Claudine Robinson went to work for Ada S. McKinley Community Services in 1979. Her job title: Director of Foster Care Services. She received a letter confirming her appointment. The letter stated, "Please be advised that tenure is achieved after the successful completion of six (6) months of service with our Agency."

Claudine Robinson also got a copy of McKinley's Personnel Policies Manual, which said that employees qualify for permanent employment status after completion of the six-month probation period. The manual presented other information, including grounds for disciplining or firing errant employees, and the procedures McKinley would follow in taking such actions. For example, permanent employment status could be suspended "as a result of unacceptable conduct or job performance." The employer had to notify the employee in writing, with supporting reasons, and allow sufficient time for the employee to respond. The manual went on to say that all disciplinary action—including even oral reprimands—"shall be based on objective evidence." Employees could be discharged for "willful insubordination, gross misconduct or other failure to meet Agency standards." In such cases, discharge could be effective immediately.

Robinson completed her six months' probation and went on to work for the social service agency for ten years. In 1989, McKinley fired Robinson. Robinson sued, claiming that the termination breached the terms of the 1979 hiring letter and the employee manual.

McKinley played its ace. A new Personnel Policies Manual had been published in 1986. By then, it was becoming fashionable to include disclaimers. McKinley's disclaimer read as follows:

---

[1] *Robinson v. Ada S. McKinley Community Services, Inc.*, 19 F.3d 359 (7th Cir. 1994).

> The Agency reserves the right to modify or change any of the pro-
> visions of this manual at any time without notice to employees.
> This manual is intended as a general reference guideline for its em-
> ployees; however, the Agency may at times depart from the guide-
> lines set forth herein, when it deems such departure to be warranted
> by the circumstances. Nothing contained in this manual is or shall
> be construed to be a part of any agreement or contract between the
> Agency and its employees.

That, the employer thought, took care of that. And the first court that heard the case[2] agreed, holding that the 1979 letter and manual did not constitute an offer of employment on anything other than an at-will basis. The court said that the terms "permanent employment status" and "tenure" were just a convenience for the employer, distinguishing employees entitled to benefits from those not entitled to benefits. Robinson's complaint was dismissed.

Claudine Robinson appealed. McKinley argued that the 1979 manual and letter did not constitute an employment contract—and, even if they did, the 1986 disclaimer effectively modified the previous contract.

The Seventh Circuit rejected *both* arguments.

What Makes a Handbook a Contract?

The appeals court decision spells out the factors that make an employee handbook or other policy statement into a binding contract:

1. The company document must contain language that would reasonably lead the employee to think an offer had been made.

2. The statement must be presented to the employee in such a
   way that the employee is aware of the contents and reasonably
   believes it to be an offer.

3. The employee must accept the offer by starting or continuing
   to work.

When these conditions are met, a valid contract is formed.

---

[2] United States District Court for the Northern District of Illinois.

The Seventh Circuit decided that, in the case of Claudine Robinson, all of these conditions were fulfilled, and so the 1979 manual and letter *were* an employment contract.

Why Can't the Company Cancel the Contract?

But what about the disclaimer? In 1986, perhaps acknowledging that the earlier manual might be binding, McKinley published a new booklet containing its disclaimer. The agency's argument on appeal cited an Illinois case in which a state court found that "an employer may unilaterally alter existing policies to disclaim those policies in order to prevent contractual obligations from arising . . . ."[3] The state court held that the employee was bound by the disclaimers inserted in the manuals after his hiring.

In Robinson's case, the federal court refused to buy that proposition, citing the generally recognized principle that "a party cannot unilaterally modify a contract." How should the contract be altered? The court's decision declares that "a valid modification requires an offer, acceptance, and consideration."

Robinson continued to work after the insertion of the disclaimer. The employer said that this meant she accepted the alteration. Not so, said the court; she was just doing her job under the original contract. There was no bargaining. McKinley did not give Robinson any inducement to give up her protection.

Thus, the employer was still bound by the terms of the original "contract"—the letter and manual given the employee in 1979.

The employer was pinned in a Catch-22. The original documents were a contract, and that contract could not be changed unilaterally. Never mind that the contract placed more responsibility on the employer than on the employee; that was the employer's tough luck for offering the agreement in the first place.

The McKinley agency can't be blamed for thinking that a simple disclaimer would clear up any confusion and make everything all right. Just about any employer would have thought the same thing—and there was legal underpinning for the feeling. After all, what we were talking about here was just some routine material the company (unilaterally)

---

[3] *Condon v. American Telephone & Telegraph Co., Inc.*, 569 N.E. 2d (2nd Dist. 1991).

created and passed out. Didn't the company have a perfect right to make changes whenever it saw fit?

No way, says the 1994 decision. The employer can print disclaimers *ad infinitum*. It doesn't make any difference. It's like the scene in Shakespeare's *Henry IV, Part 1*, in which the irreverent Hotspur needles the ignorant, boastful Welsh chieftain Owen Glendower:

> **Glendower:**   I can call spirits from the vasty deep.
>
> **Hotspur:**   Why, so can I, or so can any man; but will they come when you do call for them?

Circling the Wagons

Alarm bells are clanging. Innocuous (and usually ignored) booklets handed out to employees have suddenly become legal documents. If the company handbook contains promises (even implied promises), the employer may be called on to make good on those promises.

Legal departments and human resource executives want to keep the lid on the ramifications of this decision, but they are discussing it urgently. In the *Employee Relations Law Journal*, Kenneth A. Jenero sounds a warning: "The Seventh Circuit's decision in *Robinson* has potentially far-reaching and disturbing implications for employers—not only in the state of Illinois, but also in other states . . . [an employer] will forever be precluded from changing those policies without . . . employees' consent."[4]

Once handbooks and similar documents come under contract law, the employer is in a bind. A contract cannot be altered unilaterally. Putting out a new booklet with a disclaimer does not offer protection, even when the employee accepts the new booklet and continues to work for the company.

Experts say that the Illinois decision (and a constellation of similar decisions) gives nonunion employees greater rights than union employees. Collective bargaining agreements have a fixed term. The

---

[4] *Employee Relations Law Journal*, September 22, 1994, "Employers Beware: You May Be Bound by the Terms of Your Old Employee Handbooks," by Kenneth A. Jenero.

Illinois court says that the terms of the old handbook remain in force indefinitely.

Other courts have said, among other things, that every modification of the handbook is an offer of a modification of a contract of employment. By staying on the job, the employee accepts the offer.

The situation will remain somewhat fluid, perhaps for quite a while. Meanwhile, however, experts (like Jenero) offer employers advice along these lines:

- Give employees notice of a change in the handbook. Send them a letter or memo explaining the changes.

- Spell out the message that the new handbook (in Jenero's words) "is intended to supersede and replace all previous employee handbooks, manuals and policy statements, whether oral or written, issued by the employer."

- Put in a disclaimer, such as:

The handbook is not a contract or an offer to form a contract, and is not intended to create any binding contractual commitments between the employer and any of its employees; the employer and its employees retain the mutual right to terminate the employment relationship at will, with or without warning, notice, or cause. The employer retains the right to unilaterally modify, interpret, or discontinue any of the policies or procedures set forth in the handbook; and any such action will apply to existing and future employees, with continued employment representing the consideration and the employee's acceptance of the action.

- Require employees to sign a form acknowledging receipt and acceptance of the new terms.

The Weakness in the Defenses

There are problems (from the employer's point of view) with this defense. For one thing, by making such a big deal of the changes, the company signals that it feels it does have a contractual relationship with employees. Jenero alerts employees to a more fundamental flaw. By asking employees to accept the "new" contract, the company implies that the employee may choose to reject the modifications and continue working under the "old" contract. However, the author concludes, "employers should at least be in a better position to argue that any employee who continued in employment, without expressly rejecting the proposed modifications, implicitly accepted the modifications. The only other hope for employers is that [the Illinois decision] either will be limited in its particular facts or will not be followed at all."

Building Your "Stealth" Contract

That's what specialists are telling employers about the unexploded contractual mines that may lie in their old employee handbooks.

What does it all mean to you?

1. Start Thinking in Terms of Your CONTRACTUAL Relationship

You hope that you will never be fired, that there will never be a battle over your termination pay, and that your relationship with the employer will continue in productive cordiality.

You only need contractual protection in case of trouble. Then, you may need all the help you can get.

Help begins with knowledge. The more you know about developments affecting you, the better prepared you are to defend yourself in the clinches.

You should know about anything of substance that affects your compensation, job status, retirement, severance, or chances of getting a fair deal in a dispute. That includes having a general idea of what the courts are saying.

This doesn't mean you're going to sue anybody. Starting a lawsuit is the absolute last resort. However, just knowing about the legal resources that *might* be available to you can serve as a potent bargaining tool. The main thing to bear in mind is that you *already have* a contractual relationship with the company. True, it is not written up in one neat document. It is scattered through various documents—some of which you consider unimportant, or never think of at all, or don't even know about.

This is your *de facto contract*—or, if you prefer, your *stealth contract*.

2. Save Those Old Handbooks

The situation is still evolving. New court decisions may provide greater clarity—or, as is often the case, the courts may confuse the situation further.

But one thing is clear. Experts consider old employee handbooks a problem for employers because the statements in the handbooks can be construed as binding promises.

That holding puts the employee in the enviable position of having a unilateral pact, in which the employee gives up nothing of substance in exchange for the assurances in the "contract."

This *does not* mean you're invulnerable. It *does* mean that the nondescript policy booklet is a potentially useful part of your stealth contract.

Save all your old employee manuals. Have you thrown away the one you were given when you joined the firm? You may not even have looked at it. No doubt it came in a package with various other pieces of paper that are provided to new hires at all levels. (An incoming executive vice president feels little in common with a mailroom messenger being hired at the same time; but the provisions of the implied contract apply to the highest rank as well as the lowest.)

Even if you didn't save your copy, the contents still apply to you. Get hold of the original booklet. The Human Resources/Personnel people know where it is. They save everything, either in a hard-copy file or a data bank. Get it. It's not confidential; there's no reason why they should not give it to you.

You'd rather not draw attention to the fact that you're getting the document? Don't make a big deal of it. Don't ask the HR Director (who probably doesn't know where it is anyway). Ask one of the midlevel people in the department—verbally, not in writing. Staff persons, conditioned to respond to requests from other departments know where things are.

The text of the handbook in the Illinois case would have applied even if the employee had not had the booklet. But if you don't have it, you don't know what's in it.

There is a more important reason to possess an actual copy of an old company policy manual. You will be able to use this document, and others, as negotiating exhibits. You definitely want to avoid going to court; Ms. Robinson has already done that for you.

3. Save All Potentially Relevant Documents

You may have a read-and-toss attitude toward your in-box, which overflows almost daily with the volume of deliveries. Instead, start saving documents that could be relevant in a future dispute. For example:

- When you agree to take a job, you receive a letter saying, "We look forward to a long and happy association . . . . We have great plans for you . . . ."

- A firm that is trying to recruit you wants you to relocate. You are savvy enough to get a relocation bonus and to have the whole arrangement described in writing.

- Your boss sends you a congratulatory memo after you've scored a success. It contains language attesting to your value to the company.

- The annual report's "Letter from the Chairman" lauds the sterling worth of the company's people and remarks on the lengths to which the firm has gone to build its workforce and keep good employees.

- Everyone in the company receives a year-end missive celebrating the ability and dedication of the people on staff.

- The company house organ runs an editorial in which the CEO-author says that every employee is entitled to the same fairness that the top brass receive.

- You have asked for some improvement in your retirement package. Your superior says it can't be done right now, but, not to worry. You send him or her a memo (and retain a copy) saying, "I appreciate your assurance that my retirement plan will be amended to provide continuing full medical coverage to me and my family. . . ."

Messages of reassurance, congratulation, and encouragement are constantly passing back and forth in an organization. Some are general; some are particularized. Some have meaning; others are pro forma expressions. They contain, specifically or by implication, *assurances*—of fair treatment, of the loyalty of the organization to its members, of safeguards and procedures in discipline and discharge. *Put them in your "De Facto Contract" file.* Maybe most of them are meaningless. That doesn't matter. Somewhere in that file may be a piece of paper (or an electronic entry) that will come in very handy in case of a dispute.

4. Get Your Job Description in Writing

Do you have a job description? Where is it? Have you looked at it lately? Pull it out of that desk drawer. Is it up-to-date? You may find, to your surprise, that your job description has not kept up with your status and your responsibilities.

People don't look at a job description every day to figure out what they are supposed to do. They know what they're supposed to do, and so does everybody else. But the job description can be a very important part of your *de facto* contract.

Here's a brief quote from the employment contract between Harold E. Layman and Blount, Inc., which appears in its entirety in Appendix 3:

> Duties: Executive shall serve the Company in a full-time salaried position designated by the Company. The position is to be defined using a written job description . . . .

Get and file an up-to-date job description. If you don't have one, Human Resources should have one. If none exists, work one out.

5. Document All Pay, Perks, Bonuses, and Other Rewards

The intricate nature of most executive compensation plans (and components of plans) today makes it all but certain that they exist as written documents. Make sure yours is in writing—complete and up-to-date.

Keep past documents as well. They are all part of your contractual relationship with the company.

6. Set Up a Clip File

In your daily reading of the business and general press, keep your eyes open for items bearing on your rights as an employee. Never mind that you don't ever expect them to apply to you; clip them anyway. Typically, a reader of *The Wall Street Journal* would clip such stories as "Age-Bias Law Can't Be Used in Suits Charging Pension Violation in Layoffs" (April 21, 1993); "Seminars Teach Managers Finer Points of Firing" (April 26, 1995); "Boss May Be Personally Liable If Firing Violates Disability Law" (May 2, 1995).

Clip relevant articles from magazines as well. Your computer (with a modem), gives you access to a wealth of databank material that you can access by topic. There are a variety of such services. The author of this book makes particular use of Dow Jones News/Retrieval; the ZiffNet business and magazine databases, available on CompuServe; and the resources available on America Online.

And, as elsewhere in this book, we urge familiarity with *Executive Compensation Reports*, the newsletter and source for executive compensation information.

7. Don't Sign Your Rights Away

Realizing that they cannot unilaterally modify an implied "just cause" provision or other implied provisions, some companies take another tack. To shore up their contention that an employee's continuation on the job is assent to the modification, they ask for a signed receipt of the new booklet or document carrying the altered policy and disclaimer.

One employee wrote the following on such a receipt form: "I have received the Handbook but do not agree with the comments above [namely, that his employment with the company was at-will]."[5]

There are various ways to avoid signing such a receipt. One way is just to ignore it; the firm may not wish to make a federal case of getting your signature. Another is to go in the other direction and treat the

---

[5] *Id.*

requested signature as if it were a profoundly important step. Ask what it means: "Why a signed receipt for a little booklet?" Ask what will be done with the receipt. Then say you'll think about it.

8. Keep Getting Everything in Writing

As we urge elsewhere in the book, get all happenings, comments, and records in writing. (You'll find ongoing suggestions here about how to do that.) When, for example, a top executive says that you are doing fine, see if you can get him or her to put the high marks in a memo; or send a memo of thanks for the reassurance, which you then spell out.

The point of building your *de facto* contract is not to adopt a "victim" mentality. Nor is it to prepare a lawsuit. You hope you never need to use it. But, if the crunch comes, you have good negotiating material that might make a clear statement: You know your rights.

7

How Long Should the
Contract Run?

The usual length of time covered by an employment contract is
three to five years. The agreement should always specify the
termination date. Here's a typical term-of-employment provision:

> The Company has employed and now employs the Employee upon
> an active full-time basis, as Executive Vice President and Chief
> Operating Officer, subject to the order, supervision, and direction
> of the Board of Directors of the Company and any officer senior to
> [him/her] and the Employee has accepted and agrees to remain in
> the employ of the Company in the aforesaid capacity upon the
> terms, conditions, and provisions herein stated from the effective
> date hereof (April 1, 1996) through March 31, 1999, unless sooner
> terminated as hereinafter provided.

Note that this clause also covers the employee's full-time status
and titles, and that it refers to the possibility of earlier termination
under subsequent provisions of the contract. The language covering
reasons for early termination is crucial; we'll discuss it a little later in
this book.

Some contracts are automatically renewed from year to year by
language like this: "This agreement shall be extended for an additional
year on June 30 of each year unless either party gives the other written
notice of termination."

Any deviation from the usual three- to five-year term raises some interesting questions. If the employer presses for a shorter term, the manager may wonder how deeply the organization is committed to him or her. A manager in a strong negotiating position—sure that this is the company for the long haul—may push for a maximum term. This tactic can backfire. Years hence, the situation changes. The manager receives an attractive offer. But the contract gets in the way of the move. There must be extraordinary reasons to want a very long-term deal (say, ten years). The manager must be sure that this is *the* place for an indefinite career stay, and that the assured tenure is needed, to do what needs to be done.

Severance payments (salary continuation) will usually be higher under a five-year contract than under a three-year contract. If a manager thinks his or her job may be in jeopardy—for whatever reason—within the next few years, the longer term takes higher priority.

When an individual wants the job but isn't in a position to make a really good deal going in, he or she may try to keep the term of an agreement as short as is reasonably possible, so as to be able to achieve great things demonstrating great value—and negotiate a richer package when the initial pact runs out.

The relationship between term and amount of compensation can be used as a trade-off in the negotiation: the manager "concedes" on a shorter term (the longer term wasn't a must anyway) in exchange for more favorable stock options.

When you think about the term of the contract, you touch on a variety of subjects:

- Long-term career strategy.
- Confidence about one's ability to succeed in the job.
- The nature of the challenge to be faced.
- Immediate and long-term prospects for the company.
- Possibilities of merger and takeover.
- State of the industry.

Ordinarily, the employer will suggest the term. The suggestion may be automatic, arising from the fact that the company always thinks of, say, three-year arrangements; or it may be the result of some calculation. The executive should not accept the suggested term as a given; rather, he or she should think through the question beforehand.

Variations from the Norm

Most employment agreements run three to five years, but there are exceptions. Michael Eisner's 1989 contract with Disney (which is exceptional in a number of ways) runs for ten years: "The term of this Agreement shall commence as of January 10, 1989 and shall terminate on September 30, 1998."

Here's another variation, from an agreement (signed in 1994) between Blount, Inc. and Senior Vice President/CFO Harold E. Layman (Layman was 47 when he signed):

> 5.0   Term: The term of Agreement shall be for a period beginning on the effective date of this agreement and ending two years prior to the date of the Executive's 65th birthday.
>
> This Agreement is a contract of employment at will. This means that employment will continue only so long as both Company and Executive want it to do so. Subject to the minimum notice requirement set forth below, Executive is free to quit at any time at his discretion and Company is, subject to the severance payment provisions of Paragraph 7.0, free to terminate Executive's employment at any time at its discretion. The Agreement may be terminated by the Executive or the Company upon 30 days' written notice. If the Agreement is terminated for reasons other than normal retirement, death, total disability, Cause (Paragraph 9.0(d)), or voluntary termination, the Executive shall be paid as described in Severance Payment (Paragraph 7.0).

(The entire text of this contract is in Appendix 3.)

Why the Employer May Want a Longer Term

When a company asks for a longer term (five years or more), it's reasonable to assume that it wants an extended relationship, without having to renegotiate often. The firm is expressing its confidence in the manager. However, the firm is not necessarily saying it has big plans for the manager. For example, a corporation that plans to make an executive head of a subsidiary within two years may assume realistically that a new and more lucrative agreement will have to be made at the time of the promotion, so the term of the present pact may be short. However, let's say the company's goal is to be sure that an important (although not high-profile) task is handled reliably. It may want to tie up, for as long as possible, the person who can perform that task. In suggesting a long-term agreement, the company may be saying, "We have big plans for you." But it may also be saying, "You're not the greatest, but you're useful and reliable. Once we're sure you'll be doing your thing for a while, we can think about other matters."

In the negotiation, probe beneath the surface. Ask what plans the company has for you. By listening to what is said—and what is *not* said—get as good an idea as you can of how the company sees your future.

Why the Employer May Want a Shorter Term

One overriding reason for the employer to push for a short-term agreement is *unwillingness to make a commitment.* In many cases, the company is not sure whether the manager will work out. A second factor may be impending change in the company, which may make the manager's services less desirable. For instance, suppose the job to be filled is marketing director for the consumer goods division. If the firm is considering de-emphasizing consumer goods, it will want to avoid a long-term commitment to a marketing specialist.

Precedent is another reason for the company's preferring a shorter term. Even if the employer has every confidence in an employee, and big plans for the employee's future, there is still the question: "What will the other managers think?" The specter of hordes of managers demanding five-year contracts may overshadow the company's commitment to one individual.

Why the Executive May Want a Longer Term

A manager who is in a strong bargaining position will want to push that advantage to the limit by securing the most favorable possible terms, extending over the longest possible period. To ensure the continuation of the manager's services, the company may be willing to make some attractive long-term concessions.

The manager should also have in mind the size of the termination agreement. The longer the term of the contract, the longer the period over which termination payments will be made—at least, that is the general rule.

The individual's view of the challenges and opportunities that lie ahead is probably the biggest factor in opting for a longer rather than a shorter term. Let's say the manager is confident that he or she can turn a struggling division around, but it will take some time. In these circumstances, the longer the better.

Why the Executive May Want a Shorter Term

The employee may be confident of accomplishing a lot in a short time, thus creating a more favorable bargaining position. Right now, he or she can't get the desired deal. The best strategy is to accept what is offered but keep the term of the pact to a minimum.

When you're negotiating from strength, get the best deal over the longest possible period. It doesn't make much sense to lock yourself into a mediocre deal for a long time, unless job security is at the top of your priority list.

Taking an Effective Negotiating Posture

If the manager wants a long-term contract and the company offers two years, the logical question is: "Why?" The employee can say something like, "I'm surprised that you want to negotiate all the aspects of this arrangement and then limit it to just a couple of years. I have to ask myself why. One reason could be that you foresee big changes in the organization. Is there a change-of-control possibility? If that were the case, you wouldn't want to make any long-term commitments."

The employee bargains on the assumption that the company's aversion to a long-term commitment is *general*, not confined to this particular case. The employer can hardly say, "No, we have no problem with long-term deals as a rule; with you, though, we want to keep it shorter." The rejoinder is likely to be reassurance: "No, there are no big changes of that kind down the road."

Having said this, the employer must offer a reason. One standard ploy: "We never sign more than a two-year agreement."

Your research (and we hope you have done your homework) may suggest that this blanket statement doesn't quite hold water. This is not the time to challenge it directly. Instead, push the "Why?" question. It's a bit tough for an employer to make a convincing case for avoidance of an extended commitment. Companies that are trying to hire people are hardly likely to admit doubts about competence. Nor is it easy to stick to a position that nothing longer than two years is possible. Your opposite number is apt to feel the need for a better reason than "We've always done it that way." Such insistence makes the company look rather stodgy.

Right now is when you get an idea whether the term of the contract is a big issue. If it's not, the employer will agree to a longer term or will suggest that the discussion move on to other points, returning to the term of the contract later. If you feel that, in the subsequent discussion, the employer is willing to talk objectively about signing a longer-term pact, you have no reason not to table the point for the moment.

However, let's say the employer wants to sweeten other parts of the deal—salary, bonus, and so on (but *not* severance)—to get you to buy into a minimum term. An alarm bell should go off in your head. What's going on here? Is it possible that the company just wants some short-term work? Is somebody waiting in the wings for your job?

Be wary of trading a shorter term for bigger pay. The company doesn't have to pay you if you get fired—unless the severance arrangement says so.

If the company insists on a minimal term, you should bargain hard for a bigger severance package: "OK, I'll buy the idea that you won't go for five years, or even three, because that's not the way you do business. That leaves me with a bigger risk factor. I'm sure we won't have any trouble taking care of that. We can just augment the severance arrangement. Since it's not likely to come into play, then it won't make that much difference to you."

Negotiate hard for the kind of severance package you would get on a five-year contract.

If you are moving into a new job, and the employer insists on a short term without offsetting it by providing a larger severance deal, think carefully about the implications. You may still want the job; but your reality check shows that the firm may not be contemplating an extended relationship.

You're taking a chance. Try for an up-front, lump-sum bonus that will compensate you in part for the risk. If you keep running into a stone wall along each of these fronts—term, severance, up-front bonus—you *must* ask yourself why. No matter how much you need or want this job, consider the implications.

Negotiations over employment agreements can provide some useful insights. When they suggest that you should take off the rose-colored glasses, do so.

Setting the Tone for the Negotiation

In most contract negotiations, the term is not likely to be the big issue. You may find the employer offering an acceptable term. But this doesn't mean you should take it without question. If you're offered three years, try for five. The company may not be willing to go for five, but might compromise on four. And even if you wind up agreeing to three years, you may be able to gain some bargaining advantage on other points. At the very least, you will have signaled that you've come to bargain seriously and you intend to take nothing for granted.

The same rules don't apply, though, if you want a shorter term than the company wants. You're in an altogether different position, and you must be ready to justify it.

The standard reason for seeking a shorter term is that you think you can get a better deal—with this company or another—within, say, a couple of years. You want the advantage of a contract, but you don't want it to tie you down for too long.

You don't tell this to your adversary. That would be neither tactful nor productive. Even if you are able to force the shorter-term deal, you leave a residue of resentment and suspicion. The assumption is that you're looking around for another job; so the company looks around for someone who might take your place. If you stay on and no one else is hired, the suspicion that you may just be using the company as a career pit stop continues.

Even if that's your plan, avoid giving that impression. For one thing, you may find yourself wanting to stay with the firm longer than you thought you would. And why stir up needless resentment and suspicion? That atmosphere will make it harder for you to do a good job and build an impressive track record.

Your best bet is to acknowledge that you figure on being able to make a better deal *with this company*. Say, "Frankly, I think that what I hope to do for you is going to make me more valuable to you, and worth more to you, in a fairly short period of time. When that happens, I'd want to be able to sit down with you in a position where we're both free to talk it over. But maybe I can't do the job for you. If that happens, you don't want to be stuck with me because of a piece of paper. I don't see that happening, and that's why I'm willing to take the risk. But, all in all, it makes sense for us to agree to a two-year deal . . . ."

Winning a point in a contract negotiation is not everything. You still have to live with the job and the company. If your bosses are unexpectedly adamant about a particular term, be alert to the implications. But if other things are more important, don't make a major issue out of it at the beginning. You can always return to it, after bargaining on the other issues.

These Days, Length of Contract Is Important

Ken Cole publishes *The Recruiting & Search Report.* He is also an author and search consultant. Within the past three years, he has dealt with more than 100 executives earning between $100,000 and $800,000+. Cole says, "Because of downsizing and restructuring, it's more important than ever to get a contract that covers the longest possible term. I show my clients how to negotiate for two years' severance after termination for reasons other than cause. The agreement must cover Change of Control."

If you can't get two years, advises Cole, settle for one year. If you have options and/or stock grants, insist that they all vest within the severance period.

Ken Cole is a good source of information on compensation trends. Reach him at:

P.O. Box 9433
Panama City Beach, FL 32407
904-235-3733

8

How Your Job Is Defined in the Contract

The Duties section of an agreement can become very important if the employer claims that the employee has not been carrying out the duties called for, or if the employee claims that the company is meting out treatment or assigning duties that are at odds with the agreement.

A useful Duties section gives, along with the job title, a capsule version of what the individual is supposed to do. Some clauses are quite general; they say, in effect, that the person does what the company wants. Other clauses are more specific about the responsibilities of the job and the reporting relationships.

Here are a few examples.

The Company hereby agrees to employ the Executive, and the Executive hereby agrees to accept employment with the Company and agrees to serve, upon the terms and conditions herein contained, as the Company's Executive Vice President, Chief Administrative Officer, and Secretary.

[From Michael D. Eisner's contract with Disney]

Executive shall be employed by Company as its Chairman and Chief Executive Officer. Executive shall report directly and solely to the Company's Board of Directors (**"Board"**).

151

Executive shall devote his full time and best efforts to the Company. Company agrees to nominate Executive for election to the Board as a member of the management slate at each annual meeting of stockholders during his employment hereunder at which Executive's director class comes up for election. Executive agrees to serve on the Board if elected.

The Company hereby employs Executive to serve as Senior Vice President–Chief Financial Officer of the Company. Executive shall have such responsibilities and authority as may from time to time be assigned to Executive by the President, the Chief Executive Officer of the Company or by the Board of Directors.

Whereas, the Board of Directors of the Company has requested the Executive to accept appointment to the offices of Chairman, President and Chief Executive Officer of the Company, and President and Chief Executive Officer of the Subsidiary, and the Executive has accepted such appointment subject to the terms of this agreement (the "Agreement"), the parties in consideration thereof have agreed as follows:

1. Employment
The parties hereby confirm their intention that during the term of the Agreement set forth in paragraph 2 below, the Executive shall be employed as Chairman, President and Chief Executive Officer of the Company, and President and Chief Executive Officer of the Subsidiary, with overall charge and responsibility for the business and affairs of each, subject at all times to supervision by the Board of Directors of the Company or the Subsidiary, as the case may be . . . .

Duties During the Period of Employment
Employee shall devote his full business time, attention, and best efforts to the affairs of Employer and its subsidiaries during the Period of Employment and shall have such duties, responsibilities, and authority as shall be consistent with the position and title of Chairman of the Board of Directors and Chief Executive Officer. Employee may engage in other activities, such as activities

involving charitable, educational, religious, and similar types of organizations (all of which are deemed to benefit Employer), speaking engagements, and similar type activities, and may serve on the board of directors of other corporations approved by the Board of Directors of Employer, in each case to the extent that such activities do not materially detract from or limit the performance of his duties under this Agreement, or inhibit or conflict in any material way with the business of Employer and its subsidiaries.

The Corporation hereby employs Mr. Pierce during the term of this Agreement, subject to his election as such by the Board of Directors of the Corporation (hereinafter called the "Board"), as Executive Vice President of the Corporation.

Mr. Pierce shall report to one or more of the persons holding the following offices, as shall be determined by the Corporation from time to time: (a) Chairman of the Board; (b) the President.

The office of Executive Vice President of the Corporation shall have the responsibilities set forth in Paragraph (a) of this Article FIRST or such responsibilities as may be assigned to such office by the Board, and/or the Chairman of the Board, and/or the President of the Corporation, provided, however, that the responsibilities assigned to such office shall be of a character and dignity appropriate to a senior executive of the Corporation.

. . . Responsibility for all activities of the Television Division, including news and sports, the owned television stations, Video Enterprises and theatrical motion pictures. In the areas for which such position is responsible, no officer except the Chairman of the Board and/or the President shall be superior in authority to such position.

Mr. Pierce's principal office shall be at the Corporation's headquarters.

Most books on management practice insist that there should be a job description for every job. But the descriptions applied to executive positions, if they exist at all, are likely to be incomplete or misleading. This is probably no drawback at all for the talented manager; his or her contributions are apt to be judged in terms of results, not how well a particular pattern was followed. Today, we see great emphasis on stating what executives are supposed to accomplish, without precise definition of their authority, responsibility, or parameters of operation. This is a logical—if not always helpful—outgrowth of the popular concept of Management by Objectives.

Now and then, we see an employment contract that applies objective measurement to the job. Take, for example, the following excerpt from a contract between Blount, Inc. and Harold E. Layman, the company's Senior Vice President and CFO, dated January 1, 1994:

> 1.0   Purpose and Employment: The purpose of this Agreement is to define the relationship between the Company, as an employer, and Executive, as an employee. By the execution of this Agreement, the Company employs Executive and Executive accepts employment by the Company.
>
> 2.0   Compensation and Benefits: Based on the Executive's performance, the compensation in effect on the effective date of this agreement and as adjusted from time to time by the President and Chief Executive Officer and approved by the Compensation and Management Development Committee of the Board of Directors of the Company, and the Executive's position with the Company, the Executive shall be entitled to and the Company agrees to provide any and all basic benefits which are generally provided by the Company to its similarly situated employees. Further, the Executive shall be entitled to and the Company agrees to provide any and all working facilities, perquisites and incentives which are in effect on the date of this agreement and as may be adjusted or eliminated from time to time at management's discretion.
>
> 3.0   Duties: Executive shall serve the Company in a full-time salaried position designated by the Company. *The position is to be defined using a written job description and be subject to the Hay Compensation Position Evaluation System or other systematic evaluation systems that the Company may employ.* [Emphasis added]

The Hay Evaluation System is a method of job evaluation developed and applied by the Hay Group, a worldwide human resources management consulting organization, with corporate headquarters in Washington (DC), and U.S. headquarters in Philadelphia.

Get That Job Description Out of the Drawer!

Managers can live their entire working lives without ever worrying much about how their jobs are defined, except in terms of the results they are supposed to achieve. Sometimes, however, the job description becomes important because the employer tries to change the nature of the job of a person who is covered by a contract. Some companies have tried to humiliate managers by giving them ignominious and demeaning tasks while continuing to pay the specified amounts. They hope the executives will get fed up and quit. This kind of underhanded maneuver, relatively rare but unfortunately far from unknown, is made possible by vague Duties clauses like this one:

> Executive shall devote his full time and best efforts to the Company and to fulfillment of the responsibilities called for by his position, which shall include such duties as may from time to time be assigned by the Company.

There is nothing in this language that would prevent the company from assigning the duties of coffee messenger, gofer, or cleaner of the washrooms. True, this would be going too far, even for the most hard-boiled of employers, but the potential is there.

Take a good look at the Duties clause and ask yourself: "What could they make me do under this? What *couldn't* they make me do under this?" Some contracts offer a little protection by such wording as: "provided that such duties are reasonably consistent with Executive's education, experience, and background."

All right. If you've graduated from St. Paul's, Yale, and Wharton, if you have spent twenty years rising to the heights in your profession, and if you are acknowledged by one and all as a person of distinction, you won't be assigned to latrine duty. But the words "reasonably consistent" and the elasticity of the three criteria winding up the sentence provide a fair amount of leeway for the employer. The most obvious course for an employer who wanted to force you out would be demotion. From Vice President, Marketing, you are suddenly demoted to Sales Manager, Northwest Region. This involves a difficult relocation and a considerable reduction in status, but you might have a tough time arguing that it is inconsistent with your "education, experience, and background," particularly if the company can show that people with similar backgrounds have occupied similar jobs.

To protect themselves against such contingencies, employees might negotiate for a provision worded like this:

> Company agrees to employ Executive for [term] at Executive's present management position or at a higher responsible management position with Company.

This is somewhat better, but it is far from ironclad. The employer might still try a sideways move or create a position ("vice president for contingency planning") that is not a demotion but is a nothing job.

Being kicked sideways brings just as many frustrations and embarrassments as being demoted, but it is not so apparent to the world at large. You still have a title. There may be gossip in the industry that the firm has stuck you in a Mickey Mouse spot, but that probably won't reduce your attractiveness to other companies as much as a demotion would. You may hate to take the empty position, but you can spend your time looking for another job while you collect your paychecks.

In the contract excerpts at the start of this chapter, you'll find various employee safeguards against unpleasant treatment. This language, for example:

> . . . shall have such duties, responsibilities, and authority as shall be consistent with the position . . .

That's fine, as long as they don't change the position. The following language offers greater protection:

> . . . shall have . . . such responsibilities as may be assigned . . . , provided, however, that the responsibilities assigned to such office shall be of a character and dignity appropriate to a senior executive of the Corporation.

By specifying treatment "appropriate to a senior executive of the Corporation," the agreement covers perks big and small as well as the more substantial areas of employment.

Companies sometimes harass managers who have contracts through "torture by transfer." This is becoming less prevalent as executives—now more insistent on the lifestyle aspects of the agreement—build in assurance of being able to work in their preferred locations, safe from being uprooted. You can attain this assurance by inclusion of language like, "The Company agrees to employ the Executive at its corporate headquarters [address] or another location acceptable to the Executive."

A further refinement of the contract may specify present and/or future titles (vice president, executive vice president, president, and so on). This approach would keep the employer from dreaming up a meaningless title, but it does not ensure the manager's status and function. Employers who want to make it tough for a manager with "title protection" may keep the title but change the reporting routine. He or she can be told to report to someone who has an inferior title and a lower spot on the totem pole.

This ploy can be particularly effective because it attacks the individual in a vulnerable spot—his or her innate sense of status. "Pecking order" is by no means confined to the barnyard. We may sometimes be ashamed of our impulse to seek status, but we are driven by it nevertheless. Status-seeking exists in all cultures. In a particular New Guinea tribe, the people wear no clothes. However, the men wear sheaths the color and shape of carrots on their penises. The bigger the "carrot," the higher the status. In that part of the world, the biggest carrot takes the place of the corner office.

A contract can safeguard against status destruction by specifying the reporting channels: "Executive shall report to the persons holding the following offices: (a) Chairman of the Board, (b) President. . . . In the areas for which such position is responsible, no officer except the Chairman of the Board and/or the President shall be superior in authority."

People who are negotiating employment agreements should build in safeguards against being marginalized. Typically, the protection consists of a provision relating to reporting channels. A contract stating that the person will report directly to the Chief Executive Officer does not guarantee that the CEO's door will always be open, but it will at least limit the employer's ability to relegate the individual to a lower rung of the ladder.

These recommendations offer specific protections against certain kinds of harassment. No contract can give you a complete defense against attacks on status. The company may not be able to demote you or change your reporting relationship, but it can still try to diminish you by other means. One such means is the "task force assignment." The task force is a positive and useful tool for bringing a diverse group together to combine their talents toward the solution of a particular corporate problem. The members of the task force are persons who would ordinarily not work with each other, and who, after the purposes of the task force are achieved, may never work with each other again. The strength of the approach is that it encourages the members of the group to interact without feeling confined by the organization chart.

An employer might pervert this technique to impose a *de facto* demotion. The person is assigned to the group and told to report to someone who is distinctly junior—and, perhaps, someone whose supervision might be especially galling. Refusal to participate, especially if the company has used the task force approach before, might give the employer grounds for dismissal.

Along with specifics like job title and location, the contract can provide a good measure of protection in somewhat broader areas: assigned tasks and reporting relationships, for example. It cannot keep a really determined employer from making life tough for you. But a well-drawn employment agreement is likely to make any employer think at least twice before trying to drive out an unwanted executive through status amputation.

As the practice of negotiating employment agreements becomes more common and applies to a greater number of positions, these contracts are apt to contain more complete job descriptions. After all, a good job description—including title, reporting relationships, level in the organization, location, duties, responsibilities, and authority—helps employer and employee.

Some senior managers give lip service to job descriptions but resist them in practice. They're afraid the job description will set up barriers that limit innovation. That's bad; but a well-written job description can define the job without being restrictive.

Resourceful executives will want to create their own job descriptions—or at least shape the job descriptions that will be applied to them. The first step is to find out how the company views the job. If, for example, you've been approached by an executive search firm, ask the headhunter about the job description that has been given to him or her.

Author and consultant Auren Uris provides this "executive sketch," used by a search firm on an assignment:

THE POSITION

Operations manager, reporting to the vice president and general manager of the division. He/she will be directly responsible for the profitability of this division through his/her subordinate organization. This includes:

General sales manager
Plant managers at branch plants
Product engineers

Specific responsibilities include:

A. Production

(1) Production, forecasting, deliveries

(2) Inventory controls, purchasing

(3) Manufacturing costs

(4) Quality of products

B. Sales

(1) Sales programs for automotive products in OEM and resale markets

(2) Sales forecasts to permit plant scheduling and control

(3) Advertising programs

(4) Customer contacts

C. Profits

(1) Profit forecasting

(2) Pricing policy

D. Engineering

Product improvement, modification, and development through engineering research

E. Personnel

(1) Constructive employee relations

(2) Maintenance of adequately trained personnel to protect the company and permit advancement of qualified persons

QUALIFICATIONS

A degree in mechanical engineering or business administration is preferred, although the equivalent in manufacturing experience will be considered. Although the person selected will have charge of operations, the emphasis will be placed most heavily on manufacturing know-how. He/she must be a good manager and be able to anticipate production problems with practical solutions. He/she must be thoroughly familiar with the manufacturing of small, low-unit-cost, high-volume products and be conversant with the demands of automotive OEM sales as well as aftermarket needs.

OPPORTUNITY

There will be ample opportunity for the person selected to demonstrate his/her ability to run this division in his/her own way and to qualify for greater responsibility with the parent company. Compensation is composed of an attractive salary, profit-sharing bonus, and stock options.

Should the Contract Include a Job Description?

There are pluses and minuses to the inclusion of a job description in the contract. On the downside, the employee might fear that the employer can find contract-voiding loopholes in the enumeration in detail of specific responsibilities. For instance, the company points to the line about "constructive employee relations" and declares that the manager has not fulfilled this somewhat vague prescription. You can clear up this objection with language to the effect that "the foregoing describes areas of responsibility which are typical to the position. It is not to be interpreted as limiting in the sense that the responsibilities must be confined only to the areas prescribed, nor is it to be interpreted as indicating standards for satisfactory performance." The standards for satisfactory performance, if they are to be included, will be described in terms of results rather than areas of activity.

Don't take the job description given to the headhunter—or any job description crafted by the employer—and simply include it in the employment agreement. In preparing to negotiate a contract, collect information on which to base strategy and tactics. The job description is a useful piece of information. Furthermore, the existence of the job description benefits employer and employee. Like other provisions that may be negotiated into the contract, it is a commonsense measure that facilitates relations between executive and company, contract or no contract.

The positive benefit of incorporating a modified job description into the contract is that it offers protection against excessive change in the conditions of employment.

If you and the company agree to include a job description in the contract, then you must make sure there is provision to modify the description whenever you're promoted.

Defining the Future

Many agreements say that the employee is expected to handle chores that "may from time to time be imposed" by the top brass. What if those chores are demeaning or trivial? Or if they squash your status?

You can try to forestall such treatment by negotiating for language that sets out guidelines for treatment in any future assignment as well as in your present post. One provision might state that the executive cannot be assigned to report, even temporarily, to someone of inferior rank. (They're unlikely to promote a messenger to senior vice president just to humiliate you.) Other provisions might refer to the proportion of time that the manager might reasonably be expected to spend on duties outside those of his or her accustomed position, and the assurance that participation in unusual activity (e.g., a task force) does not mean the individual can be locked out of the channels that go with the regular job.

Provisions of the contract that define the job's responsibilities, scope, title, and reporting channels—as distinct from those that specify the performance expected in the job—are provisions that you hope you will never have to refer to. They are essentially protective devices that would come into play only under the most extreme circumstances. Your position is that these provisions cover very remote contingencies. Furthermore, you know that the persons you are dealing with today would never treat you that way. However, circumstances change and strange things happen. So why should there be any objection to the provisions?

One more point: Be sure you think these contingencies really *are* remote. If you think you are in urgent need of such protection in a contract, reconsider your willingness to work for this outfit, contract or no contract.

Protection Against Unwanted Transfers

You like the job and you like the location—an agreeable lifestyle, a pleasant climate, cultural and recreational opportunities, good schools for the kids, a nice home, all the things that go to make up a good place to live.

Then one day they tell you you're going to Siberia—or the company's equivalent. With today's multinationals, "Siberia" might be anywhere in the world.

You might conclude that a relocation is worthwhile because it means a promotion and more money. But you'd like to have a choice. You don't like being told, "Take it or leave it."

When young managers sign on to work at a new firm, they might not give much thought to location. They're footloose, willing to go anywhere. As they put down roots in the community, establish relationships, maybe start a family, that feeling changes. They've never been transferred, so they don't feel vulnerable.

But they are vulnerable.

Right from the start, it's worthwhile to think about a restriction on the right of transfer. Or, if you didn't think about location before, but are thinking about it now, you will want to negotiate for an appropriate safeguard.

One line may do it: "Executive's principal place of work shall be at the Corporation's headquarters."

Headquarters change, so that can be elaborated:

> During the Employment Period it is understood that the Company expects to maintain its principal place of business in [location]. If the requirements of the Company, as determined by its Board of Directors, make it desirable to relocate the principal offices of the Company to another location during the Employment Period, the Executive will be consulted in advance of any such relocation.

If the provision were to end here, allowing only that the executive be "consulted in advance," the company might feel it could fulfill the agreement by means of a pro forma notification. To give it teeth, the provision should carry something like the following:

> The Executive will not be required to render services hereunder outside the New York metropolitan area without her approval. Whether or not such approval is given, the Executive shall be entitled to the compensation provided for in Paragraph 2 . . . .

A shorter way of putting it:

> Unless the Executive otherwise consents, the principal place of the Executive's employment shall be within a 50-mile radius of Princeton, New Jersey . . . .

Working at Home

The computer and modem, inevitably to be joined by picturephones and other advances in telecommunication, make it possible for many people to do just about all their work at home.

It's a good idea to insert such a permission into your agreement, even if you don't work at home much right now. Your situation and inclinations may change. But your top management or board of directors may become uncomfortable when people spend a lot of working time away from the office.

Here is a brief provision, quoted from the contract between William J. Agee and Morrison Knudsen Corporation, that can safeguard your freedom to work from your home:

> Executive also shall have the right to perform his duties out of any of his personal residences, provided that such right does not result in behavior or actions injurious to the Company.

You can ensure the contractual privilege of working at home with this type of provision, but you will not necessarily keep some folks from eyeing you askance. When Morrison Knudsen collapsed under Agee's leadership, one of the bitter criticisms was that Agee shunned the firm's headquarters in Boise, Idaho, preferring his luxurious links-side villa in Pebble Beach, California, from where he and Mary Cunningham, his wife, held court.

Agee's highly publicized misadventures aside, however, at-home work is a rising tide for the future. Ensure yourself the chance to take advantage of it.

Moonlighting

You may want to give yourself the freedom to do some spare-time work—consulting, speaking, writing, and other activities. And you may want to be free to serve on the boards of other companies. If so, make sure the contract does not preclude these types of outside activity. Here is language that gives you fairly wide leeway (note the tactical use of the key word "substantially"):

> Executive agrees to devote substantially all of his time and energy to the performance of the duties of the position so long as his employment in that position continues. Notwithstanding the above, Executive shall be permitted to serve as a Director or Trustee of other organizations, provided such service does not prevent Executive from performing his duties under this agreement.

When you're offered a contract, look in the "Employment" or "Services" section for language that might be interpreted as severely limiting any outside activity. Here are two examples of this kind of language, which you should try to get rid of:

> During the term of this Agreement, the Executive shall devote [his/her] total time and energy to the business and affairs of the company . . . .

> The Executive hereby accepts such employment and agrees to devote [his/her] full working time and best efforts to the service of the Company . . . .

Loosen up the language to look more like the following two excerpts:

> During the employment period, the Executive agrees to devote *substantially all of [his/her] normal business time and attention* (reasonable vacations and periods of leave excepted) to the affairs of the Company and the promotion of its interests . . . .

> Executive agrees that at all times during the term thereof, [he/she] will devote all of [his/her] undivided time *during customary business hours* to the business and interests of the company.

These days, a lot of people moonlight. Managerial moonlighting can include such activities as teaching, consulting, running a part-time business like a mail-order firm, bookkeeping and financial counseling, programming, writing, selling (in noncompetitive areas), and so on. Some freelancers work off-the-books.

An employment contract might try to preclude moonlighting by inserting a paragraph like the following:

> Executive shall devote [his/her] *full-time and best* efforts to the Company and to fulfilling exclusively the duties of [his/her] position, said duties to be assigned by the Company . . . .

The stoppers for the would-be moonlighter are words like *full-time* and *exclusively*.

When you see wording like this, try to negotiate it out. You may not be thinking about outside work right now, but you might want to think about it in the future. Let's say you get a really good idea that you'd like to try out while keeping your day job. You don't want to be in the position of having to skulk around, doing it secretly.

Some companies are adamant about opposing all forms of moonlighting. Others may allow it to happen by turning a blind eye, but they'd like to retain the right to forbid it.

If you just try to eliminate a few problematic words (like *full-time*), you're apt to run into considerable opposition. Two other tactics will work better:

1. *Eliminate the whole paragraph, along with others.* Any contract is likely to contain a number of pro forma paragraphs that are, basically, just ballast. Suggest that several of them be deleted ("They don't mean anything, and they just clutter it up."). Include the "best efforts" paragraph ("If you didn't think I would give you my best, you wouldn't hire me.").

2. *Level with them.* Say, "I'm going to be working around the clock to meet the goals we've talked about. But someday, down the road, I might want to do something on the side, something that would in no way impact on my effectiveness—would, in fact, sharpen it. Of course, *with* your agreement. But this clause, if it means anything, means that is forbidden. I don't think you intend to do that. Can we delete it?"

Your Bargaining Posture

You have no current plans to freelance. Success in your job is all-important, and you will be devoting great efforts to that end. You'll be working long hours, and on weekends, but you will not be working on the company's business twenty-four hours a day. You don't imagine that anybody in the company does that, nor do you think the company expects it.

The company will benefit if you are always sharp and at your best. Can you be at your best if you just play golf in your spare time? Or would it be better if you keep your edge and develop your skills by exercising your mental muscles on other challenging tasks? A team is better off when an athlete works out on his own.

You would, of course, engage in no off-job activity that competes with the company or that in any way could damage the company's interests. (Why would you do that—especially if, as is likely, you are a stockholder?) Your freelance work, if you ever engaged in any, would be like ongoing training. The company doesn't have to pay for it; in fact, the company benefits in another way, because that additional income makes you a little bit more secure financially and more able to tackle the challenges of your job with peace of mind. At the same time, emphasize that the money you will make is minimal; that's not your main motivation. You are doing it to keep busy in leisure time and to develop yourself. It's like a paid hobby. (It's important to play down the money end, because you don't want the employer to think you enjoy a substantial outside income.)

Be ready to point out the ways in which certain kinds of freelance work will make you more valuable to the company—by helping you enhance particular skills, by giving you another string to your bow through the addition of new abilities, by widening your circle of contacts, by getting and adapting ideas from entirely different fields.

Some employers maintain that volunteer community work is all right, but they don't want employees engaging in paid activities. Your response: "I'm already involved in a number of community activities. I want to expand these activities, in areas that will do the company the most good. There's no question of my taking on any paid jobs—whatever they might be—any time soon. Down the road, at some point, you and I might agree that it's worthwhile to sharpen my skills in the real world of work. All I'm saying is, why shut off that avenue now?"

Evidence You Can Cite

If you've been around the company for any length of time, you've probably learned about various people who—steadily or occasionally—moonlight. *Never name names.* Just say, "Since other people in comparable jobs do freelance work, I know the company has no policy against it."

You might think of quoting Peter Drucker as an authority on the beneficial nature of freelancing: "Business organizations should be more tolerant of the manager who develops an outside interest; indeed, they should encourage it." Drucker says that the manager benefits when he or she has "a genuine, true, major outside interest. . . . It not only develops your strengths, it helps to protect you against the inevitable shocks."

Trading Off

Your initial bargaining position is that any limitation on outside activity should be removed from the contract.

Unless you have some lucrative outside prospects lined up right away, you will not want to fight to the death for this. (If the freelance possibilities are *that* great, why take the job?) You'll settle for some modification. Point out that the rigid language would keep you from, say, writing an article for a trade publication. Since that would be good exposure for the firm, they shouldn't forbid it.

Reasonable employers will allow some limited off-the-job activities, as long as they don't conflict with your real job. They're likely to listen to reason, and you may wind up agreeing to language like this:

> The Executive will engage in no paid activity for any competitor of the Company or any organization in a related field.

At the proper moment, you should be ready to "concede" and agree to such a provision. The advantage of a clause that excludes certain kinds of activities is that, by implication, it allows other activities. Be careful not to allow the employer to stick in a "but not limited to" phrase, which has the effect of making the forbidden activity one among many, with the rest unspecified.

Job Definition: Important, But Not Life-or-Death

Negotiation over the various aspects of the Duties and Job Definition parts of the agreement will almost never be central. And, if the employer refuses to give an inch on these parts, you will then decide whether you can live with them. If you *can* live with a situation that makes it impossible for you ever to do anything outside the confines of your job, then you go along gracefully—but not without trying for a quid pro quo.

9

Compensation

Salary, Stock Bonuses, and Alternate Plans

Money is the centerpiece of an employment contract. Some employment contracts simply specify the minimum salary, leaving bonus arrangements and other details to be described in separate documents (which become, in effect, part of the contract).

Here's a typical section from a contract (between Del E. Webb Corporation and a senior vice president). Note that although it does not spell out the bonus rate, it does, up front, specify one perk; membership in a country club.

> *Compensation:* (a) The Employee's minimum base salary shall be [amount] per annum, payable as nearly as possible in equal semimonthly installments (except to the extent that Employee may have elected to defer payment pursuant to the provisions of the Company's Executive Deferred Compensation Plan or such other deferred compensation plan of the Company as may be in effect from time to time) subject to adjustment (but not below the minimum base salary provided above) in accordance with the regular procedures established by the Company for salary adjustments.
>
> (b) The Employee shall participate in any incentive compensation plan, pension or profit-sharing plan, stock purchase plan, annuity or group benefit plan, medical plan and

other benefit plans maintained by the Company for its executive employees, in accordance with the terms and conditions thereof. In addition, the Company will provide the Employee with a suitable automobile and an active membership in a suitable country club of the Employee's choice.

Here's another way of covering the salary part of the deal. It is quoted from the pact between Alumax Inc. and CEO C. Allen Born. (The contract was prepared by Pearl Meyer & Partners; increasingly, specialized firms design employment agreements, because the agreements are so complex.) This contract states the employee's current salary, requires annual review, and provides for raises.

5. Current Cash Compensation

Employer shall pay to Employee during the Period of Employment a base annual salary of not less than $750,000 (or such greater amount as may have been approved by the Board of Directors in its sole discretion), payable in substantially equal monthly installments during each calendar year, or portion thereof, of the Period of Employment; *provided, however,* that Employer agrees to review such base annual salary annually and in light of such review may, in the sole discretion of the Board of Directors of Employer, increase such salary, taking into effect such factors as it deems pertinent.

The following excerpt, from the contract between Paramount Communications Inc. and Executive Vice President Donald Oresman, dated June 23, 1989, handles salary *and* bonus briefly. As we shall see, it's the stock plans that get wordy.

3. Salary

3.1 The Executive shall be entitled to receive a base salary, effective July 1, 1989, at a rate of $650,000 per annum, payable in accordance with the Company's payroll policy from time to time in effect.

3.2 The Company may, in its sole discretion, increase the Executive's per annum base salary.

4. Bonuses

4.1 The Executive shall be eligible to receive bonuses on the terms specified in the Paramount Corporate Annual Performance

Plan and on the terms specified in the Paramount Long Term Performance Plan, or any successor plans.

4.2 The Company may, in its sole discretion, grant bonuses to the Executive in addition to those bonuses granted in Section 4.1.

Now here is a section that wraps up all of the elements of compensation, including perks. It's not short, but it is a lot more concise than many other pacts that cover similar ground. The section is from a contract dated November 8, 1993, between Provident Life and Accident Insurance Company of America and J. Harold Chandler, who had been recruited to serve as President and CEO. Note that the contract follows a current trend by specifying the level of ownership of the company (2 to 3 percent) to be accomplished via stock grants and stock options.

Section IV

COMPENSATION, BENEFITS AND PERQUISITES

For all services rendered by the Executive in any capacity during the Period of Employment, the Executive shall be compensated as follows:

A. Base Salary

The Executive will receive a Base Salary at an annual rate of $650,000.00 for the Period of Employment. For any period thereafter during which this Agreement remains in effect, the Executive's Base Salary may be increased consistent with recommendations from the Compensation Committee of the Board, but Employer shall have no obligation hereunder to effect such increases. At least annually, the Compensation Committee will review the Executive's Base Salary for competitiveness and appropriateness in the industry. In no event, however, will the Executive's Base Salary on or after November 8, 1994, be less than an annual rate of $650,000.00. Base Salary will be payable according to the customary payroll practices of the Employer and will be subject to all required withholding for taxes.

There are two somewhat unusual features of the above paragraph. The contract seems to go out of its way to assert that the company doesn't have to follow the recommendations of the Board's compensation committee. Without speculating on the reasons why such language appears in this agreement, we might observe that one should question such wording. The other point of particular interest is that the contract specifies that, once a year, the salary will be reviewed in the light of what similar executives in the industry are being paid.

B. Transition Bonus

In addition to the other payments referred to in this Agreement, the Employer agrees to pay to the Executive a transition bonus of $130,000.00. Said bonus will be payable in cash as soon as administratively practical following November 8, 1993, but not later than December 31, 1993.

C. Special Bonus

In addition to the other payments referred to in this Agreement, the Employer agrees to pay the Executive a special bonus equal to $170,000.00. Said bonus will be paid in cash not later than December 31, 1993.

The "transition bonus" and "special bonus" are up-front signing bonuses.

D. Annual Incentive Bonus

In addition to the other payments referred to in this Agreement, the Executive shall be entitled to participate in an annual incentive bonus plan. The amount of the Executive's participation and the benefits paid under the incentive bonus plan shall be based upon goals recommended by the Executive and approved by the Compensation Committee. For the years ended December 31, 1993, and December 31, 1994, the minimum amount payable to the Executive under the annual incentive bonus plan is $200,000.00 annually. The annual incentive bonus plan payments ("Annual Incentive Bonus") will be paid in cash and the payment for the year ended December 31, 1993, will be paid not later than December 31, 1993.

It's always advantageous to set the goals—or at least to take part in setting the goals—on which your bonus is based.

Note that this manager can't lose; he is guaranteed a bonus of at least $200,000. When negotiating with a company that has an established bonus scheme, it can be useful to take the position that you don't want a special plan set up for you; all you require is a guaranteed bonus.

E. Restricted Stock Grants

In addition to other payments referred to in this Agreement, the Executive will be granted 29,216 shares of Class B stock of the Employer subject to certain restrictions relative to vesting. 7,304 of such shares shall vest and be delivered annually on December 31, 1993, December 31, 1994, December 31, 1995, and December 31, 1996, provided that the Executive is still employed by Employer on such dates. Prior to vesting, the Executive will be entitled to receive dividends and vote the unvested shares, but will have no other ownership rights therein.

F. Stock Option and Other Equity Grants

It is intended that the Executive have the opportunity to attain an ownership position of 2%–3% of the outstanding stock of the Employer. In furtherance of this goal and in addition to the other payments referred to in this Agreement, the Executive shall be entitled to receive option grants at fair market value and/or other equity grants to purchase the stock of the Employer totaling approximately 1,000,000 shares over 10 years. The first such award will be for 190,000 shares with a date of award of November 8, 1993, and will be made pursuant to the provisions of the Stock Option Plan of 1989. An additional award of 110,000 shares will be made no later than January 10, 1994, and will be made pursuant to the provisions of the Stock Option Plan of 1994.

The foregoing will become 100% vested two years following the date of grant and must be exercised within five years following the date of grant. The Executive will have the right to exercise the options by payment in cash or the delivery of shares of Employer stock owned by the Executive or some combination of cash and stock. In furtherance of the above referenced intent for the Executive to attain the desired level of stock ownership, the Executive will develop and recommend to the Compensation Committee of the Board a plan under which the remaining options and/or equity grants will be made in subsequent years.

Here is a good example of the strong trend toward setting goals in terms of specific levels of stock ownership by executives.

G. Retirement Plans

The Executive shall be eligible to participate in the Employer's Retirement Plan for Salaried Employees (the "Qualified Plan") and the nonqualified Supplemental Executive Retirement Plan (the "SERP").

The Employer will provide an additional supplemental retirement benefit (the "SRB") to the Executive calculated pursuant to the formula contained in the SERP, using as Compensation in the benefit formula the Executive's Base Salary, unrestricted by the limitations contained in Section 401(a)(17) of the Internal Revenue Code of 1986, as amended (the "Code") and including the Executive's years of service with his prior employer as Service in the benefit formula. The Executive's right to receive the SRB will vest 10% per year of service, provided that the Executive remains employed by the Employer for five (5) years.

If Executive's employment is terminated prior to such five (5)-year period, none of the SRB benefits will vest, except as may be otherwise herein provided. Any SRB benefits will be reduced by the benefits paid under the Qualified Plan, the SERP and any qualified or nonqualified retirement benefit paid to the Executive by the Executive's prior employer.

These days, top executives who move to other companies are being "made whole" through compensation for what they are leaving behind.

H. Health and Welfare Benefits

During the Period of Employment, the Executive shall be entitled to participate, under the terms and conditions thereof, in any group life, medical, dental or other health and welfare program generally available to management personnel of the Employer which may be in effect from time to time during the Period of Employment; provided that nothing herein shall require the Employer to establish or maintain such plans. Any tax liability which these benefits create for the Executive will be the sole responsibility of the Executive.

The Nuts and Bolts of Executive Compensation: Key Definitions

Here are terms you run across frequently in compensation negotiations. The brief definitions given here have been supplied by Frederick W. Cook & Company, the nationwide compensation consulting house. Note that a full-value grant conveys the actual stock itself, not just the option to buy.

Full-Value Grants

Performance Units. Grants of cash allotments or dollar-denominated units whose payment or value depends on performance measured against predetermined objectives over a multiyear period.

Performance Shares. Grants of actual shares of stock or stock units whose payment depends on performance measured against predetermined objectives over several years. (These are similar to performance units except that the value paid fluctuates as stock price changes.)

Restricted Stock. Grants of actual shares of stock or stock units subject to restrictions and risk of forfeiture until the employee has worked for the company for a specified period. Typically, dividends or dividend equivalents are paid out during the restriction period. These full-value grants are based solely on employment, not on performance.

Performance-Accelerated Restricted Stock Award Plans (PARSAPs). This hybrid also involves grants of restricted stock (see above). However, if the employee meets certain performance goals, some or all restrictions may lapse early. If the objectives are not met, the restrictions are in force until the employee has remained with the company for the specified time. Also known as *performance-accelerated restricted stock* (PARS) and *time-accelerated restricted stock award plans* (TARSAPs).

Dividend Rights. Rights to receive dividends (or their equivalent) paid on a specified number of company shares, usually granted in combination with other grant types.

Stock Purchase Opportunities. Rights to buy shares of company stock either at prices below market value ("discount purchases"), with financing from the company or a third party ("market value purchases"), or through securities convertible into common shares ("convertible securities").

Formula-Value Grants. Grants based on a value determined by a formula other than the market; final value delivered may be either the appreciation over an initial grant value, or the value of a full formula-derived "share."

Appreciation Grants

Stock Options. Rights to purchase shares of company stock at a specified price over a stated period, usually five or more years. Typically, the option price is 100 percent of market value at the time of the grant; however, there may be variations.

Performance Stock Options. Options on which some aspect of the vesting or exercise price depends on meeting specified performance criteria. Options with performance vesting provisions typically become exercisable at or near the end of the option term (regardless of performance), to secure favorable accounting treatment under current rules.

Restoration (or "Replacement" or "Reload") Stock Options.   Options granted as a result of exercising stock options using already-owned shares in a stock-for-stock exercise. The size of the typical restoration grant is equal to the number of shares used to pay the exercise price. The new exercise price is set at the then-market value and a term equal to that remaining on the original options.

Premium Stock Options.   Options with an exercise price above market value at the time of grant. Premiums can range anywhere from 10 percent to 80 percent over market value.

Discount Stock Options.   The opposite of premium stock options. The exercise price is *below* market value at the time of grant.

Indexed Stock Options.   Options whose exercise price may fluctuate above or below market value at grant, depending on the company's stock price performance relative to a specified index (e.g., S&P 500) or the movement of the index itself. Indexed options differ from performance options in that the exercise price of the indexed option typically remains variable until the option is exercised.

Stock Appreciation Rights (SARs).   Rights to receive the increase in the price of the company stock since it was granted. There are three types of market-based SARs:

1. *Tandem SARs.* Rights to receive the gain on a stock option in lieu of exercising the option. The exercise of one cancels the other.

2. *Freestanding SARs.* Rights to receive the gain on a "phantom" stock option. (The phantom option carries no specific termination date. It lists the employee as owning a certain number of shares, with the grants running from one to ten years or more. The employee chooses the time to exercise the option and receives cash or stock for whatever appreciation has occurred.) Freestanding SARs are granted independent of stock options; therefore, the exercise of an option, if any, does not cancel the SAR.

3. *Additive SARs.* Rights granted in addition to a stock option. In most cases, the exercise of the underlying option triggers the SAR payment. The two are paid simultaneously (unlike a tandem SAR, where the exercise of the stock option cancels the SAR payment, and vice versa). Additive SARs are typically used to offset income taxes on a related stock option gain, as well as the tax on the SAR payment.

The Trend Toward Stock Ownership

The big item used as incentive compensation in most executive pay plans today is company stock. The basic message is: Do a good job and you will earn more. What you earn will be tied, more closely than before, to performance. What you receive is less likely to be cash, and more likely to be a bigger and bigger piece of the company. And you're not apt to get that bigger piece of the company right away; a substantial portion of it is future compensation, available to you only if you stay with the firm and continue to do a good job.

Frederick W. Cook & Company conducts annual surveys of incentive grant practices among the 200 top U.S. industrial companies (in terms of revenues). The 1994 survey showed that 99 percent of the top 200 companies use long-term incentives. Berkshire-Hathaway and FINA were the only firms not reporting any long-term grant usage. Stock option usage "is almost universal with 98 percent of this year's [1994] companies granting options."

An important reason for the switch away from high executive salaries is a 1993 tax provision that, in effect, bars a public company from deducting pay of more than $1 million to each of its five top officers unless that pay is based on stockholder-approved (via the board) performance criteria. If the company can't pay the CEO and his or her policy-level team huge salaries, then it pays them in another way—increasingly, in stock, distributed in various ways.

What applies to the top five officers applies to managers in the lower echelons, so companies have instituted broad-based stock plans. Compensation-via-stock rewards improved performance, satisfies tax law, and gives stockholders and employees a mutual interest in building performance.

What Do Options Really Cost?

When a company grants options, it incurs a cost. But because it is impossible to reckon that cost exactly, corporate financial reports have simply ignored the cost. This has made stockholders and analysts unhappy. In 1994, the Financial Accounting Standards Board (FASB) considered a proposal to force companies to calculate the cost of stock options according to an approved formula—and then to deduct the cost of the options from profits!

Business interests erupted in a storm of protest that was not generally front-page news but was tempestuous among corporate leaders and financial executives. They knew very well that the requirement would make severe inroads on their bottom line, their earnings report, and the prices of their stock. The holders of options might, in many cases, confront the spectacle of share prices that would be sinking because of the very fact that the options had been granted.

The FASB retreated to its fallback position. The cost of options need not be put in the earnings report. It will, however, be carried in a footnote.

Critics claim that the FASB took a dive on the issue; that the footnote, though potentially embarrassing, will be ineffectual; and that the compromise allows companies so much leeway in computing "cost" that the actual cost will be minimized. The FASB rejected the simple approach of valuing an option according to its exercise price, its duration, and the current market value.

Corporations have come to rely on stock options as a mainstay of executive compensation and motivation. They heaved a sigh of relief when the FASB backed off.

However, there is still unhappiness in powerful quarters about the "hidden" cost of options. And, if and when the political and economic climates change, more stringent accounting requirements may yet force companies to deduct the cost of options from their reported profits.

Millions from Mickey

Michael Eisner's ten-year contract with Disney (signed in 1989) comprises a large stock option component (see Appendix 2). At the end of fiscal 1994, before the Cap Cities merger, Eisner held $107.4 million in vested grants and $64.5 million in unvested grants. The Disney board, spurred by the rich harvest reaped by its CEO and other executives, decided that, henceforth, options would be granted only at the time of hiring; when the executive was promoted; or when all previous options were vested or within a year of vesting.

Stock options, the company said, remain the best long-term incentive compensation for senior officers.

Your Reward Is Risk

Cash on the barrelhead is a certainty. A share of stock represents a risk. If you own stock in your own company, you hold at least some part of your financial fate in your own hands. But, by and large, unless you command the giant stature of a Michael Eisner and are able to sway an industry, the value of your stock depends on the efforts of others, along with the state of the industry and the general economy.

Bear the risk factor in mind when you deal with stock options. If your company shares the current enthusiasm for stock as compensation, and for setting targets for stock ownership by executives, you may not have much choice. Just remember that what goes up comes down.

Participants, of course, don't receive stock certificates instead of checks in their pay envelopes. By and large, these plans provide stock *options*, not outright grants of equity.

Incentive stock options (ISOs) are the staple of some plans. ISOs started to move toward the top of the charts in 1981, when the Tax Reform Act made the device attractive to employees by reducing the tax rate on capital gains; by decreeing that no taxes need be paid until the stock was actually sold; and by ensuring capital gains treatment for shares held for one year or more. The legislation entailed various restrictions on how long the recipient had to wait before exercising the option, and how soon the options had to be exercised after the recipient left the company.

The Tax Reform Act of 1986 cut the capital gains advantage of ISOs considerably, leading companies to rely more heavily on "nonqualified" stock options (NSOs). NSOs are free of the restrictions imposed by the laws, but NSOs do not have a capital gains advantage.

The pendulum swung again in 1993, when federal tax legislation increased the value of capital gains treatment of options. At that time, says one compensation specialist, NSOs were running 4–1 ahead of ISOs in popularity. Why not? The company receives a tax advantage with NSOs, and if there is little difference to the executive, then NSOs seem the logical choice. But now that ISOs provide a distinct tax break for the recipient, firms are using them to a greater degree. The ISO costs the company more than the NSO, but it's a better break for the employee; and the motivating power of that better break for the employee makes the difference for some firms. Others still prefer NSOs. Many provide a mix.

Broad-Based Stock Plans

Broad-based stock plans provide stock as compensation to a great many people in the organization, not just (as was once the case) a "privileged" few.

Early in 1995, *Executive Compensation Reports* (ECR) analyzed the broad-based option programs of eight major corporations. Here, encapsulated, are their findings.

1. Baker Hughes Inc. 1993 Stock Option Plan

All domestic employees (including management), along with nonemployee directors, are participants. The plan involves ISOs or NSOs, with maximum ten-year terms. The initial grant (100 NSOs to each domestic employee) vests on the third anniversary after the grant date. Options can be exercised for three years after retirement or disability, and for one year after death. Vested options can be exercised for up to three years after voluntary resignation (unless extended by the board). Grant sizes vary at the board's discretion.

2. Best Buy Inc. 1994 Full-Time Employee Nonqualified Stock Option Plan

Participants are selected from among full-time, nonofficer employees. Approximately 7,500 are eligible (out of a total workforce of 15,200).

The grants involve NSOs with four-year terms. Grant size is 100 shares. The board decides on frequency. Vesting is 50 percent one year after the grant date; the remainder is vested two years after the grant date. Initial grants: 100 shares each, to 4,700 persons.

3. General Mills, Inc. Stock Option and Long-Term Incentive Plan of 1993

All employees with more than three years of service are eligible; the company expected 50,000 persons (out of a workforce of 121,300) to participate over the plan life. The grants are in the form of NSOs (maximum term = ten years and one month); stock units are restricted.

Frequency and size of grants are at the board's discretion. In fiscal 1993, more than 30,000 employees received regular stock options; the average grant size was 110 shares. Vesting takes place at least five years after the grant date.

4. Helene Curtis All-Employee Stock Option Program

All regular full- and part-time employees (approximately 3,200 persons) participate in a plan involving ISOs with ten-year terms. Frequency is one-time. Grant size is 100 shares, vesting five years after the grant date. Payment may be in cash, shares, or "other considerations."

5. Kellogg Co. 1993 Employee Stock Ownership Plan

More than 16,000 employees are eligible for this plan, which involves NSOs, stock bonuses, performance shares, performance units, SARs, and "other awards." The initial grants, at board discretion, distributed around 900,000 units to more than 8,000 employees. Initial grants vest three years after the grant date; vesting accelerates upon retirement, death, or disability, and options then can be exercised within one year; vested options can be exercised up to three months after resignation. Payment can be in cash or, at the committee's discretion, in unrestricted shares or through a brokerage arrangement.

6. Merck, Inc. 1991 Incentive Stock Plan

All regular full- and part-time employees (more than 47,000) may receive ISOs, NSOs, SARs, restricted shares, or performance shares. A subprogram, the "World-Shares Stock Option Plan," granted broad-based options. The board decides on size and frequency; in 1993, the grant amounted to 300 shares to each "worldwide employee." Grants vest after five years and expire ten years after the grant date.

The plan provided that only vested options could be exercised after death, retirement, or termination without cause, for a period determined by the committee. The committee can accelerate vesting.

7. PepsiCo SharePower Stock Option Plan

Full-time workers participate in an NSO plan with a maximum term of ten years. Approximately 75,000 persons receive grants (out of a total workforce of 430,000, including 325,000 U.S. employees). Each grant is calculated as 10 percent of the participant's gross earnings (including annual bonus and overtime) for the preceding year, divided by the option exercise price (fair market value of the common stock on the grant date).

Each grant includes five option shares or more. No grant can exceed 10 percent of the total shares authorized under the plan. The kitty is 4 million shares, 1.5 percent of outstanding common stock. Vesting is 20 percent on each anniversary date. "Cashless" exercise of options is allowed.

8. Toys "R" Us 1994 Stock Option and Performance Incentive Plan

The plan can involve ISOs, NSOs, SARs, restricted shares, performance shares, performance units, stock awards, and tax offset payments. Nonmanagement employees appear to receive only NSOs.

Options generally become exercisable after four years and nine months. Although NSO exercise prices may be as low as 90 percent of fair market value, the company stated (according to ECR) that all grants have been priced at fair market value on the grant date.

The Benefits of ISOs

If you are a manager—a younger manager, in particular—the offer of stock options constitutes admission to "the club." The company thinks enough of you to provide you with the same perk the top brass gets.

Viewed objectively, the incentive stock option (ISO) is by no means perfect. The most obvious point is that the value of the stock must go up for the exercise of the options to be worthwhile. The price you agree to pay is fixed. If it's $30 a share, you can buy the stock (up to the specified limit) for that price after the waiting period (say, two years) has expired.

The "locked-in" aspect of the deal takes some of the pressure off. When the two-year period ends, the stock may be drifting at about $35, so there's no particular profit in buying it. But the market is bullish, and the company stock is rising with the tide. It reaches $40, then $43. Participants wonder: Should they cash in, or wait?

Some people stay out of individual stocks. They can't read the future. They don't feel they are spending quality time when they sit around staring at graphs and numbers in the newspapers and on their computer screens. Instead, they invest in mutual funds, leaving it up to someone else (hopefully, an expert) to handle the risk.

But then these market-averse persons get stock options and are placed in the unpleasant position they've been trying to avoid. The "buy now or wait" decision can be just as tormenting as the "buy or sell" decision.

Some option holders experience another frustration. They watch the stock price climb steeply, but they can't cash in because the requisite time has not expired. As the happy date approaches, however, the stock price declines. Without ever owning the stock, they feel they've lost money.

There is a further obstacle: getting the money to exercise the option. By putting up the shares as collateral, you can get a bank loan, but the interest on the loan reduces your profit. The company may offer a lower-than-going-rate loan. This borrowing locks you in more solidly; the firm is now your creditor.

There are pluses and minuses to taking a company loan as a perk. It is sufficient to note here that a company loan, if available, should not necessarily be snapped up.

The "cashless" approach to exercising options is designed to make the process easy and relatively painless. The typical cashless transaction works almost like an SAR. You call a broker and say you want to exercise a certain number of options. Using power of attorney granted to it earlier, the brokerage house handles the entire deal and sends you a check.

ISOs are important perks that are getting more important every day. Now let's look at a potentially troublesome aspect of the practice: "underwater options."

Underwater Options

What happens if the stock price sinks, so that there is never going to be a chance that the options are worth anything?

These "underwater options" have, from the beginning, been among the biggest drawbacks and dangers in using equity as compensation. The problem is fairly widespread. *Executive Compensation Reports* (ECR) found that top executives in 11 percent of its database companies held some underwater options at the end of 1993, and ECR inferred in February 1995 that the percentage had probably gone up in 1994.

At first—when stock options were, by and large, confined to a few top executives—some corporations didn't worry about underwater options. When the shares disappeared below the surface, they simply dredged them up again. They "made whole" the recipients by repricing the grants.

But, asked institutional investors and other observers, where is the motivating factor in all this? The idea of giving people large option grants is to impel them to do everything possible to drive the share prices up. If, when the stock sinks, the executives are rewarded anyway, then we are back in the bad old days when top executives continued to rake in mounting bonuses even while their companies showed big losses.

Reproaching underwater options has now gone out of fashion.

But, at the same time, companies have tended toward broad-based option plans. It's one thing if the CEO's options fail to appreciate; after all, the CEO is highly paid to take that risk. But when the company has given large numbers of its people option grants as compensation, declining share values take on another coloration altogether. To a middle manager without policy responsibility, an underwater option is like counterfeit money in the paycheck.

To cope with this difficulty, companies are dealing with underwater options in ways other than repricing. One popular approach is to exchange new options for old. The value of the new options is not set arbitrarily; rather, it is keyed to the value of the older options through a formula that retains the value of the original grant. Furthermore, companies are setting performance criteria for the exchanging of grants. In yet another move to allay criticism, corporations are excluding the topmost managers from the exchange offer.

Another recourse is to lengthen the life of the grant. In one example given by ECR, Safety-Kleen Corporation moved to restore the incentive value of underwater options granted before 1990 by extending their expiration dates to November 30, 2004.

In 1993, Chiquita Brands allowed 800 nonexecutive officers to exchange options whose fair market value had sunk to 50 percent under the exercise price. The maximum exchange ratio was 2-for-3.

In September 1991, Merck celebrated its centennial by awarding stock options to every employee, down through its assembly-line workers. The employees were pleased, and Merck took satisfaction in making a generous gesture that was also a good human resource move. Then the stock price dropped. People were devastated. They felt they had lost money, or that the company had taken a benefit away from them. Two years later, in an effort to rehabilitate morale, Merck made duplicate option grants at the lower market price.

Shoney's directors took a different approach. They declared that the decline of share prices was due to factors beyond management's control; therefore, underwater grants from 1992 and 1993 could be exchanged for the same number of new ones at present market value. The company's top three executives were left out, but they received additional options representing 50 percent of the underwater grants.

IBM's board—facing the problem of underwater options from 1987 through 1992—voted to allow the sunken treasures to be exchanged for new grants at fair market value on an average basis of 2.5-for-1. Executive officers did not participate.

Underwater options can happen anywhere. Household-name companies such as Bristol-Myers, Ford, and Coca-Cola are not immune. When we buy stock in a company, we know we are taking risks. We must remember that there is risk in options-as-compensation as well.

What Goes Up Must Come Down—Or Must It?

Corporations are dealing with underwater options in a variety of ways. Don't despair if you see your options slide beneath the surface. Others are in the same boat (or submarine). You're probably *not* going to have to forget about the options altogether. Something will be done.

But as you negotiate the part of your package involving options, you may want to raise the question: If the value of the stock goes down, what will the company do about it?

The issue of underwater options relates to a larger issue—the long-term wisdom of relying so heavily on stock as compensation.

The debate over heavy reliance on stock options takes place within the broader context of a debate about the overall amounts that executives are paid. Graef ("Bud") Crystal, a prominent commentator on corporate compensation, maintains in a recent book[1] that managers are paid too much. This happens, he says, because of greed and an unbalanced corporate governance process that lets senior executives set their own pay.

Crystal gives expert underpinning to the more general feeling among politicians and ordinary citizens that the amounts paid to high-flying executives are outrageous. Corporations have tried to allay this criticism through payment in stock (grants or options) instead of cash.

This approach, too, says Crystal, has been abused. The size of option grants is out of control. He cites various companies that give top brass options to the tune of millions of shares.

The American Compensation Association, based in Scottsdale, Arizona, issues useful white papers on the question. Writing in the *ACA Journal* (Autumn 1992), George B. Paulin and Frederic W. Cook reflect, "There are problems with executive compensation, and it is good to debate them. The public, employee and shareholder perceptions of executive compensation are not good, and those perceptions

---

[1] *In Search of Excess: The Overcompensation of American Executives* (New York: W.W. Norton & Co., 1991).

need to be changed if public corporations are to be allowed to retain the freedom to compensate executives under a free-enterprise system."

Heavier reliance on stock-as-pay has been the answer. Increasingly, companies have chosen stock options, rather than stock grants, as their vehicles. And this is setting off alarm bells with a different tone.

In the mid-1990s, a number of authoritative voices were being raised in warning about the reliance on options. Pearl Meyer, President of Pearl Meyer & Partners, Inc., the New York-based executive compensation consultants, said, "In their haste to hop aboard the option bandwagon, Boards are overlooking the problems inherent in basing too large a portion of executive pay on tomorrow's stock prices. Several emerging trends threaten to scuttle the unqualified success of options as a compensation vehicle—and forward-looking Directors would be wise to step back and avoid excessive reliance on options as their primary performance carrot."

Stockholder and government pressure pushed companies away from high salaries and bonuses as means of compensating managers. However, the long-lasting bull market of the 1980s and 1990s has provided the magic for the option boom. Meyer observes, "Buoyed by a decade of steeply rising stock prices, top-performing executives have willingly traded current cash income for extraordinary option gains while stockholders applauded Boards for the realignment of executive pay with shareholder value."

These have been heady days for a lot of top executives loaded with climbing shares. On May 10, 1995, *The Wall Street Journal* carried a story headlined "Chip Executives Are Cashing In As Shares Soar." The story, by Michael Gonzalez, highlighted stock sales by a number of insiders at surging technology companies. Texas Instruments Chairman Jerry Junkins sold 61,986 shares on April 25, 1995, a day when the stock closed at $101.25. Nine insiders at Sun Microsystems sold a total of 180,000 shares in April 1995. In the same month, seven Intel insiders "dumped a total of 245,544 . . . ."

Pearl Meyer: "We believe those heady days are about to end. In designing compensation programs, Boards and executives need to remember that the other side of reward is risk, and start preparing for the downside, because it's coming. We've seen more than a threefold increase in the market averages over the past ten years, including the Dow

Jones industrials' rise from 1,200 to over 4,000 [well past 5,000 as of this writing]—and it may be foolhardy to plan on a movement of this magnitude in the next several years to again foot the bill for our pay programs."

In a sense, options are compensation "on the cheap." Companies are using the bull market to bolster the illusion that the options are the equivalent of a sure thing. That, says Meyer, is dangerous:

> Options can and should remain a most important element in executive compensation packages . . . especially for cash-strapped high-technology and start-up firms that depend on equity rewards as a way to attract top talent.
>
> But to maintain executive pay parameters that are truly performance-based and uphold the idea of a management stake in the company, options should not be the main course. *Boards need to implement diversified equity plans that also award performance-based, full-value shares, not just options.* In that way, key employees who have surpassed performance benchmarks will get to be immediate owners with a real piece of the action in their businesses.
>
> Such compensation vehicles will exact a real cost on companies' bottom lines and may appear less attractive to Directors. But that's a fair price for the free ride companies have had on the option bandwagon for so long. Compared to the cost in employee morale devalued by worthless options, it's a fair deal.

We have cited Pearl Meyer's warnings about options because they are pertinent in the broad sense—and because, in negotiating your particular compensation package, you should try to reduce the risk proportion (as represented by options, in whatever form) while increasing the reward portion.

Special Stock Option Grants: An Example

Before we discuss tactics to be used in negotiating stock option deals, let's take a look at how it was done by two executives in one company. This example highlights some of the issues to consider in bargaining about options.

In February 1994, Enron Corporation renewed the contracts of Chairman/CEO Kenneth L. Lay and President/COO Richard D. Kinder. The contracts, renewed for five-year terms, set minimum salary levels: $900,000 for Lay and $660,000 for Kinder. Each received a special stock option grant: 1.2 million shares for Lay, 1 million for Kinder. The options vested 20 percent on the grant date. If the company achieves 15 percent annual growth in earnings per share, the remaining 80 percent vest in three equal increments on the first, second, and third anniversaries of the grant date. Otherwise, the two executives have to wait until six years and ten months from the grant date to exercise the options.

If either leaves before full vesting, he can exercise the vested shares through February 7, 2001, while relinquishing the unvested options.

ECR notes that "both officers were given 'advances' ($5-mil for Lay, $3-mil for Kinder) plus additional loan commitments ($2.5-mil and $1.5-mil respectively) in order to purchase company common." Lay and Kinder are required to put up stock and personal property as collateral for the loans, which bear varying interest rates. ECR reports: "If the stock pledged as collateral for the advances becomes insufficient to cover the amount of the advances and outstanding interest, the officers were to be liable for up to one-third of the advance and all of the loan interest." In the case of death or disability, the slate is wiped clean (Enron purchased insurance to cover this contingency).

Deciding on the Right Amount of Risk

When a company makes stock options a major part of your compensation package, you must ask yourself some pertinent questions:

- What happens if the shares go underwater?
- How much risk am I willing to take?
- Is the company stock likely to continue going up?
- How stringent are the vesting requirements?
- If I leave, how much can I take with me?

- Will the company help me pay for the shares? How?
- If I take a company loan, to what extent does it lock me in?
- What other forms of compensation are possible?
- What is the ideally balanced compensation plan for me?

If the company has a broad-based option plan, you will be offered options as a matter of course. In addition, you may be offered a big option package as a major component of your pay arrangement.

How to "Position" the Option Component

When a company offers NSOs or ISOs galore as part of the compensation package, your counterpart in the negotiation will take the position that the offer is very generous. It not only bestows on you a surefire source of wealth, it makes you an owner of the company.

As an employee, your position should be a little different. You're all for ownership. You're willing to risk a lot on the company's future. You look forward to holding a considerable amount of company stock. But there are various ways to acquire that stock.

Think of the options as an "of course" perk, not a big deal at all—as much to be expected as health insurance or a pension plan. This posture is easier when the company has a broad-based stock ownership plan, but it can work with any firm that offers stock options.

Anticipate the Offer

The company negotiator may be saving the stock option plan as the clincher. Bring it up first, casually: "I know you provide stock options, and I'll expect the size of my option plan to be commensurate with the job. You also have a good major medical, I'm told."

The employer will resist the notion of classifying stock options with the health plan, arguing that it is anything but routine and, indeed, is a fabulous concession.

Here is the moment at which you introduce some reality. Your first point is that the stock has to go up for the option to be worthwhile. The

employer responds that, of course, the payoff depends on stock performance, but that, after all, is the criterion of excellence, and you are part
of a team that will achieve that level of excellence, and so on.

You look forward with pride to being part of the team. But your
professional pride also requires that you be compensated in accordance
with your standing. "I know you don't think that the only way you can
get me to do a good job is to dangle the option carrot in front of me."
You see stock options as a reasonable part of the package, but you don't
want it to dominate the package.

Ask Pertinent Questions

One pertinent question is: "What if, for reasons totally out of my
control, or anyone else's control, the stock price goes underwater?" If
that has happened before, the employer will explain what was done:

Ow! Those Golden Handcuffs Pinch!

Companies use stock options to keep valuable talent from
leaving. Executives should be fully aware of the strings
attached to options, and think through the possible
consequences of violating the letter or spirit of the
agreement.

For example, *The Wall Street Journal* (December 6,
1995) reported that IBM was suing Bruce Claflin, a former
PC executive. IBM claimed that Claflin breached his
contract by exercising a profitable bundle of stock options a
month before quitting to join Digital Equipment Corp. The
potential profit for the executive was around $1 million.

The IBM program specifies that, if the employee
leaves within six months of exercising his or her options,
IBM can ask for its money back. IBM demanded repayment
from Claflin, who refused. Hence the lawsuit.

---

exchanges, extensions, and so on. Now, you have established that the shares do not inevitably increase in value.

Another question is: "How do I pay for the stock?" The grant is not much use to you if you can't convert at the optimum time. Can the company ensure that you will have the requisite funds?

Specify Alternatives

The company wants you to own stock. Fine. Why not give you stock outright, instead of going the option route? After all, stock options still don't cost the company all that much to issue. You will probably not want to put it this way, but they are paying you with possibilities and promises rather than with cash.

Another alternative is the SAR, which is a quicker and neater way to motivate you to get the share prices up, and to reap the fruits of your labors.

Does the company proposal feature NSOs? Why? NSOs are good for the company, but ISOs allow you favorable capital gains treatment.

Work Toward a More Favorable Option Package

- If the proportion of option to actual pay (in salary, bonus, or stock) is too high, build up the "cash on the barrelhead" component.

- Try to get the most favorable terms for exercising your options. Negotiate for a shorter vesting period and a longer conversion period.

- If you have decided you want a company loan to buy the stock when the time comes, ask for it.

- Try to get the loan at no interest, or at minimal interest.

- Get the employer to commit to a satisfactory plan to "make you whole" if the stock goes underwater.

- Are there incentive criteria? For more shares, or quicker vesting? Negotiate those thresholds to the lowest possible point.

Pertinent Option Provisions from Contracts

This excerpt from a 1993 contract concerns options:

6. Stock Options

(a) Grant

Immediately following the Commencement Date and the end of the 120-Day Period . . . Employer shall grant to Employee non-qualified stock options (the "Options") to acquire shares of common stock, par value of $.01 per share, of Employer ("Common Stock"), in an aggregate amount equal to 625,000 shares multiplied by a fraction, the numerator of which is 15, and the denominator of which is the 120-Day Average Price. . . . Employer and Employee agree that the number of shares of Common Stock subject to the Options and any other options granted or to be granted by Employer to Employee under the . . . Long Term Incentive Plan during any period of five consecutive years following the Commencement Date shall not exceed 1,500,000 shares.

(b) Exercise Price

The exercise price of each of the Options (the "Exercise Price") shall be equal to the 120-Day Average Price.

(c) Vesting

The Options shall vest at the rate of 20 percent per year on each of the first five anniversary dates of the Commencement Date; *provided, however,* that (i) Options that have not previously vested shall vest immediately, and all restrictions and risks of forfeiture shall lapse, upon (A) the death or Disability . . . of Employee, (B) Employee's retirement on or after age 65, (C) Employee's retirement on or after age 62 but before age 65, if Employer's Board of Directors, in its sole discretion and without taking into account any vote of Employee, approves the immediate vesting of such options upon such retirement, (D) termination of Employee's employment without Cause . . . or by Employee with Good Reason . . . or (E) a Change in Control . . . and (ii) Options that have not previously vested shall not vest, and shall be immediately forfeited by Employee, upon (X) Employee's retirement before age 65 unless Employer's Board of Directors, in its sole discretion and without taking into account any vote of Employee, approves the immediate (or future) vesting of such Options upon any such retirement on or after 62, or (Y) termination of Employee's employment by Employer with Cause or by Employee other than with Good Reason.

(d) Term

Vested Options may be exercised only within the first ten years after the date of grant.

(e) Exercise

Except as described below, an Option that is vested may be exercised only by (i) written notice of intent to exercise the Option and (ii) payment or deemed payment of the Exercise Price to Employer (contemporaneously with delivery of such notice) in cash or Common Stock of equivalent Fair Market Value. In its sole discretion, the Committee may permit the Exercise Price to be paid in the form of awards issued under the Employer's compensation plans, or other property (including notes or other contractual obligations of the Employee to make payment on a deferred basis, such as through "cashless exercise" arrangements, to the extent permitted by applicable law). Common Stock utilized in full or partial payment of the Exercise Price shall be valued at its Fair Market Value . . . on the date of exercise. In the event of a Change in Control, in lieu of acquiring the shares of Common Stock covered by the Options, to receive, and the Employer shall be obligated to pay, the Change in Control Settlement Value . . . with respect to shares of Common Stock up to the number of shares covered by the Options, which amount shall be paid in cash.

Keying Options to Specific Goals

Options can be granted as incentives for quite specific achievements. The following excerpt (from a December 1987 contract between Allegis and CEO Stephen M. Wolf) refers to the completion of a corporate move. (Note the reference to a separate Stock Option Agreement, which, of course, becomes part of the contractual arrangement.)

3. Inducement for Employment

As an inducement for the Executive's entering into the Agreement and undertaking to perform the services referred to in the Agreement, the Executive will receive:

> (a) a nonqualified option (the "Option") to purchase 250,000 shares of the Company's common stock at an exercise price of 100 percent of fair market value of such shares on the date of grant pursuant to and on the terms to be set forth in a Stock Option Agreement, substantially in the form of Appendix 1 attached to the Agreement (the "Stock Option Agreement"), such option to be granted pursuant to the Company's 1981 Incentive Stock Program (the "Stock Program"), subject to the following terms and conditions: (i) the Option shall be granted within 60 days following (x) completion by the Company of its proposed disposition of Westin Hotel Company, the Hertz Corporation, Hilton International Co., and Covia Corporation, and (y) the application of substantially all of the net proceeds thereof to distributions to the shareholders of the Company or other applications presently under consideration by the Company . . . .

Grants of Stock

The company wants you to be an owner. Stock options are one way of accomplishing this. As we've pointed out, options have distinct advantages for the employer.

Maybe you'd prefer to be granted stock. It still comes with strings attached. But suppose you're *given* the stock; you don't have to pay for it. Here's an example of a contract provision covering grants. The contract's golden handcuffs call for return of some of the stock if the recipient leaves the company early.

Restricted Stock

10.1 *Grant of Stock.* In consideration of the covenants of the Executive under this Agreement and his services to the Company, the

Company has transferred to the Executive ... 50,000 shares of Company Common Stock ... and is transferring to the Executive, effective [date] 150,000 shares of Company Common Stock, $1.00 par value per share. . . . The Executive shall have absolute ownership of the Shares including the right to vote the same and receive dividends thereon, subject, however, to the terms, conditions and restrictions set forth below.

10.2 *Restrictions.* (a) If the Executive's continuous employment with the Company shall terminate for any reason (excluding death, Permanent Disability, discharge by the Company without Cause or termination of employment by the Executive after a Change in Control) . . . [The contract proceeds to specify—on a yearly basis, five years into the future—how many shares the executive must give back in the case of departure before the five-year term. The longer the stay, the fewer shares have to be returned.]

When the employee can choose to defer some of the stock grant, the deal is even more useful and flexible. Here's a stock grant contract section covering such issues as deferral and change in control of the company.

STOCK UNITS

(a) Grant

Immediately following the Commencement Date and the end of the 120-Day Period, [the company] shall grant to Employee units of compensation (the "Units") each of which shall represent the right to receive compensation paid in the form of one share of Common Stock and the aggregate number of which shall equal $189,370 divided by the 120-Day Average Price.

(b) Vesting

The Units shall vest at the rate of 20 percent per year on each of the first five anniversary dates of the Commencement Date. . . .

(c) Deferral of Payment

By the end of each calendar year immediately preceding the calendar year in which any proportion of the Units are scheduled to vest . . . Employee shall file with [the company] a written election form in which Employee shall elect the date or dates on which the shares of Common Stock represented by such units shall be paid out to Employee; provided, however, that all vested shares of Common Stock shall be paid out to Employee no later than any Change in Control.

Any dividends paid on vested shares of Common Stock between the date of vesting and the date of payment shall be paid out to Employee when such shares are paid out to Employee.

(d) Change in Control

In the event of a Change in Control . . . the Employee shall be entitled to elect, during the 60-day period immediately following such Change in Control, to surrender shares of Common Stock received pursuant to this Agreement . . . and receive, in full settlement thereof, and [the company] shall be obligated to pay in cash, the Change in Control Stock Value . . . .

The Joy of Being Grossed-Up

Various elements of today's executive compensation packages can wander into taxable territory. For example, your option vests and you find that you owe taxes as a result.

Some companies agree to "make whole" executives who find themselves in this position. The arrangement is called the "gross-up" provision. Here, for instance, is the relevant section from William Agee's contract with Morrison Knudsen:

8. TAX "GROSS-UP" PROVISION

If any payments due Executive under this Agreement result in Executive's liability for an excise tax ("parachute tax") under Section 49 of the Internal Revenue Code of 1986, as amended (the "Code"), the Company will pay to Executive, after deducting any Federal, state or local income tax imposed on the payment, an amount sufficient to fully satisfy the "parachute tax" liability. Such payment shall be made to Executive no later than 30 days prior to the due date of the "parachute tax."

The tax situation can get complicated. In some cases, companies have to gross-up the gross-up, because the first gross-up itself incurs tax liabilities.

You want this kind of protection. Negotiate a gross-up provision into your contract.

Buying Into the Company

Payment in stock—largely through grants or options—is likely to continue to be the coin in which executives receive a good deal of their pay. Stockholders can feel that the interests of the company's managers are identical with their own. Stock prices are a measure of performance, so plans that deal heavily in equity can be seen as closely geared to performance. Stock is a malleable and quantifiable entity; it lends itself to golden handcuffs and strong incentive.

It's almost never a good idea to rely exclusively on ownership of company stock in providing for the future. Apart from other retirement benefits provided by the company, astute managers salt away appropriate amounts of money through 401(k) plans.

Negotiate the stock component of your contract with an eye toward quick vesting; stock grants rather than options; easy terms for execution of options; and the lowest possible thresholds for profitable conversion.

How Much Now, How Much Later?

Deferred compensation plans are a tried-and-true staple of executive compensation. When the compensation being deferred is in the form of money, it is placed in an interest-bearing account. You can draw on it after retirement, when your taxes are lower.

The concept of deferral of compensation now manifests itself prominently in stock grant and stock option plans. Companies use the deferral as golden handcuffs.

H&R Block provides executive officers and key people with the chance to defer up to 35 percent of salary each year, over periods of four to eight years. Aggregate deferrals cannot exceed 280 percent of salary. For each dollar deferred by the individual, the firm contributes 50 cents. Contributions vest depending on length of service.

In 1994, H&R Block started a supplemental plan. Block people can defer an additional 280 percent of salary. There is no matching 50-cent contribution.

If deferral is an option, decide beforehand how much you want to defer, and under what conditions. If possible, don't box yourself in on deferral. You may not want to do it now, but it may become more attractive later.

---

100 Percent Deferral

Harnischfeger Industries urges executives to defer up to 100 percent of their payouts in the form of stock shares. The carrot? A 25 percent discount when the bonus amounts are converted to shares (based on average closing price of the common stock for the final month of the bonus year).

Bonuses

Stock options have become major components of the compensation package. High base salaries have gone out of style because of tax legislation, and because an astronomical salary is an easy target for critics.

Not long ago, fat bonuses were handed out by some top managements as if they were gifts from the gods, without reference to performance. Complacent boards of directors sat and nodded.

That day is gone, thank heaven. But bonuses still loom large as a way to pay managers.

Some companies have broad-based bonus plans. Whirlpool's program covers around 3,400 people. Individual bonus targets run from 10 percent to 100 percent of base pay. Employees earn bonuses depending on results with respect to:

- Corporate and/or business unit goals (measured in terms of ROE and ROA or RONA, respectively).

- Individual goals.

The Whirlpool plan has been modified to establish different criteria for executive officers. For one thing, their bonuses no longer involve individual performance evaluations. Their maximum payouts are capped at 150 percent of base pay; the general bonus cap is 225 percent of base pay. Payouts are made in cash. Participants may defer up to 75 percent of the payout.

This plan exemplifies the essential bonus approach. There is usually a bonus pool. Criteria relate to how people earn their bonuses (one of your key negotiating areas). Today, the criteria may well be return on equity or some other measure of increase in share value. However, yardsticks vary widely. For example, some plans depend, at least to some degree, on employee satisfaction. Finally, one plan establishes standards for determining the amount of payout—for example, percentages of base salary. (Salary is important in itself and as a bonus-booster.)

At Wells Fargo & Company, the bonus pool (reports ECR) "is funded each year with an amount by which net income exceeds the target ROE for the year, as set by the Management Development & Compensation Committee." Nobody can get more than 30 percent of the bonus pool.

At Paine Webber, up to fifteen executive officers and key people were qualified to participate in the 1994 Executive Incentive Compensation Plan, which set pools based on percentage of profit. No individual could get more than 33 percent of the pool. A Compensation Committee may reduce the award pool or scrub it entirely. And the Committee can kill the award to any participant, for any reason.

MCN Corporation (a Michigan utility) uses quite different criteria to determine, in some degree, bonuses for its executives:

- Employee satisfaction, as determined by a survey.

- Customer satisfaction (also via a survey).

- Safety (measured in lost workdays).

These yardsticks account for 30 percent of bonus payouts. The other 70 percent is keyed to achievement of the utility's authorized rate of return.

Shopko Stores has a bonus plan and separate performance measures for each of three categories:

1. Corporate: Corporate financial, including net income, comparable store sales, and ROI.

2. Merchandising managers: "Ad-In-Stock," which measures the percentage of out-of-stock items on a selected advertisement.

3. Store operations and professional services managers: Customer satisfaction, as measured by surveys.

Turner Broadcasting's agreements with top executives specified salaries and "maximum" bonuses each year until 1997. For example, ECR found that Turner's January 1, 1994, contract with Vice President–Entertainment (later to become President, Turner Entertainment) Scott M. Sassa set the following salary and bonus levels:

	Salary	Bonus
1994	$805,000	$645,000
1995	$845,000	$680,000
1996	$890,000	$715,000
1997	$940,000	$750,000

Each bonus amount is 80 percent of salary. However, ECR reports, Sassa's contract, along with those of Executive Vice President Terence F. McGuirk and Vice President–News W. Thomas Johnson (later to become President, CNN), was amended so that the bonus figure is now the *target* award. Sassa can earn 150 percent of the target.

Issues in Negotiating Your Bonus Deal

"We have a generous bonus plan," says the company spokesperson. You wonder: "Will it be generous to *me?*"

Research on a company's various disclosure documents may turn up some interesting insights. If you can't find out what you need to know, ask some useful questions about the company's bonus plan. Here are some of the things you should query.

How Evenly Are the Bonuses Distributed?

Overall, a firm may hand out to its managers what seems like a large amount in bonus money. But closer inspection shows that, as George Orwell observed in *Animal Farm*, all animals are equal but some are more equal than others. For example, an electronics company with annual revenue of around $2 billion rewards its five most senior executives with bonuses ranging from 62 percent to 84 percent of salary; the average is 70 percent. Twenty other officers receive bonuses averaging 15 percent.

What Are the Yardsticks?

Bonus plans can be keyed to all sorts of criteria, from stock prices to customer satisfaction. In some companies, bonuses are still distributed partly (or even entirely) at the discretion of a committee of the board of directors or of the top management. (Occasionally, there is little or no difference in these entities.) If you have any say in the matter, you want to choose and shape criteria that favor you. If you're running a division and you expect that division to do well, it's reasonable to say, "You want me to concentrate on improving my unit's bottom line. I'm willing to incur the risks in doing that by keying my bonus to unit performance. And if I'm successful, I want to reap the rewards."

If there is no advantageous way for your performance to be used as a bonus yardstick, hitch your wagon to the highest rising star: "This is a team operation. If I do a good job, the company [or strategic business unit] does better. It seems logical for me to be rewarded when that happens."

How Much Influence Do You Have over the Criteria?

The bonus plan may be presented to you as a monolithic package, unvaryingly applied to all participants. But don't take its status for granted. Ask, "Does everyone in this Key Officer Incentive Plan have exactly the same language in his or her agreement? Including the numbers?" If there is any variation, then you can negotiate for lower thresholds and higher percentages.

How Sensitive Is the Bonus Plan to Uncontrollable Forces?

Some compensation plans make bonuses vulnerable to slight downturns in the economy or the industry, or to the agendas of institutional investors, or to a mixed bag of forces beyond your control (and sometimes beyond anybody's control). Investors frequently "punish" a stock because the earnings report, although very good, did not meet certain quite unreasonable "expectations."

In judging a bonus plan, apply the "worst case" approach. Think of the various "What ifs?" Bring them up in the negotiation. Ask how you're protected: "Let's say I accomplish all my objectives—but something happens and the threshold isn't reached. Am I wiped out for the year? That's a disincentive."

Bargain for a situation in which you are ensured at least a minimum bonus.

How High Is the Fence?

Some bonus plans can look very lucrative until you scrutinize the threshold criteria. Examine all the elements that go into deciding the size of your bonus—or whether you get one at all.

Why Not Adjust the Fence to Suit Yourself?

Some of the most effective incentive plans are built around performance review programs in which the employees participate in establishing the standards.

To the degree possible, be an active player in setting the standards that will be applied to you. In working out those criteria, don't always try for the lowest level. Surprise your counterparts by setting a *higher* goal for yourself in an area where you're confident of achievement. Then bargain hard for lower fences in other areas.

Keep It Clean

Focus on the paramount points in negotiating a contract. Don't wander down bypaths or load the agreement with needless provisions. Ask yourself: "Is this really important? Won't I get it as a matter of course?"

Excessive attention to trivia can hurt your bargaining tactics on the main issues. And, as we shall see, inclusion of a lot of superfluous provisions can sometimes come back to haunt you. If, for instance, things turn sour and the employer wants to break the contract, the more provisions it includes, the more opportunity the employer has to claim you have violated some aspect, however minor, of the pact.

10

New Performance Measures and Compensation Yardsticks

We are in the midst of a revolution in executive compensation. The idea of *really* connecting executive performance with executive pay (which always received a lot of good word of mouth but was frequently ignored) has taken hold.

In firms where bonuses once depended on the subjective feelings of top management and board members, managers now earn incentive rewards according to how they measure up to certain announced yardsticks. The yardsticks can vary from annual earnings to customer satisfaction. Occasionally, very senior managers hold in their own hands the means of meeting the incentive goals. More often, it's a team process; if enough members of the team do a good job, there will be money in the pot for a payout.

In the past few years, stock price has loomed up as the measurement of choice. Previously, companies were judged by other criteria—reliance on the yearly bottom line was the standard for a long time. We now agree, more or less, that reliance on annual earnings (or similar numbers) is inadequate—or at least incomplete—as a measurement of true performance and of the real worth of the enterprise.

The popularity of stock price to gauge how well a company is doing has not, of course, grown in a vacuum. Stockholders—in the form of big institutional investors—have become the 600-pound gorillas of performance assessment. How often, during earnings-report season, do we witness the spectacle of Wall Street bloodbaths in which a corporation announces substantially higher earnings—but the earnings are not high enough to satisfy the big shareholders, who sell with a vengeance.

Using stock price as the yardstick is, in many ways, logical. It is a comprehensible measurement of how well the organization is doing now. And, by a reasonable extension of logic, it makes sense to pay managers on the same basis. Indeed, influential shareholders insist on it. They are interested in the market value of their holdings right now. They want a CEO, along with a team of senior officers, who have that target always in their crosshairs. So why not reward them if they boost share value?

The Unreliable Yardstick

From the moment that stock price began to assume its present importance, some observers have pointed out the shortcomings of the approach, especially when the executive compensation system is linked in lockstep with the measurement.

These questions arise:

- Is stock price the best yardstick for company performance?
- Are managers motivated best when they are paid in stock?

Take the second question first, using the present vogue for stock options as an example.

Stock options are an effective and flexible tool for accomplishing a number of tasks. They lend themselves to use as golden handcuffs. The compensation plan, through staggered vesting, always has another bundle of options hanging out there as carrots. Although recent accounting changes now require that the cost of options be reported as a footnote on the annual statement, that "cost" can apparently be computed rather loosely. So, in the view of some, options are a "cheap" form of executive pay.

And then there is the clarion call of entrepreneurism.

By mandating an increasing degree of stock ownership among its executives, a company is not only tying those executives more closely to the firm, today and tomorrow; it is also infusing them with the entrepreneurial spirit. According to this view, the more a manager becomes an owner, the more he or she will be motivated to do a good job.

There is great pride in ownership. But—according to this theory of motivation—the biggest spur to doing a superb job is money.

This idea flies in the face of theories that have been the bedrock of worker motivation since early in the 20th century. Psychologist Abraham H. Maslow (described by Peter Drucker as "the father of humanist psychology") showed that human wants can be ranked in a hierarchy. When lower-order wants (food and shelter, for example) are satisfied, they become less important. Economic wants rank toward the bottom; the highest needs of humans are for self-fulfillment.

Another eminent psychologist, Frederick Herzberg, gave us the "hygiene theory." In Herzberg's view, economic rewards are not motivators; they are hygiene factors. If they are not met—for example, if the individual is paid too little—they deter us from doing a good job.

Building on Maslow and Herzberg, human resource specialists have based their programs on the idea that people, and especially managers, are motivated by such factors as the challenge of the job, recognition of accomplishment, and so on. And indeed, these approaches have panned out. No good manager works intensively at his or her job solely for the money.

But this view of motivation defines money strictly in its capacity to buy things. Money—in the sense of magnitude of compensation—is more than that. It is a way of keeping score. Eisner, Gerstner, Welch, and other outstanding corporate leaders are not always thinking about where the next buck is coming from, but they strive hard for the biggest packages of bucks because these are the markers that show who is winning the game.

However, even when we acknowledge the importance of money as a marker—and thus, as a motivator—we have good reason to question the notion that astronomical pay packages invariably produce the best motivational results. Harvard University President Derek Bok had these comments: ". . . the idea of tying compensation to what happens to the company stock troubles me because there are so many reasons why the stock in the company might go up that have very little to do with the performance of the CEO. . . . I am also troubled by the assumption that we can't trust CEOs to do their best for their organization unless we attach very large rewards to performance. . . . To me, the idea that well-chosen leaders will not make every possible effort to improve and benefit their organization unless hundreds of thousands of dollars are riding on the result is remarkable and doesn't correspond with any experience that I've had."[1]

But, let's face it, corporations use stock—and stock options—as compensation to motivate the stockholders rather than the managers. Here's how Avon CEO James E. Preston puts it: "Avon's compensation philosophy is that everyone in the company—not just senior management, but everyone—should have their compensation reflect the performance of the company. . . . I felt very strongly that if we were going to regain our credibility with investors and potential investors, we would have to take some very concrete steps and make some tangible moves that would signal to current and potential investors that this was a new era for Avon, that we would put the interests of shareholders first and foremost . . . . That is what precipitated my going to the compensation committee and saying that, for the next five years, I want no increase in my base salary, I want to reduce my target bonus from 65 to 50 percent of salary and I want an exchange for stock options."[2]

Looking for Better Ways

Stock options' move to the forefront in the compensation sweepstakes is not a permanent situation. Even the proponents of stock options admit that there are real drawbacks in this approach. They keep looking for better ways of measuring company performance—and of paying the managers who run the company.

---

[1] "Defining Reasonable Pay for Executives," an exclusive interview with Derek Bok, conducted for the American Compensation Association by William T. ("Tim") Haigh, Managing Director, W.T. Haigh & Co., published Autumn 1994.

[2] "Linking Compensation to Shareholder Interests," an exclusive interview with James E. Preston, conducted for the American Compensation Association by Rose Marie Orens, Partner in KPMG Peat Marwick's New York Performance and Compensation Consulting Practice, published Winter 1994.

The unattainable ideal compensation plan would involve a transcendentally sensitive instrument, working off implants in the manager's brain and in other locations, taking as input all the relevant factors, and providing a second-to-second measurement of performance. This sci-fi scenario—nightmarish to most, but sort of neat-sounding to a few—will never become reality. Experts keep probing toward approaches that do a more accurate job of gauging the real worth of the organization and the real contribution being made by the organization's managers.

One such approach is *total shareholder return* (TSR). TSR goes beyond stock price as a yardstick by cranking in stock dividends. A 1994 American Compensation Association research report studied a number of companies on the basis of this measurement. For the purposes of the study, TSR was defined as share-price appreciation plus reinvested dividends during the past five years.[3]

A relatively small number of firms have tried the total shareholder return method. They calculate the company's TSR over a specified period, and then compare it to a benchmark TSR figure, calculated for a peer group of companies.

In August 1995, ECR reported on a number of companies using TSR. Goodyear linked three-year performance share awards to its TSR as measured against the TSR of the other twenty-nine Dow Industrial companies through 1992. National City Corporation links three-year cash awards to a peer group. Lockheed compared its TSR to the S&P 400 and a peer group, and paid out three-year awards accordingly. (The plan ended when Lockheed merged with Martin Marietta.) Lincoln National Corporation terminated its use of TSR after the 1990–1992 cycle, during which, says ECR, "its TSR ranked at the 66th percentile in a peer group."

TSR has many enthusiastic partisans. Ralph Horn, President/COO of First Tennessee Corporation, told the editors of ECR that the bank's TSR-oriented approach to performance evaluation and executive pay worked better than previously tried methods because, for one thing, TSR is easy to understand. The company sets a TSR goal as measured

---

[3] John D. Bloedorn and Peter T. Chingos, "Executive Pay and Company Performance," published by ACA, Autumn 1994.

against the TSRs of competing banks. Hit the target and your shares vest early; otherwise, they don't.

TSR's relative simplicity contrasts with our next topic: EVA.

EVA—The "Hot" Yardstick

Another measurement system has come into prominence recently. It's called economic value added (EVA).

EVA's preeminent champion is Stern Stewart & Co., the New York consulting firm. Stephen F. O'Byrne, Senior Vice President and head of the compensation consulting practice at Stern Stewart, describes EVA as "a measure of economic profit after all costs, including the cost of the equity capital employed in the business. . . . Conventional accounting measures of performance, such as net income and earnings per share, reflect the cost of a company's debt capital, but they do not reflect the cost of the company's equity capital, because they are designed to be measures of the residual income available to equity-holders." This is "useful information to lenders evaluating their credit risk or to shareholders assessing their wealth, but it does not provide a useful measure of company or management performance."

EVA is "today's hottest financial idea and getting hotter." So said an influential article in *Fortune*.[4] Marquee-name companies have bought into the concept. They include Coca-Cola, Quaker Oats, AT&T, Briggs & Stratton, and others. Coca-Cola CEO Roberto Goizeta was an early enthusiast. So was AT&T CEO Robert Allen and CSX Corporation CEO John Snow. Quaker Oats leader William Smithburg said, "EVA makes managers act like shareholders."

Getting Paid the EVA Way

Executive compensation plans based on this new approach pay out bonuses (in cash, stock, or options) keyed to improvement in the EVA for the business unit in question.

---

[4] Shawn Tully, "The Real Key to Creating Wealth," *Fortune*, September 20, 1993.

Typically, the EVA pay scheme involves a rolling three-year bonus pool. Senior managers are assigned shares—say, 5 percent of the pool to the CEO, 3½ percent for the executive VP level, and so forth. Each year, one-third of the pot is distributed—*if the EVA goals are met.*

What happens if the EVA goals are not met? Then the participating executives find themselves in a "negative bonus" situation. The slate is not wiped clean. During the next period, the previous EVA deficit has to be made up before the managers can even begin to make a run at the next target.

So, as EVA's proponents say, managers are taking real risks. At the same time, say the EVA fans, these managers are not encouraged to set lower goals so that they can chalk up big bonuses more easily. The method by which EVA is calculated rules out that ploy.

When EVA rules your paycheck, you are in the entrepreneurial position. You are taking risks, just as if you were the sole owner of the company. And you can't, for example, skimp on necessary capital improvements to increase immediate bottom-line profit, because the EVA calculations detect and penalize such artifices.

Simple Idea—Complicated Calculation

G. Bennett Stewart III, senior partner at Stern Stewart, was quoted in *Fortune* (May 1, 1995): "[D]espite these widely reported successes, only a handful of companies today are getting EVA right. What we've seen in the rush toward EVA is that many companies don't know how to implement it and therefore aren't getting nearly its full benefits."

In essence, EVA is simple. Economic value added is net operating profit after taxes—*and after deducting the cost of capital.* "Capital," says Stewart, "is all the money tied up in such things as heavy equipment, real estate, and computers, plus so-called working capital—mainly cash, inventories and receivables. The cost of capital is the minimum rate of return demanded by lenders and shareholders, and varies with the riskiness of the company. When you are making more money than your cost of doing business plus your cost of capital, you are creating wealth for your shareholders."

This is a straightforward definition that would make it fairly easy for any business to compute its EVA—*if* it knew its capital cost. Stewart observes that many businesspeople "don't know their true capital cost, and some don't even consider it."

Why is it so hard? Because figuring out the true cost of capital involves formulas like the following, provided by Stephen O'Byrne:[5]

Calculating the cost of capital (C)

$$C = (P_e \times COE) + (P_d \times (1 - \text{tax rate}) \times r)$$

where

P_e is the proportion of total capital represented by equity,

COE is the cost of equity,

P_d is the proportion of total capital represented by debt,

r is the effective interest rate in the company's debt.

The expected return on a security in an efficient market, comments O'Byrne, "will be a linear function of its nondiversifiable risk." This principle is embodied in the following capital asset pricing model (CAPM):

CAPM

$$E \times R = Rf + \text{beta} \times (E \times Rm - Rf)$$

where

$E \times R$ is the expected return on a security,

Rf is the risk-free rate of interest,

beta is a measure of the security's nondiversifiable (or market) risk,

$E \times Rm$ is the expected return on the market as a whole.

Note that beta shows the sensitivity of the security's return to changes in overall market return. A beta of 1.0 means that a 1 percent increase in the market return increases the security's return, on average, by 1.0 times 1

[5] Stephen O'Byrne, "EVA and Management Compensation," *ACA Journal*, (Summer 1994).

percent, or 1 percent. A beta of 1.5 means that a 1 percent increase in the market return increases the security's return, on average, by 1.5 percent.

Having navigated the shoals and rapids of these equations, you are ready to figure out EVA:

Calculating economic value added

EVA = NOPAT − (c × capital)

where

EVA is economic value added,

NOPAT is net operating profit after tax,

c is the company's or business unit's weighted average cost of capital,

capital is the total debt and equity capital employed in the business.

For example, if a business with a 12 percent cost of capital has a $50 million NOPAT on a total capital base of $400 million, EVA = $50 million − (0.12 × $400 million) = $2 million.

Practical Problems with EVA

EVA is complicated. The calculations can make your eyes glaze over.

But, say critics, there's more wrong with EVA than arcane arithmetic. It's too hard to apply. The big difficulty comes when you try to *allocate* the cost of *all* the capital among divisions of a company with centralized staff and manufacturing functions and other capital assets that are shared among the units.

One expert (a leading advocate of EVA) cites the example of a large entertainment company (you can supply the name), which produces animated films and also runs theme parks that feature characters from the films as their main attractions. How do you divide up the cost of capital?

Compensation consultant Tim Haigh reflects the opinions of many in concluding that EVA as it stands now is not workable in multidivision organizations. The company must be simple and homogeneous, so that the division of the cost of capital can be done coherently.

And then there is the problem of making an EVA-based compensation plan intelligible to managers. Haigh comments, "In my world, simpler is better."

Strikingly, the leading proponent of EVA—Stephen O'Byrne of Stern Stewart—*agrees* with a central point made by the critics. Talking with the author of this book in August 1995, O'Byrne said that, to work effectively, the EVA approach should be used in a "freestanding" unit—a business entity that does not share large capital costs with other divisions. The more centralized the company, the less likely that EVA will work.

The Continuing Search for Pay–Performance Linkage

EVA in its present form is not likely to be applied in many firms. As it stands now, managers will not be dealing with an EVA compensation plan any time soon.

Nevertheless, as Tim Haigh says, "You can't argue with the concept." Measuring a company's *real* value, by giving correct consideration to *all* relevant criteria in their proper relationships to each other, is an idea whose time has come—and whose stay will be lengthy. At this moment, business thinkers are trying to build better yardsticks.

And when those yardsticks are applied to companies as a whole, they will be applied to compensation of managers.

We are likely to see intensification of the trend toward adopting the EVA *concept*—alongside attempts to devise more practical ways to gauge company performance and pay those who guide the company's destinies.

Here's an example. Briggs & Stratton adopted the EVA idea at the outset. In 1994, Stephen O'Byrne gave this description:

> Briggs & Stratton Corp. recently adopted a leveraged stock option (LSO) plan that provides for the grant of premium (i.e., out-of-the-money) options on Briggs & Stratton stock based on the size of each executive's EVA bonus. Each year, an executive receives a premium option with a five-year term on stock with a market value equal to ten times the executive's EVA bonus.
>
> The Briggs & Stratton plan is equivalent to doubling the EVA target bonus and requiring that half the bonus be invested in

a 10-to-1 leveraged stock purchase, but it uses the matching grant structure to avoid current income tax liability on the reinvested bonus. The exercise price of the option is based on the future value of the debt that would be incurred to finance the leveraged stock purchase. The exercise price of the five-year option is equal to 90 percent of the current stock price multiplied by $(1 + r)^5$, where the interest rate r is set 1 percent above the long-term bond yield. The LSO plan is the only stock-based compensation for senior executives of the company, including corporate executives.

In June 1995, ECR noted that Briggs & Stratton's EVA "approach has been successful—B&S reported Return on Capital of 17.3% and Return on Equity of 26.8% for fiscal year 1994 (ended July 3) and has outpaced both the S&P 500 and the S&P Machinery Index since 1992 (a $100 investment in the company was worth $456 after the five years ending with FY 94)."

Other companies are getting good results with various modifications of TSR and EVA. Cincinnati Milicron keys yearly bonuses and three-year incentive awards to return on capital, paying a special cash bonus of 25 percent of salary if 50 percent of the maximum EVA is reached. Clark Equipment, reports ECR, "uses ROC in a matrix with net income to generate incentive awards for business unit execs. Avery Dennison Corporation, whose plan had focused solely on Return on Total Capital objectives, modified its approach to reward executives on ROTC and Earnings per Share, weighted equally. Also, the company's top executives can earn up to an additional 100% of salary on the basis of comparison of Total Shareholder Return with the TSR of a peer group."

In the months and years ahead, we'll see modifications of existing measurements—and perhaps one or two brand new measurements.

The Bottom Line—You'll Be Paid in Stock for Measurable Performance

The linkage between executive pay and organizational performance is here to stay. You can expect that firms will keep on looking for ways to make that linkage stronger. For some organizations, especially where incentive pay has been geared to the price of stock, this need not mean a radical change. "One of EVA's most powerful properties," says Shawn Tully, "is its strong link to stock prices." Tully quotes James Meenan, CFO of AT&T's long-distance business: "We calculated our EVA back to 1984 and found an almost perfect correlation with stock price." Stock prices parallel EVA more closely than do other yardsticks, such as earnings per share or return on equity.

You may have neither the time nor the inclination to follow the minutiae of the latest theoretical thrusts toward finding the perfect measure for company performance. It's important, however, to understand that, along with downsizing, organizations are constantly seeking better ways of gauging just how well they are doing—and how much each manager is contributing. Theories and formulas look like ivory tower abstractions—until you realize that they're being used to decide your fate, to judge whether you are a "keeper," and to figure out how much your company is going to pay you.

Follow the trends in performance measurement. They constitute some of the most important rules of your career game.

11

Provisions for Termination

People who are about to marry rarely spend much time reading the divorce statutes. They don't think about divorce at all. Those canny souls who get their partners to sign prenuptial agreements are in a distinct minority.

The contractual provision for severance pay is the "prenuptial agreement" of the job relationship. Both parties hope the relationship will be long and happy. But if the employer becomes disenchanted, the employee needs protection. That protection is provided by an agreement, in writing, that the company, if it fires the person, will pay a specified sum of money to that person.

Language is important in every part of the contract. It is especially important in the termination/severance provisions. One word in the definition of "Termination for Cause" can give the company grounds for dismissing the individual without paying a red cent of the amount specified in the employment agreement.

Contractual Language

Let's look at the ways in which this subject can be covered, and how you can work toward language that is more favorable to you.

Here's a section from a contemporary contract:

5. *Termination.* This Agreement may be terminated on the following terms:

    a. *Termination Upon Death.* In the event of Executive's death during the Term of Employment, this Agreement shall terminate immediately.

    b. *Termination Upon Disability.* The Company shall have the right to terminate this Agreement, and have no further obligation to Executive under this Agreement, upon the "Disability" of Executive by providing ten (10) days' written notice to Executive. "Disability" as used in this section shall mean any illness or any impairment of mind or body that (i) renders it impossible or impracticable for Executive to perform his duties and responsibilities hereunder for a continuous period of at least four months or (ii) is likely to prevent Executive from performing his duties and responsibilities hereunder for more than six (6) months during any eighteen (18)-month period, each as determined in good faith by a physician selected by the Board of Directors. Any refusal by Executive to submit to a medical examination for the purpose of certifying disability under this section shall be deemed to constitute conclusive evidence of Executive's disability.

There are two potential problems here.

1. The word "impracticable": "any illness . . . that (i) renders it impossible or *impracticable* for Executive to perform his duties . . . ."

What does "impracticable" mean? Let's look at the sad example of a manager who has been injured in an automobile accident. He is confined to a wheelchair. The company deems it "impracticable" for him to get around the factory floor. Is this "disability"? Can the company terminate the agreement?

There are laws and regulations covering treatment of disabled workers. But why get involved in invoking them? Delete the word "impracticable" or any similarly vague words.

2. Medical judgment as to disability is left to a physician selected solely by the board of directors. As the employee, you should have

more input. You're better off with the following language, from another contract:

> Any question as to the existence of the Total and Permanent Disability of the Executive as to which the Executive and the Company cannot agree shall be determined in writing by a qualified independent physician mutually acceptable to the Executive and the Company. If the Executive and the Company cannot agree as to a qualified independent physician, each shall appoint such a physician and those two physicians shall select a third who shall make such determination in writing.

That arrangement is somewhat elaborate, but you might be grateful for it if the unhappy situation ever comes up.

Dismissal for "Cause"

The definition of "cause" can be the key provision in case of a dispute over severance. Consider the following:

> *Termination for Cause.* The Company shall have the right to terminate this Agreement, and have no further obligation to Executive under this Agreement, for "Cause" after giving written notice of termination to Executive.

"Cause" can cover a multitude of sins—or just one sin. It can be very broad, making the employee vulnerable to summary dismissal in a variety of circumstances. Or it can be narrow, requiring a serious, precisely designated transgression.

Let's look at an example:

> ["Cause" shall mean] (i) the breach by Executive of any material provision of this Agreement and the failure by Executive to cure such breach within fifteen (15) days after receipt by Executive of written notice of such breach; (ii) the engaging in any dishonest or fraudulent conduct in the performance by Executive of [his/her] duties and responsibilities hereunder; (iii) the willful

and continued failure by Executive to substantially perform [his/her] duties and responsibilities hereunder and the continuance thereof for a period of five (5) days after receipt, by Executive, of written notice of such failure; (iv) unsatisfactory performance by Executive of any significant duty or responsibility and the failure of Executive to improve such performance to a satisfactory level within ninety (90) days after receipt by Executive of written notice of such unsatisfactory performance; (v) the commission by Executive of any act of material misconduct which is injurious to the Company, including, without limitation, the theft or misappropriation of funds or the disclosure of trade secrets or other confidential or proprietary information . . . ; (vi) the commission by Executive of (A) a crime involving an act or acts of dishonesty or moral turpitude or (B) a felony.

First of all, there is too much here; too many loopholes have been created for the company. One plus factor for the employee is the insertion of modifiers like "material," "willful," or "substantial" when describing conduct that would justify breaking the contract for cause. But, overall, this is a provision that the employee should work to change. Look again at (iv), which mentions unsatisfactory performance. *Who decides the performance is unsatisfactory?* The wording practically describes an "employment at will" situation rather than one in which the employee is protected by a contract. Probably, in the particular case of this company and this employee, there is no suggestion that the firm will break the contract.

Now look at another contract excerpt:

(c) *Termination by the Company for Cause*

    (i) The employment of the Executive under the Agreement may be terminated by the Company or the Subsidiary for "Cause."

    For this purpose, Cause shall mean that the Executive has:

    (A) committed a significant act of dishonesty, deceit, or breach of fiduciary duty in the performance of the Executive's duties as an employee of the Company or the Subsidiary;

(B) grossly neglected or willfully failed in any way to perform substantially the duties of such employment;

(C) acted or failed to act in any other way that reflects materially and adversely on the Company or the Subsidiary.

This is better, but it still has problems. The excerpt contains a pet provision of those who draw up contracts: the part about reflecting adversely on the company. You must try to banish this kind of "soft," subjective language.

If You Blow the Whistle, a Contract Helps

Nicole Eskenazi, Executive Vice President of Bernard Chaus Inc., an apparel company, accused certain other employees of taking kickbacks, forging expense reports, having conflicts of interest, and shirking work.

The company fired Ms. Eskenazi, who then sued for $5.2 million, claiming breach of contract. She said the company had failed to give her a scheduled performance review; had ended her severance pay after seven months instead of twelve months; and had declared that her right to exercise stock options had expired.

Bernard Chaus Inc. settled the lawsuit with Ms Eskenazi.

Women's Wear Daily, September 3, 1994, "Ex-VP Settles With Chaus in $5.2M Suit For Breach," by Carol Emert.

Revisiting Eisner/Disney

Because of its length, detail, and unique features, Michael Eisner's contract with Disney gives us an interesting look at various aspects of agreements. Here's what that pact says about termination.

10. Termination by Company

(a) Company shall have the right to terminate this Agreement under the following circumstances:

(i)   Upon the death of Executive

(ii) Upon notice from Company to Executive in the event of an illness or other disability which has incapacitated him from performing his duties for six consecutive months as determined in good faith by the Board.

(iii) For good cause upon notice from Company. Termination by Company of Executive's employment for "good cause" as used in this Agreement shall be limited to gross negligence or malfeasance by Executive in the performance of his duties under this agreement or the voluntary resignation by Executive as an employee of the Company without the prior written consent of the Company.

> *Employment contracts are like weddings; neither party is likely to be thinking much about a possible breakup. Nevertheless, the exact wording of the "cause" or "good cause" provision is one of the more pivotal aspects of the deal.*

(b) If this Agreement is terminated pursuant to Section 10 (a) above, Executive's rights and Company's obligations hereunder shall forthwith terminate except as expressly provided in this Agreement.

(c) If this Agreement is terminated pursuant to Section 10(a) (i) or (ii) hereof, Executive or his estate shall be entitled to receive 100% of his base salary for the balance of the term of this Agreement, together with the bonus provided for in Section 4(e) hereof. Company may purchase insurance to cover all or any part of its obligations set forth in the preceding sentence, and Executive agrees to take a physical examination to facilitate the obtaining of such insurance. If the physical examination shows that Executive is uninsurable, such death and disability benefits shall not be provided (except for the bonus), and Executive shall receive only normal Company levels of death and disability benefits.

(d) Whenever compensation is payable to Executive hereunder during a time when he is partially or totally disabled and such disability (except for the provisions hereof) would entitle him to disability income or to salary continuation payments from Company according to the terms of any plan now or hereafter provided by Company or according to any Company policy in effect at the time of such disability, the compensation payable to him hereunder shall be inclusive of any such disability income or salary continuation and shall not be in addition thereto. If disability income is payable directly to Executive under an insurance policy paid for by Company, the amounts paid to him by said insurance company shall be considered to be part of the payments to be made by Company to him pursuant to this Section 10, and shall not be in addition thereto.

11. Termination by Executive

Executive shall have the right to terminate his employment under this agreement upon 30 days' notice to Company given within 60 days following the occurrence of any of the following events:

(i)   Executive is not elected or retained as Chairman and Chief Executive Officer and a director of Company.

(ii)   Company acts to materially reduce Executive's duties and responsibilities hereunder. Executive's duties and responsibilities shall not be deemed materially reduced for purposes hereof solely by virtue of the fact that Company is (or substantially all of its assets are) sold to, or is combined with, another entity provided that (a) Executive shall continue to have the same duties and responsibilities with respect to Company's entertainment and recreation, filmed entertainment, and consumers products business and (b) Executive shall report directly to the chief executive officer and board of directors of the entity (or individual) that acquires Company or its assets.

(iii) Company acts to change the geographic location of the performance of Executive's duties from Los Angeles California Metropolitan area.

There have been cases in which an employer has tried to force an employee to break the contract unilaterally, through humiliation, reduction in status, relocation to "Siberia," and other tactics.

12. **Consequences of Breach by Company**

(a) If this Agreement is terminated pursuant to Section 11 hereof, or if Company shall terminate Executive's employment under this Agreement in any other way that is a breach of this Agreement by Company, the following shall apply:

(i) Executive shall receive a cash payment equal to the present value (based on a discount rate of 9%) of Executive's base salary hereunder for the remainder of the term, payable within 30 days of the date of such termination.

(ii) Executive shall be entitled to bonus payments as provided in Sections 4 and 5 above (it being understood, however, that all such bonus payments, if made pursuant to this clause, shall be paid in cash regardless of whether or not such payments exceed the Cash Limit).

(iii) All stock options and Restricted Stock granted by Company to Executive under the Plan or granted by Company to Executive prior to the date hereof shall accelerate and become immediately exercisable.

Severance pay—how much, how soon, in what form—is a key element of the contract. This agreement gives Eisner the assurance of instant cash in massive amounts, plus the privilege of exercising all his stock options.

(b) The parties believe that because of the limitations of Section 11 (ii) the above payments do not constitute "Excess Parachute Payments" under Section 280G of the Internal Revenue Code of 1954, as amended (the "Code"). Notwithstanding such belief, if any benefit under the preceding paragraph is determined to be an "Excess Parachute Payment" the Company shall pay Executive an additional amount ("Tax Payment") such that (x) the excess of all Excess Parachute Payments (including payments under this sentence) over the sum of excise tax thereon under section 4999 of the Code and income tax thereon under Subtitle A of the Code and under applicable state law is equal to (y) the excess of all Excess Parachute Payments (excluding payments under this sentence) over income tax thereon under Subtitle A of the Code and under applicable state law, provided that the Company shall not be obligated to make a Tax payment in excess of the value of 6.6667 Compensation Years. For the purposes hereof, the value of a "Compensation Year," including stock options and bonus entitlements, is defined as equal to two times the base salary set forth in Section 3.

> *A lot of the verbiage here is designed to cushion Eisner against the possibility that Uncle Sam will look askance at the payout. As golden parachutes became an antitakeover weapon (rather than merely recompense for ousted managers), the IRS and the SEC took steps designed to stop practices deemed excessive.*

13. Remedies

Company recognizes that because of Executive's special talents, stature and opportunities in the entertainment industry, and because of the creative nature of and compensation practices of said industry and the material impact that individual projects can have on an entertainment company's results of operations, in the event of termination by Company hereunder (except under Section 10 (a)), or in the event of termination by Executive under Section 11, before the end of the agreed term, Company acknowledges and agrees that the provisions of this Agreement regarding further payments of base salary, bonuses and the exercisability of stock options constitute fair and reasonable provisions for the consequences of such termination, do not constitute a penalty, and such payments and benefits shall not be limited or reduced by amounts Executive might earn or be able to earn from any other employment or ventures during the remainder of the agreed term of this Agreement.

> *The optimum is to keep 100 percent of the severance even if you get an even higher-paying job the moment you leave.*

Your Negotiating Posture

Your ideal accomplishment would be to eliminate the "for cause" provision altogether. This being impractical, you want to restrict the "cause" language as narrowly as possible, to take away from the employer the leeway to break the contract unilaterally for unimportant reasons.

Don't assume that the employer has put this language in the contract to trap you. Language gets into employment agreements for a host of reasons:

- It is "standard" and nobody questions it.
- Neither side pays much attention.
- The attorney who drew up the contract likes to put in items that will probably never come into play but, if implemented literally, can be devastating to the employee.

Even when you're confident that the employer doesn't mean to use the provision against you, you must still work to get it out of the document. Conditions and attitudes may change. You may soon find yourself dealing with different circumstances and different people. The very existence of loose language in the "cause" provision is an enticement to an employer to try to get rid of you. Maybe you could win a lawsuit; but it's a lot better if there is never any attempt to terminate you for dubious reasons.

Work over the "cause" language. Don't attack it directly, as if you intended to do bad things and didn't want to get caught. Instead, use questions:

- Can you tell me what this means?
- How would it work out in practice?
- Who decides?
- What constitutes "unsatisfactory performance?"
- Can you give me a few examples of what this sentence is meant to cover?
- How often have you exercised this clause?

By carrying certain provisions to their extremes, you can reduce them to absurdity. For example, "Now, here it specifies 'failure to conform to company policies.' The company has a policy against theft of company property. That's a good policy, of course, and, if anything, it should be enforced more vigorously than it is now. But suppose I stick a yellow pad in my briefcase and take it home. The yellow pad is company property. Does that constitute 'cause'?"

Probably the answer will be some variation of, "That's ridiculous."

You agree. Now you pick up another phrase: "What about 'failure to perform assigned tasks'? Let's say I'm assigned to handle a conference call with the distributors every week. One week we have an emergency in shipping. I'm down there straightening it out. Have I violated the agreement?"

"Of course not," is the answer. But that's your point: This language is so vague and sweeping that it could be construed to cover such things. "I know you don't mean it that way. You agree that it's ridiculous. We don't need this. Let's get rid of it."

You acknowledge that the company should have the right to terminate you for a really serious offense. That "offense" should be indisputable, major, and precisely describable. Here's the kind of thing you want:

> "Cause" shall mean gross misappropriation or theft of company funds, or conviction of a felony.

The company may also want wording that allows firing you if you absolutely louse up on the job. In this provision, the wording protects the company and the employee:

> The Company may terminate this Agreement in the event of repeated and demonstrable failure on the part of the Executive to perform the material duties of Executive's management position (as described in Paragraph 2) in a competent manner, and failure of the Executive to substantially remedy such failure within 30 days of receiving specific written notice of such failure from Company.

This "cause" paragraph ensures that the termination can be triggered only by really bad performance. It has to be demonstrable. The manager's performance is measured against the standards of the job description included in the contract.

Here's another acceptable provision:

> The Company may terminate the Agreement in the event of repeated and demonstrated failure to carry out the reasonable instructions of Executive's superiors (as designated in Paragraph 4),

provided such instructions reasonably relate to, and are not incon-sistent with, the Executive's management position and standing; or any failure to carry out a material instruction of the said supe-riors which is not remedied by Executive within ten (10) days of receiving written notice of such failure from the Company.

Note the key modifiers: "repeated," "demonstrated," "reasonable." The agreement specifies the persons who can give the employee in-structions. And it says that those instructions must be consistent with the manager's position—not demeaning and not trivial.

Both of the above recommended examples require notice in writing.

Bad-Mouthing Breaks the Pact

A broadcasting company fired a manager, who threatened to sue. The company said that if the manager agreed not to sue, the company would provide only positive references. However, one company executive slammed the terminated manager, who went to court and won $3.4 million.

Written Notice

A requirement that the company give you reasons, in writing (and in ad-vance), for termination "for cause" may be one of your most powerful protections.

It's one thing for a member of the top brass to say to a manager, "This just isn't working out." It's quite another thing to actually docu-ment the unsatisfactory performance. Employers are usually reluctant to put the reasons for firing a manager into writing. With good reason. There is the possibility of a lawsuit. And then there is the problem that, when forced to spell out the reasons for dissatisfaction, the employer can't come up with anything substantial, or maybe anything that the employer wants to admit, especially on paper.

Therefore, a clause like the following is useful:

> *Notice of termination.* Any termination, by the Company or by the Executive, shall be communicated in writing to the other party. In case of a termination by the Company for Cause, the Notice of Termination shall set forth in detail the facts and circumstances claimed to provide a basis for such termination.

The above clause would have even sharper teeth if the employer were obligated to provide it *in advance of termination.* As it stands now, the employee gets the notice of termination along with a list of reasons for it. It's much better to know in advance that the move is pending, and why the company claims it is entitled to make it:

> *Advance notice of termination.* With respect to any termination by the Company for Cause, the specifics of the Cause shall be communicated to the Executive in writing at least thirty (30) days before the date on which the termination is proposed to take effect. Executive shall be given the opportunity to correct or respond . . . .

Documenting Your Performance

Your contract will contain language relating to your performance in the job. You will have negotiated to eliminate loopholes and ambiguities in that language to make sure that there are no grounds for terminating the contract "with Cause" because you are alleged to have broken some minor rule, or because of some vague and subjective opinions about how you're doing your job.

Think ahead. Imagine the "worst case": The company claims that because you have failed to fulfill your obligations under that provision, the company is relieved from its obligation to pay severance.

That contingency seems remote. Think about it anyway. If somebody claims you've been doing an unsatisfactory job under the terms of the contract, how can you refute the charge?

By documenting your performance.

No doubt your files contain most of the documentation you need. Put the relevant material together in your own personal and confidential folder. If you use a computer for the job, use your own computer, not one that is accessible by others.

In your documentation file, assemble and keep current the quantifiable data: budget objectives for your unit, for example, along with actual performance against those objectives.

Nobody's perfect. Where you fall short, collect material that puts the deficiency in perspective. This is particularly important if you fall short of agreed-on objectives. Get the figures for other divisions and for the company as a whole. If you missed budget by 3 percent and nobody else came closer to hitting the target, this does not make you a paragon, but it goes to show that you did your job at least as well as everyone else. If your performance equals or exceeds that of competitors or the industry average, your proof material is enhanced. It is unlikely that you can put together complete figures, particularly for competitive firms; the idea is to get whatever you can. Collect everything that seems significant. If a particular fact does not support your case, you don't have to use it.

Read and clip the company's annual report and its official press releases. Within its walls, a firm may be blaming a particular individual for bad performance; publicly, however, the firm may be casting a rosy light on the person's performance, or claiming extenuating circumstances.

Collect data that help to explain failures. For example, when the budget is being put together, you make certain requests that are turned down; on others, you receive substantially less than you asked. Make sure your requests are in writing, with full supporting material. Get the turndown in writing as well.

Go beyond the numbers. Keep a file of correspondence that acknowledges your contributions, sheds light on your importance to the company, reflects top management's confidence in you, hints at bigger things in the future, and so on. A lot of positive comment flows around in some offices. People tend to dismiss it as pro forma lubrication, and so it is. But it can come in handy if anyone ever turns around and says you're doing an inadequate job.

Keep your performance reviews. These are often couched in positive—occasionally, fulsome—terms. Insiders know that; but the top brass might find it hard to tell a judge or jury that they didn't mean a word they said.

Judge? Jury? Court? Yes. The whole thrust of documenting your performance against the standards established in the contract is to prepare for the "worst case," the remote possibility that you might have to sue to get fair treatment. You don't think that can happen; nobody ever does. And, although the "unthinkable" doesn't happen often, it does happen. It's well to be prepared.

In practice, companies are more likely to use the *threat* of termination for cause to try to get an individual to compromise on a lower-figure settlement of the contracted severance amount. This can be intimidating. You're not in the best emotional condition, the company is better able to afford a court battle than you are, and so on.

If you've documented your performance as described above, you can counter with the *threat* of court action against the company. Your carefully prepared file, plus your familiarity with the issues, shows that you are serious.

The situation may deteriorate into a game of Chicken. Companies don't like wrongful-dismissal suits, even when they think they can win them. And you certainly don't want to go to court. Apart from the expense and anguish, you exhaust your valuable time and energy, and you diminish your attractiveness to potential employers.

A well-furnished documentation file can help you head off this miserable situation.

In building your file, be comprehensive. Include items that may seem insignificant, even ridiculous: items in the house organ, puff pieces in the trade press, routine letters and memos.

Include company handouts, especially the orientation booklets and materials given to all new employees. You may have ignored this stuff. Don't. As explained in Chapter 6, "The *De Facto* Contract," courts are finding that the statements made in these booklets can amount to contractual promises to employees.

Chances are that you'll never have to use this file in court. It has other uses, however. For one thing, you can use it in negotiating your next raise. A judicious selection of the contents of your support folder can serve as impressive proof material.

Writing Conflict Resolution Methods into the Contract

The strength of a contract lies in the general agreement that it is legally binding and enforceable in a court of law.

But you want to avoid going to court. So does the company.

There can be all kinds of questions and disagreements about sections of an employment agreement. Most of these disagreements don't require any formal legal process. The parties iron things out through reasonable discussion. (That's another purpose for keeping a documentation file and learning as much as you can about contracts.)

But what if a serious dispute can't be settled this way? For example, the basis for computing a bonus payout can get pretty complicated. It's to the advantage of both parties to build into the contract a provision for resolving complex financial issues relating to incentive compensation. Here is a section embodying a method for settling differences in this area:

> In case of any dispute between the Executive and the Company as to the amount of additional compensation payable to the Executive in respect of any fiscal year, determination of the amount so payable by the independent public accountants at that time retained by the Company, made at the request of any party, shall be binding and conclusive on all parties hereto.

Assuming that the accounting firm is a reputable organization, you should be comfortable with a provision like this. If you can't trust the company's accountants, you shouldn't be working there.

Other differences have to be settled in other ways. As we have noted, one of the most frequent causes of bitter controversy is the question of termination "for cause," or the related question of whether an individual terminates voluntarily or is forced out by the employer.

Of such disputes, lawsuits are made. Some companies try to discourage employees from seeking legal remedies by inserting provisions like the following:

> In the event that any action, suit or other proceeding in law or in equity is brought to enforce the provisions of this agreement, and such action results in the awarding of a judgment in favor of the Company, all expenses of the Company in conjunction with said action shall be payable by the Executive.

"Loser pays all" is a powerful deterrent to legal action. You should vigorously resist any such provision.

The Arbitration Clause

There are better ways to settle disputes. Your contract should carry a provision for arbitration. The standard forum for argument and resolution is provided by the American Arbitration Association, a nonprofit organization that maintains panels of arbitrators and administrative services for judging labor and commercial disputes. Here is a typical arbitration clause:

> Any controversy or claim arising under this Agreement shall be settled by arbitration in accordance with the Rules of the American Arbitration Association then in effect. The controversy or claim shall be submitted to three arbitrators, one of whom shall be chosen by the Company, one of whom shall be chosen by the Executive, and the third of whom shall be chosen by the two so selected. The party desiring arbitration shall give written notice to the other party of its desire to arbitrate the particular matter in question, naming the arbitrator selected by it.
>
> If the other party shall fail within a period of 15 days after such notice to have given a reply in writing naming the arbitrator selected by it, then the party not in default may apply to the American Arbitration Association for the appointment of the second arbitrator. If the two arbitrators chosen as above shall fail within 15 days after their selection to agree on the third arbitrator, then either party may apply to the American Arbitration Association for the appointment of an arbitrator to fill the place so remaining vacant. The decision of any two of the arbitrators shall be final and binding upon the parties hereto and shall be delivered in writing signed in triplicate by the concurring arbitrators to each of the parties hereto. Judgment upon the award rendered by the arbitrators may be entered in any court having jurisdiction thereof.

Notification is an important adjunct. Typically, a contract may specify the notification process this way:

> Any notice, request, or other communication required or permitted pursuant to this Agreement shall be in writing and shall be

deemed duly given when received by the party to whom it shall be given or three days after being mailed by certified, registered, or express mail, postage prepaid, addressed as follows:

If to the Company:

> The Stonesong Press, Inc.
> 211 East 51st Street
> New York NY 10022
> Attention of the Secretary

If to the Executive:

> John J. Tarrant
> 6789 Erdgeist Drive
> Anywhere NY 10456

Any party may change the address to which communications are to be mailed by giving notice of such change in the manner provided above.

Arbitration makes sense. Occasionally, a corporation with legal counsel on staff or on retainer will prefer to keep the arbitration clause out, assuming that if the only recourse is legal action, the company is vastly better prepared for it than the employee.

Don't agree to that omission. Top management of the company is unlikely to have any reason to avoid arbitration. There should be general agreement that it's a commonsense way to resolve disputes.

But If You Need a Lawyer . . .

You hope you'll never have to go to court because of a dispute with your employer. If you do, you may want an attorney who has experience in this area.

Laws vary from state to state. Sometimes, one of the key issues in employment disputes is deciding the state under whose laws the suit will be tried (unless this contingency is covered in the employment agreement).

You may want to get in touch with the National Employment Lawyers Association, a nonprofit, professional membership organization of more than 2,500 lawyers from around the country who represent employees in employment matters. To request a state listing of employment lawyers, you can send a written request and a *self-addressed, stamped, business-size envelope to:*

National Employment Lawyers Association
600 Harrison Street
Suite 535
San Francisco CA 94107

Allow four to six weeks for a response.

Including Benefits in the Severance Agreement

Let's say the company terminates your employment agreement. There's no dispute; they pay you the full severance.

But you have no health insurance.

Executives who have had health insurance plans for their entire working lives are often shocked at the size of the premiums when they're forced to foot the bill themselves. Try to remain tied into the employer's health plan (and other benefits) for as long as possible after termination. You may someday welcome the inclusion of a paragraph like the following:

> Following termination of this Agreement, and unless and until the Employee accepts full-time employment with another company, the Company shall provide and continue to provide to the Employee such insurance benefits (including medical and life insurance) as the Company generally provides for any group or class of employee of which the Employee would have been a member if his employment had continued.

That's the ideal. If you can't (as is likely) persuade the company to continue coverage indefinitely, bargain to make it as long as possible. You have cards to play. The company maintains the plans anyway, so this is a relatively low-cost benefit. And the company does not relish the thought of a former employee in severe financial difficulty.

Here is a provision from a contemporary contract that is worth emulating in your next contract. It touches all bases and provides continuing coverage for up to three years.

If the Period of Employment terminates . . . as a result of a voluntary termination by Employee with Good Reason, or a voluntary termination by Employer without Cause, then Employee will be entitled to receive only: . . .

(v) maintenance in effect for the continued benefit of Employee and his dependents for a period terminating on the earlier of (A) three years after the date of termination of employment and the date on which Employee reaches age 65, or (B) the commencement of equivalent benefits from a new employer of:

(A) all insured and self-insured medical and dental benefit plans in which Employee was participating immediately prior to termination, provided that Employee's continued participation is possible under the general terms and conditions of such plans (and any applicable funding media) and Employee continues to pay an amount equal to Employee's regular contribution for such participation; and

(B) the group and individual life insurance and disability insurance policies of Employer then in effect for Employee; *provided, however*, that if Employer so elects, or such continued participation is not possible under the general terms and conditions of such plans or under such policies, Employer shall, in lieu of the foregoing, arrange to have issued for the benefit of Employee and Employee's dependents equivalent benefits (on an after-tax basis); provided further that, in no event shall Employee be required to pay any premiums or other charges in an amount greater than that which Employee would have paid in order to participate in Employer's plans and policies . . . .

This same contract provides benefits for three months after termination for cause.

Tap into the Company's Firing Strategy

Your company probably has a policy, formal or informal, on how to fire people.

More companies are thinking about it—because, as *The Wall Street Journal* told its readers, "Big bosses often demand big money when they sue over lost jobs. . . . There has been a rising tide of unfair dismissal suits filed by ousted executives."[1]

To forestall wrongful dismissal suits, companies are installing litigation-alternative programs. Typically, these programs apply to a wide range of employees, although the purpose may be to combat court action by senior managers. Chrysler's program, instituted in June 1995, calls for a group of managers to hear the employee's complaint. The employee can appeal to a panel of human resource managers; and, finally, to an outside arbitrator whose decision is binding.

Arbitration is the key to the lawsuit-avoidance strategies of most companies. Most companies don't go as far as Rockwell International, which, in 1992, gave nearly 900 top managers a choice: accept an arbitration agreement or give up your stock options. River Oaks Imaging and Diagnostic went further, ordering staff people to sign arbitration agreements if they wanted to keep their jobs. This, said a federal judge, is going too far. The court threw out the proposed policy.

Some plaintiffs' attorneys decry the strategy, saying that managers should not give up their right to sue, and maintaining that fired managers are likely to get a better break from a jury than from an arbitrator.

That may be true; but the lawyers (perhaps understandably) overlook the delay and agony that managers go through when they sue for wrongful dismissal.

This author maintains that an arbitration clause is a good idea for most people. The issue is decided quickly and unambiguously. You suffer less pain. And you avoid damaging yourself (unjust though the damage may be) in the eyes of other potential employers.

Nevertheless, your firm may be getting worried about lawsuits—perhaps worried enough to send managers (including you) to one of the newfangled firing seminars that are springing up across the landscape.

---

[1] *The Wall Street Journal*, June 28, 1995, "Companies Try to Prevent Fired Executives From Suing," by Joann S. Lublin.

At these sessions, managers hear that they should document the case against the employee; handle the termination personally and in private; choose the right time (say, a morning in midweek); and so forth.

Find out as much as you can about the company's approach to firing. If they want to send you to a seminar, by all means attend.

Until now, maybe your company doesn't have an arbitration agreement with you. Top brass may come to you and ask you to sign one. Use it as an opening to win concessions elsewhere. If you don't have a full-blown employment agreement, take advantage of the situation to bargain for one.

Make sure your arbitration agreement provides for a truly impartial and orderly process. The model language in this book is a useful guide.

Getting the Most You Can Get in Severance

Bargain hard for a liberal and comprehensive severance deal. Consider issues like the following:

- If you relocated to take the job, will the company pay to move you back (if you so choose)?
- Will the company buy your house if you can't sell it?
- Do your bonuses continue during the severance period?
- Do you have the option of a lump-sum payment?
- *Will the company pay for meaningful outplacement service?*

The last might be the most important issue. Whatever the circumstances of your termination, you want all the help you can get in landing another job. Negotiate a provision that lets you use an effective outplacement specialist.

At the hiring stage, neither party is thinking all that much about the ending of the association. That may give you an advantage. If you negotiate, calmly but with determination, for an optimum severance package, the employer may agree to quite a few of your conditions, because they are predicated on a contingency that doesn't seem likely to come about.

12

Golden Parachutes

We don't hear the term "golden parachute" as much as we used to. But that doesn't mean you no longer need protection against the consequences of a change in control of your company. Quite the contrary. You need it more than ever. So let's take a look at new departures and new strategies in golden parachutes (GPs).

As the wave of corporate mergers and acquisitions swept over American business, starting in the 1970s, the "golden parachute" was born.

At first, GPs were hefty insurance policies given by top managers to each other as protection against a dreaded change of control (COC). Later, the concept was adapted to make it a protection against unwanted takeovers, the notion being that the takeover could be made so expensive that the would-be devourer would be deterred. We saw the rise of "tin parachutes," giving payouts to *all* employees, or all salaried employees, in case of a COC.

The "poison pill" approach has not been remarkably effective in staving off takeovers. Golden parachutes continue to be standard parts of the employment deals of managers. These days, GPs are often given to people well down the chain of command, not just to a handful of top officers. One reason for this expansion is the difficulty the top officers had in defending the GP as a perk confined to an exclusive club.

Executive Compensation Reports (ECR) noted in 1995 that almost 80 percent of the companies in its database provide some form of COC-related protection. Typically, the parachutes carry "double triggers," meaning that the employee receives a payout only if he or she is terminated without cause or resigns for good reason within a specified period following the change in control.

Pickens Sheds His Parachute

In September 1995, T. Boone Pickens disclosed that he was abandoning the big parachute strapped onto him by Mesa Inc., of which he was chairman.* Pickens's parachute came under heavy fire from Marvin Davis and others involved in a bid to take over Mesa. Pickens said he was pulling out of the program to head off stockholder challenges that might kill Mesa's plan to give severance to *all* employees who lose their jobs because of a change in control.

The Wall Street Journal, September 12, 1995, "Pickens to Give Up Golden Parachute to Head Off Mesa Holders' Challenges," by Allanna Sullivan.

A Typical COC Provision

Here's the COC section of a current contract:

Change of Control Termination

If, within twenty-four (24) months following a Change of Control, as hereinafter defined, the Executive voluntarily resigns or retires or the Executive's employment is terminated during the Period of Employment except for Disability, Death or Termination for Cause, the termination shall be deemed a "Change of Control Termination." For purposes of this paragraph . . . (a) the delivery of a notice of termination by the Employer . . . within twenty-four (24) months of a Change of Control and (b) a Constructive Discharge within twenty-four (24) months following a Change of Control will also be deemed a Change of Control Termination. In the event of a Change of Control Termination, the Employer will pay to the Executive a lump-sum payment of 299% of the Executive's average annual Base Salary and Annual Incentive Bonus during the preceding five-year period. In the event that a Change of Control Termination occurs before the Executive completes five years of service, the lump-sum payment will be valued at 299% of the Executive's average annual Base Salary and Annual Incentive Bonus during all years of service.

Additionally, any options and/or restricted stock granted to the Executive shall become fully vested as of the date of Change of Control Termination. Provided further, the Executive will receive a cash payment equal to the value of any options anticipated to be granted . . . within the three years following the Change of Control Termination . . . .

> *The COC protection extends for two years. The payout is virtually three times salary and bonus. The deal on the stock is reasonable. Now comes the "gross-up"—the reimbursement for taxes.*

If any portion of any payment or distribution by the Employer, to or for the benefit of the Executive, whether paid or payable or distributed or distributable pursuant to the terms of this Section . . . shall be subject to the excise tax imposed by Section 4999 of the [Internal Revenue] Code, or any interest or penalties are incurred by the Executive with respect to such excise tax . . . the Employer shall pay to the Executive an additional payment (the "Gross-Up Payment") in an amount such that after payment by the Executive of such Excise Tax, including, without limitation, any income taxes and Excise Tax imposed on the Gross-Up Payment, the Executive retains an amount including the Gross-Up Payment equal to the total payment hereunder without regard to the Gross-Up Payment.

> *Thus, the gross-up is additionally grossed-up.*

Definitions are important throughout the contract. Here's the definition of Change of Control:

"Change of Control" shall be deemed to have occurred if at any time or from time to time after the date of this Agreement:

(i) Any "person" or "group" . . . is or becomes the "beneficial owner" . . . directly or indirectly, of securities of the Employer representing thirty percent (30%) or more of the combined voting power of the Employer's then outstanding securities . . . , or

(ii) the stockholders of the Employer approve a merger or consolidation of the Employer with any other corporation, other than a merger or consolidation which would result in the voting securities of the Employer . . . continuing to represent . . . more than 50 percent (50%) of the combined voting power of the voting securities of the Employer or such surviving entity outstanding immediately after such merger or consolidation, or the stockholders of the Employer approve a plan of complete liquidation of the Employer or an agreement for the sale or disposition by the Employer of all or substantially all of the Employer's assets.

A Bold New Parachute

In July 1995, Chrysler's top management—electrified by the takeover threat of Kirk Kerkorian—adopted golden parachutes for its top thirty officers. But, reported *The Wall Street Journal* (July 12, 1995), "[T]hese are no ordinary golden parachutes. Instead of taking effect *after* control of a company changes, these open if a potential acquirer moves to get top executives fired *even before a takeover is completed.*"

These, then, are parachutes that open in the plane, because you don't like the looks of a guy on the tarmac who, you think, might climb into the cockpit. (At this time, Chrysler implemented a number of defensive measures, including one that tried to block former CEO Lee Iacocca—a member of the takeover team—from cashing in his stock options.)

We have been able to get the text of an interesting Chrysler document titled "Summary of Principal Terms of Key Executive Employment Protection Agreements." Here are some significant excerpts.

TERM OF AGREEMENT

On the date on which a *Potential Change of Control* or Change of Control occurs (the "Effective Date"), the Agreement becomes effective as an employment agreement between the Company and the Executive. In the event that the Agreement becomes effective on a Potential Change of Control, the Agreement will also expire at any time that the Board determines in good faith that a Change of Control *is not likely to occur*, or, at the Executive's election, at any anniversary of the Potential Change of Control . . . .

"We Don't Want You to Be Upset . . ."

The conventional rationale for the GP is that it permits senior executives to make decisions calmly and judiciously when the possibility of a takeover looms. According to this reasoning, when a top manager fears that he or she will be thrown out by the new controlling faction, that top manager will fight tooth and nail to forestall the takeover. The manager's battle to save his or her job may be detrimental to the interests of the stockholders.

Here's part of a parachute section that spells out the soothing nature of the deal.

The Board of Directors and the Compensation Committee of the Board have determined that it is in the best interests of the Corporation and its shareholders for the Corporation to agree, as provided herein, to pay you termination compensation in the event you should leave the employ of the Corporation under the circumstances described below.

The Board and Committee recognize that the continuing possibility of an unsolicited tender offer or other takeover bid for the Corporation is *unsettling to you and other senior executives of the Corporation.*

Therefore these arrangements are being made to help assure a continuing dedication by you to your duties to the corporation notwithstanding the occurrence of a tender offer or takeover bid. In particular, the Board and the Committee believe it important, should the Corporation receive proposals from third parties with respect to its future, to enable you, without being influenced by the uncertainties of your own situation, to assess and advise the Board whether such proposals would be in the best interests of the Corporation and its shareholders and to take such other action regarding such proposals as the Board might determine to be appropriate. The Board and the Committee also wish to demonstrate to executives of the

Corporation and its subsidiaries that the Corporation is concerned with the welfare of its executives and intends to see that loyal executives are treated fairly.

Here's the beginning of a golden parachute agreement signed by Richard J. Ferris, Chairman, President, and CEO of Allegis Corporation:

PRIVILEGED AND CONFIDENTIAL

April 16, 1987

Joseph T. Kane
208 Oxford Road
Kenilworth IL 60043

Dear Mr. Kane:

Allegis Corporation (the "Company") considers it essential to the best interests of its stockholders to foster the continuous employment of key management personnel. In this connection, the Board of Directors of the Company (the "Board") recognizes that, as is the case with many publicly held corporations, the possibility of a change in control may exist and that such possibility, and the uncertainty and questions it may raise among management, may result in the departure or distraction of management personnel to the detriment of the Company and its stockholders.

The Board has determined that appropriate steps should be taken to reinforce and encourage the continued attention and dedication of members of the management of the Company and its subsidiaries, including yourself, to their assigned duties in the face of potentially disturbing circumstances arising from the possibility of a change in control of the Company, although no such change is now contemplated.

This language is designed to soothe the stockholders at least as much as to ease the mind of the executive. As investors, particularly institutional investors, read about GPs in the corporation's proxy statements, they get irritable.

If your employer has issued parachutes to top executives, the company is probably a little sensitive about it. In negotiating for a better deal for yourself, you can use the argument that you deserve at least as much protection as the top brass.

Sensitivity About GPs

Late in 1994, Raytel Medical Corporation was bidding to take over Medical Diagnostics Inc. (MDI). With Raytel's tender offer looming over them, MDI's directors gave eight senior executives new golden parachutes.

The cost of these GPs became a big issue. In February 1995, the CEO of Raytel (the would-be taker-over) sent a letter to stockholders of the target company:

> MDI's Directors wrote you recently complaining that Raytel's investment advisor deliberately misled you about the size of the golden parachutes they gave John Lynch and seven other MDI executives on December 15, 1994, because Raytel's tender offer made them nervous about their jobs. . . .
>
> When the MDI directors approved these golden parachutes and other agreements, they did not know their total cost. We think that is a shocking admission, since every golden parachute dollar paid to management reduces the value of the Stockholders' Equity in MDI by the same amount.
>
> One month after approving these agreements, the MDI directors filed a brief in the federal court in Delaware, claiming they could not tell you how much of their assets they had given away to MDI management because they still did not know! Directors are supposed to be fully informed before they act.
>
> Because MDI claimed it was unable to tell you how much of your MDI assets they had given away to John Lynch and his cronies . . .

The letter goes on to further excoriate MDI's top managers and board, and includes the stirring cry, "When the MDI Board tells you they are outraged that we have misled you about their grand giveaway of stockholder assets, I'd tell them to give me a break. I hope you will join us as stockholders and continue to demand that these outrageous devices which reduce stockholder value be eliminated . . . ."

Hardball! When GPs are potentially vulnerable to attack as "outrageous devices which reduce stockholder value," managements and boards are naturally sensitive.

We will continue to see undiplomatic language about golden parachutes in takeover fights. In December 1994, California Energy Company was frustrated in its efforts to acquire control of Magma Power Company. California Energy, claiming that two inside shareholders of Magma (Dow Chemical and the B.C. McCabe Foundation) had frustrated the wishes of the noninsiders, withdrew its bid and issued a communiqué that contained the following blast:

> . . . the only steps which Dow and Magma have taken . . . are to approve poison pills, golden parachutes, and other actions to enrich management, entrench management, and sustain Dow's control of Magma.
>
> We regret that Dow and Magma have prevented a transaction which would materially benefit the non-insider shareholders in order to serve their own self-interest. The blatant breach of fiduciary obligations to shareholders . . .

Golden parachutes are a popular target. When Dickstein Partners sent solicitations to stockholders of Hills' Stores, Mark Dickstein denounced "the Hills Board's . . . total disregard for shareholder rights in adopting the poison pill, modifying golden parachutes for senior executives and a consultant who is also a board member . . . ." When Steinhardt Pensler was striving to acquire Katy Industries, Katy's dominant shareholder group was assailed for having "threatened to load the company up with golden parachutes . . ."

Stock Options in Parachutes

With executive compensation plans leaning more heavily toward stock plans, employment agreements are likely to contain specific COC provisions attached to the section of the contract concerned with the stock plan. The contract may, in addition, carry an overall COC clause.

Here's a relevant part of a contract signed with Paramount Communications.

> 10.8 *Changes in Capital Structure: Merger or Consolidation . . .*
>   In the event of a merger or consolidation of the Company with another company . . . The Executive shall be entitled to immediate receipt . . . of (a) any cash and securities other than common stock paid or issued in connection with any reorganization recapitalization, merger or consolidation . . . the Company shall make available to the Executive the certificates representing the Shares to the extent the Executive is required to submit or deliver such securities as a condition to the receipt of cash, securities or common stock.

Components of a Parachute

Among the key issues in a golden parachute are:

- The definition of a change of control.
- The window: How long do you have to pull the ripcord?
- The trigger: What has to happen to cause a payout?

Definitions of a change in control vary. Here are five recent versions noted by the invaluable researchers at *Executive Compensation Reports.*

1. Tribune Company
   - Outside 20 percent buyout.
   - Unapproved change in Board majority.
   - Sale or liquidation of the Company.
   - Merger or reorganization involving more than a 40 percent change in shareholders.
2. Farah Inc.
   - A 30 percent buyout (40 percent if by Marciano Group, which controls 9.3 percent of company).
   - Unapproved change in Board majority.

3. DSC Communications

- A 20 percent buyout.
- Unapproved change in Board majority.
- Stockholder approval of a substantive merger.
- Company's sale, dissolution, or liquidation.

4. Eastman Chemical Company

- A 25 percent buyout.
- Change in Board majority unapproved by at least three-fourths of directors.
- Reorganization, sale, merger, consolidation, or liquidation.

5. Conagra, Inc.

- Outside acquisition of 30 percent voting power.
- Unapproved change in Board majority.
- Stockholder approval of reorganization, merger, or consolidation, involving at least a 50 percent change in voting power.
- Sale, liquidation, or dissolution of the company.

We occasionally see exotic digressions, as in the case (already discussed) of Chrysler's anticipatory parachutes. For instance, an executive of Tidewater Inc. pulled the ripcord on his parachute, not because Tidewater was being acquired, but because Tidewater was *acquiring* another company, Zapata Gulf Marine Corporation. The executive may have felt his job was threatened, perhaps by somebody in the Zapata ranks. After this incident, Tidewater said the agreements would be changed to provide payouts only if Tidewater was taken over.

Some key terms should become familiar to you:

Windows—The time periods after a change in control within which the employee can exercise the privileges of the parachute. Typically, they run for two or three years (three years can be a lot better than two), but they can vary in length.

Triggers—Some parachute agreements give the possessor wide latitude in deciding to cash in and leave after a COC. Others have somewhat more rigorous criteria for the payment of severance—

for example, demotion, reduction in compensation or benefits, or relocation.

Rabbi trust—One of several possible collateral provisions. It guarantees that a parachute will be funded through money that is placed in trust and is unavailable to the executive unless there is a change in control.

Negotiating Points

Find out as much as you can about the company's approach to golden parachutes. Do as much as you can with research. Question the headhunter. And ask the employer.

There's no reason why the employer should not tell you everything you want to know about GPs in the company. But that doesn't mean every employer is happy to talk about the subject.

For example, a relatively senior manager, discussing an employment package, asks, "What's your policy on GPs?" The employer retorts, "Why do you want to know?"

Such defensiveness might stem from a number of sources. The company may have strapped parachutes on its top officers, but not on anybody else. Or, there may be faint intimations of a merger or takeover—intimations that the top brass of the company think (or hope) have not gotten around.

Either way, the executive proceeds calmly. The employer's sensitivity about GPs may provide an opening. There is no reason for you, as a prospective employee, to be apologetic about saying: "I asked about golden parachutes because they are a fact of life in compensation today, aren't they? Nine out of ten companies have them. So I assume you provide them as well."

Go on the assumption that you will be given a GP. "These days, change of control is a possibility that everybody takes into account. That doesn't mean it's going to happen, any more than an automobile accident is going to happen. Nevertheless, you carry insurance, just in case. I don't expect that I'd ever want to use my parachute. But of course I'm interested in its provisions."

If GPs are limited, ask why. "It seems as if a lot of companies are extending change of control provisions to a larger group of managers, not just a privileged few. This seems fair; if there's a merger or takeover, the effects would not be confined to just a few people."

Stress your feelings of importance to the company. "Let's see if I understand you properly. Half a dozen senior officers have protection because the company wants them to be free to make objective decisions for the good of the firm. That's an excellent reason for golden parachutes. But then you seem to be saying that people like me can be left out in the cold because our decisions don't matter so much . . . ."

Capitalize on the "It can't happen here" argument. The employer says, "There's absolutely no chance of a takeover." Instead of being skeptical, you are pleased: "That's great. So, that being the case, nobody has a golden parachute, right? It's wonderful that you and the other top people here don't feel the need for such protection . . . ."

If the answer is, "Well, a few of us have some sort of change of control arrangement as a pro forma matter, but there is no possibility, as far as anyone can see, that they would ever come into play . . . ."

You answer, "Since that's the case, there's no reason why I shouldn't have a GP then, is there? Fine. That will let me give the job my total concentration . . . ."

Your Optimum GP

The best golden parachute:

- Kicks in at a low level of change of control (say, 25 percent rather than 40 percent).
- Provides maximum benefits.
- Allows a quick, definite payout.
- Specifies ample time following COC.
- Pays out completely on stock and bonus plans.
- Affords the employee maximum latitude in deciding what to do.

If you have been able to get a good severance agreement, you have a simple negotiating point: "Instead of going into a lot of detail about a golden parachute, let's just say that if I leave or if I'm terminated for any reason within three years after a change in control, I will be entitled to the severance we've already agreed on."

Takeover is always a possibility. Bargain for the biggest and best parachute you can get. Because the top management or board you're dealing with today would not be the same after a merger or takeover, they are not, in a sense, gambling with their own money. But that doesn't mean the company can go wild in handing out GPs. There's too much stockholder and media scrutiny nowadays for that to happen.

However, by negotiating logically and tenaciously, you can enhance your protection against being demoted, demeaned, or dropped by a different controlling group.

A Postmerger Employment Agreement

Mergers and acquisitions among companies from different nations can get pretty complicated. If you're an executive of a company involved in such a merger or acquisition, the challenge of safeguarding what you've already earned and ensuring your position under the new arrangement is equally complicated.

Helen M. Feeney was VP/Secretary of AMAX, a metals and mining company. In 1993, Cyprus Minerals acquired AMAX. Alumax had been AMAX's wholly owned subsidiary since 1986. In that year, AMAX bought out Mitsui & Company, Ltd., which had been its partner in a joint venture since 1973.

The contract signed by Helen Feeney upon the occasion of the Cyprus Minerals takeover is reproduced in Appendix 4. Its text and accompanying comments will be helpful if you're facing a possible international merger.

13

Noncompete and Nondisclosure Provisions

Curtailing Your Freedom

A key segment in a growing number of contracts is the "non-compete" provision, in which the executive agrees to refrain from certain activities for a specified length of time after leaving the company.

Here's a brief version of a noncompete, from a letter of agreement:

> NON-COMPETITION
> For a period of twelve (12) months after the termination of your employment, you will not, directly or indirectly, receive any fee or render any services for or in connection with any entity that was a client of [company] during the twelve (12)-month period preceding the termination of your employment, except for clients that are acquired by [company] as a sole and direct result of your contacts and business development activities.

The above is a comparatively liberal provision. It allows the departing associate of the firm to do business with clients that he or she brought into the house. As we shall see, other provisions can be much more rigid.

Take a look at this excerpt:

> *Noncompetition*—Executive agrees that during the term of this Agreement and for a period after the termination hereof (for whatever reason) equal to the time during which payments are being made to Executive in accordance with Section 5 (d) [the severance clause under which the company makes monthly payments], Executive shall not become involved, directly or indirectly, in any business as an officer, director, employee, paid consultant, agent, representative, more than 5 percent shareholder or partner of a corporation or partnership or other business enterprise engaged in the wholesale distribution of pharmaceutical aids and sundry items.

And here is noncompete language from another contract:

> COVENANT NOT TO COMPETE
> During the term of this Employment Agreement, and for such period as the Executive is receiving payments hereunder as a result of a Voluntary Resignation or Retirement, the Executive shall not, directly or indirectly, own, manage, operate, join, control or participate in the ownership, management, operation or control of, or be employed by or connected in any manner with, any business which engages in substantially the same line of business as the Employer, whether for compensation or otherwise, without the prior written consent of the Employer. Should the Executive, directly or indirectly, own, manage, operate, join, control or participate in the ownership, management, operation or control of, or be employed by or connected in any manner with, any business which primarily engages in the same line of business as the employer, all payments under this Agreement shall cease.

The nonsolicitation provision is a close relative of the noncompete: The company limits the ability of the employee (ex-employee, really) to go after customers or to try to lure other employees away from the firm.

Here's how one contract handles this:

> *Non-Solicitation:* During the period beginning on the date of this Agreement's execution and ending two (2) years following

termination of Executive's employment with the Company, Executive shall not hire or solicit any employees of the Company or any person that controls, is controlled by, or is under common control with any other person of the Company, to work for any other Person then in competition with the Company or any of its Affiliates, or, directly or indirectly, solicit or attempt in any manner to persuade or influence any present, future or prospective customer or client of the Company or any of its Affiliates to divert his or its purchases of products or services from the company or any of its Affiliates to any person then in competition with the Company or any of its Affiliates. Executive agrees and acknowledges that [he or she] possesses valuable information with respect to customers and clients of the Company as a result of [his or her] employment and that violation of this provision would cause irreparable harm to the Company. Executive hereby specifically acknowledges the adequacy of the compensation to be paid by Company hereunder and of the other benefits provided by Company under this Agreement . . . .

Besides protecting itself from competition, the company wants to protect its secrets. Contracts often contain a nondisclosure clause:

Confidentiality
The Executive hereby acknowledges that, as an employee of the Employer, [he or she] will be making use of, acquiring and adding to confidential information of a special and unique nature and value relating to the Employer and its strategic plan and financial operations. The Executive further recognizes and acknowledges that all confidential information is the exclusive property of the Employer, is material and confidential, and is critical to the successful conduct of the business of the Employer.

Accordingly, the Executive hereby covenants and agrees that [he or she] will use confidential information for the benefit of the Employer only and shall not at any time, directly or indirectly, during the term of this Agreement, and thereafter for all periods during which severance or other amount is paid, divulge, reveal or communicate any confidential information to any person, firm, corporation or entity whatsoever, or use any confidential information for [his or her] own benefit or for the benefit of others.

Policing the Noncompetes

You can't blame companies for trying to keep their secrets or to prevent ex-employees from stealing present employees or customers. Naturally, a company is eager to give competition as few openings as possible. And when a knowledgeable executive joins the enemy, business—which is already tough—gets tougher.

The trouble, from the employee's point of view, is that noncompete clauses and their relatives place restrictions on the employee's freedom of action after the employee has left the company. Where else would a fired executive go but to another company in the same industry? Or to start his or her own company in the same business?

But the employment agreement prohibits these activities.

A few years ago, companies tried to enforce noncompete clauses, principally through the threat of court action. Courts tended to look askance at such provisions, comparing them with "involuntary servitude" or "slavery."

But even if the provisions wouldn't hold up in court, companies still managed to enforce them by making life miserable, if not impossible, for the offending ex-employee. Lawyers called the noncompete the *in terrorum* clause (meaning it scares the hell out of you).

Now, for the most part, employers have what they feel is a better way. They build into the contract a severance deal that involves payment periodically (say, monthly) over a period of, for example, two years after the contract is terminated. The noncompete period sometimes coincides with the length of the severance period.

Unique Self-Protective Provisions

Disney considers Michael Eisner unique—and uniquely able to offer effective competition. Thus the following language:

9. Protection of Company's Interests

(a) During the term of this Agreement Executive shall not directly or indirectly engage in competition with, or not own any interest in any business which competes with, any business of Company or any of its subsidiaries; provided, however, that the provisions of this Section 9 shall not prohibit his ownership of not more than 5% of voting stock of any publicly held corporation.

(b) Except for actions taken in the course of his employment hereunder, at no time shall Executive divulge, furnish or make accessible to any person any information of a confidential or proprietary nature obtained by him while in the employ of Company. Upon termination of his employment by Company, Executive shall return to the Company all such information which exists in writing or other physical form and all copies thereof in his possession or under his control.

Here is a standard restrictive covenant protecting the company.

(c) Company, its successors and assigns, shall, in addition to Executive's services, be entitled to receive and own all of the results and proceeds of said services (including, without limitation, literary material and other intellectual property) produced or created during the term of Executive's employment hereunder. Executive will, at the request of Company, execute such assignments, certificates or other instruments as Company may from time to time deem necessary or desirable to evidence, establish, maintain, protect, enforce or defend its right or title to any such material.

This clause is much more specific, protecting Disney against, say, the possibility that its CEO might leave and take a blockbuster script to another production company. The last sentence also exemplifies the well-known propensity of lawyers to use five words where one might have done the job.

(d) Executive recognizes that the services to be rendered by him hereunder are of a character giving them peculiar value, the loss of which cannot be adequately compensated for in damages, and in the event of a breach of this Agreement by Executive, Company shall be entitled to equitable relief by way of injunction or by any other legal or equitable remedies.

Hmmm. The shark shows its teeth. The company could apply for an injunction any time it wants—but spelling it out in the contract certainly sends a warning message.

When the Restriction Is the Reason for the Contract

Nowadays, an executive may be surprised when an employer—who has adamantly resisted the idea of a written employment agreement—introduces the idea. Some employers want a contract in order to ensure the tenure of a talented person. Often, a company's impulse toward contractual bonding stems from a desire for protection against competition and a need to maintain the sanctity of confidential information. The two are linked, of course; the thought of key managers going over to the enemy, taking with them an arsenal of secret information, makes CEOs lose sleep.

From the employer's point of view, the ideal situation is one in which you are bound by a restrictive agreement that focuses only on competition and confidentiality and does not bind the company to anything regarding compensation or severance. From the employee's point of view, the best of all possible worlds exists when there is a written contract ensuring pay, bonuses, options, benefits, perks, severance, GPs, and all the other goodies, with no restriction on the freedom of the employee.

The real-world contract will be somewhere between these poles.

If Your Present Employer Wants You to Sign a Noncompete

You've never had a formal contract. Now the company presents you with a restrictive agreement. Use it as an opportunity to win a broader contract.

Ask "Why"

What is the reason for making this request now? Is your job in jeopardy? Who else is being asked to sign a noncompete?

If the employer says it is just a precaution, a provision that all key people are being asked to sign, you acknowledge that they have a legitimate concern. You know important things; you would be a formidable competitor, should such an unlikely eventuality come to pass.

Exploit the Opening

But that observation doesn't mean you automatically sign. Instead, you say, "Now that the subject comes up, I can see that a written agreement is good for the company and for me as well. So let's do it right, and sign an agreement that covers all the important aspects of my job situation here. Then we can just store it away and forget about it."

And you bargain for a full-fledged contract, using some of the techniques we discuss elsewhere in this book.

When a New Employer Asks You to Agree to a Restrictive Agreement

Did you have a noncompete/nondisclosure agreement in your previous job? Are such clauses common in your industry? If so, you don't have much of a case for opposing the idea. But you can, as we discuss in a moment, work toward limiting the scope of the agreement.

If such provisions are not commonplace, your first response might be puzzlement. Why should you have to sign a piece of paper limiting your freedom after you leave the company? "I look forward to being with your firm for many years. If I were to leave for some reason, I would conduct myself ethically and honorably. Surely you don't have any reason to think otherwise?"

Gauge the employer's depth of commitment. Maybe it's more or less pro forma to ask the employee to sign the clause. If that's the case, your starting position can be, "Let's take that provision out altogether."

But if the employer insists, then the representative will tell you that the company is not casting aspersions; it is merely protecting itself. "We do this with everyone who comes in at your level."

Ask the company to explain what it wants protection from: "Revealing confidential information is one thing. If I tell you I won't disclose a secret, I won't disclose it. But as for preventing me from going to work for someone else in the industry, or starting my own business, or consulting . . . well, you're stripping me of my ability to make a living."

The usual comeback is that you will be receiving a generous amount of severance pay. However, as you've seen from the foregoing chapters, it's more complicated than that. For example, a substantial portion of your compensation may be deferred in one way or another. "I understand the idea of 'golden handcuffs,' and I have no quarrel with that. The purpose is to keep good people around; I'm pleased that you see me as an important part of the future. But let's say things change, and you decide to let me go, without me having done anything to violate our agreement. At least in that case, I should receive the severance in a lump sum, and my options should vest. After all, that is money I've already earned. And, in a real sense, I've earned the severance part of the package as well . . . ."

Negotiate for lump-sum severance payment or accelerated severance payment. Front-load as much of the severance as you can.

Obtain Trade-Offs

The firm may insist on a tough noncompete arrangement because of policy or because it thinks you would be very valuable to a competitor.

Use this tacit acknowledgment of your value as a bargaining lever. Negotiate hard for elimination or modification of the noncompete clause. If your adversary refuses to budge, then try to get concessions elsewhere: "These restrictions lock me in. They are designed to keep me from considering a better offer from the people who are most likely to make such an offer. Whether they would work or not is another matter. Have you ever run into situations where they just made people mad?

"Anyway, I have no intention of leaving here if things work out the way I think they will. But surely it's asking a lot to expect me to cut myself off from other chances in my field of expertise. If you insist on that, then I must insist on a higher base salary to make up for what I'm giving away here . . . ."

Pulling—or Blunting—the Teeth of the Restrictive Clause

Front-loading the severance package is one way to mitigate the effect of noncompete and nondisclosure provisions.

When you've done all you can on that front, work to reduce the bite of the language. If the language is overly general, work toward specificity. Say, for example, the provision reads:

> Executive agrees that during the term of this Agreement and there-
> after, Executive shall not disclose any Confidential Information, di-
> rectly or indirectly, to any person other than the Company . . . .

You can start refining this language by asking what it means: "Can you give me an example of Confidential Information? If I tell a competitor all the details of an upcoming price promotion, that's confidential. But suppose I'm at a convention and I mention the name of a distributor while I'm talking to a guy from Polaris Products. Would that be a violation? And what does 'indirectly' mean . . . ?"

Sometimes, the way to make the restrictive language more employee-friendly is to eliminate categories or sections of the clause. Take this one, for example:

> Executive shall not become involved, directly or indirectly, in any
> competitive business as an officer, director, employee, consultant,
> adviser, agent, representative, shareholder, partner or associate . . . .

This sentence combines the general and the specific. The general is embodied by that familiar usage, "involved, directly or indirectly." Try not to let language like that stand: "In these days of mergers and acquisitions and interlocking businesses, you can become 'indirectly involved' in something without knowing it. So the only point of that language would be as a kind of all-purpose ban. And what does 'involved' mean? Just talking to somebody from another business could be construed as being 'involved.' I know you would not want to do business that way. So we can eliminate that, can't we?"

Then work on the things that the company would like to include as involvement: "Buying a few shares of stock—surely that's not the same as competing. And when do you become an 'adviser?' I have friends throughout this industry. Some of them used to be my colleagues. I meet them socially, I run across them professionally, just like you do. What do you say we make this clause mean what it's supposed to mean: actually taking a full-time job with a company that is competing directly with us. Not with an affiliate, or the parent company; with the specific organization in this business. After all, that's what direct competition means."

Keep your options open—particularly the option to do consulting work.

Consultation and Noncompete

When Mark W. Perry resigned from Silicon Graphics (office equipment and services) in 1993 (where he had been Executive Vice President and Vice Chairman of the Board), he signed a consulting contract that has him doing substantially what he did before, but for just five days a month.

The arrangement pegged Perry's compensation at $13,000 per month, along with office space and secretarial help, reimbursement of expenses, and medical and life insurance. Perry also receives $20,000 per year, plus $1,000 for each board meeting he attends.

The pact contained noncompete, nonsolicit, and confidentiality provisions. This evidently did not provide a conflict when Perry became president of ViewStar, an applications software firm.

You're Fired—Now Please Sign This Contract

You've been laid off. Nothing personal about it, of course; it's just that the company is continuing to cut back. When the bottom line was skinny, the cry was, "Let's cut the fat!" The bottom line grew robust; now the motto is, "Let's keep squeezing to keep it that way."

You wish you'd had a contract that provided you with an ample severance deal. But you didn't. Now you're being let go along with a bunch of other people. Your boss says, "I wish we could do better for you, but we have to make an across-the-board arrangement that's equal and fair for everybody."

So you're going to wind up with not much in the way of severance pay.

But wait. Here you are, on your way out the door—and here is the company, waving a piece of paper at you. It's an agreement that binds you to certain things and gives you something in return.

In other words, a contract. Not an employment contract; more of an ex-employment contract.

Why now? You've been sacked; why are the sacking members of the firm asking you to sign a pact? Simple; they want to see you walk out the door empty-handed. They don't want to see you take employees, customers, or secrets with you. They can't expunge from your mind the knowledge you have acquired; but they'd like to make sure you don't use it against them.

Laid-off managers and professionals have the potential to hurt their former employers. They might lure away business, disclose confidential information to competitors, persuade other employees (those the company would prefer to *keep*) to leave the firm and join a new company or set up a new venture.

There are other ways in which the departing individual can do harm: by "stealing" customers, by giving valuable information to competitors, by doing consulting work for the competitors, or by joining one of them as an employee.

In today's world of ferocious worldwide competition, the loss of key people can hurt badly. Companies are building elaborate antidefection defenses. Their motive is self-preservation. One expert observes, "It can be terrible to lose one executive. But when several leave, a company can be devastated."

Companies can protect themselves in various ways. With respect to defections of key people (instigated by laid-off executives), employers use two general approaches. One is to lock in the key personnel through the use of golden handcuffs. The other is to deter the would-be seducer. How can the company control what a departing—and, possibly, not too friendly—employee will do? The answer is to get that departing employee to sign an agreement forbidding him or her to lure other employees away.

Sweetening the Severance

Any contract has elements of quid pro quo. How will the company make it worth your while to enter into such an agreement?

By paying you, of course. Maybe by offering extended benefits such as health coverage; but usually by beefing up your severance deal.

The following is the text of a deal offered to a laid-off manager in a large bank. Take a look at it; one day, you may receive such an offer and confront the choice that it proposes: trading a limitation on your freedom of operation for more money now. We're going to make some suggestions about how to deal with it. First, it's a good idea to become familiar with this actual example. We have inserted some observations along the way.

Dear _____

    As you have been advised, due to a reorganization and consolidation, your employment with _____ will be terminated [date].

    This letter sets forth our agreement concerning the change in your employment status and the additional benefits you will receive if you **agree to give a general release of all claims you may have.**

Here, and subsequently, emphasis has been added by the author.

    Apart from any retirement and insurance benefits to which you may be entitled, this agreement will govern your rights and obligations regarding [the company], and its parent, subsidiaries and affiliated corporations, and their respective successors, assigns, representatives, agents, shareholders, officers, directors, attorneys and employees, all of whom are collectively referred to below as the "Bank."

In case the bank is taken over by another company, the signer is still bound by the provisions of the agreement, which casts a broad net to include attorneys and shareholders.

    It has been _____'s practice to pay bridging pay determined by length of service to officers whose positions have been eliminated. Bridging pay provides for continuation of salary and most benefits until the end of the bridging period or until the officer begins employment elsewhere, whichever comes first.

"Bridging" (rather than severance) pay keeps the ex-employee on the string, offering no lump-sum option.

It has also been _____'s practice to **convert the bridging pay to a guaranteed severance payment (that is, the payment will continue to be made for the full bridging period *even if* the officer locates another position, or the payment can be taken in a lump sum) on condition that the officer execute a release.** In connection with the elimination of positions that will occur in [date], _____ will continue this practice and will offer to all officers who execute releases an additional benefit equaling one-third of what the officer would be entitled to as total bridging pay, as part of the guaranteed severance payment. The guaranteed payment may be received in a lump sum or over time, at the officer's election.

> *As we will see, there may be good reason to decline this agreement. But if the employee does agree, then it probably makes sense to take the severance in a lump sum.*
>
> *You can do what you want with the money; you, not the company, enjoys the float. And, most important, if there is a dispute, you are free from the threat of discontinued payment. They have to try to get the money back from you, which is, of course, an entirely different matter.*

In your case . . . you are entitled to six months' bridging pay and benefits exclusive of the Savings and Investment Plan (SIP) and Long Term Disability (LTD), or until [date]. This bridging pay will cease should you become employed prior to that date. In return for your accepting the terms and conditions below and releasing the Bank from all claims, you will be entitled to eight months' guaranteed severance until [date], together with continuation of benefits except SIP and LTD. You may elect to receive the severance benefit of $ _____ or eight months' salary in a lump sum, in which case your employment and benefits will cease as of the date you are paid.

> *In this case, the quid pro quo is two months' salary, guaranteed.*

In exchange for providing you with the above-referenced separation payment and benefits continuation, if applicable, **you agree to waive all claims against the Bank, and you hereby release and discharge the Bank from liability for any claims or damages that you may have against it as of the date of this** agreement, whether known or unknown to you, including but not limited to any claims arising under federal, state or local law or ordinance, tort, express or implied employment contract, public policy, or any other obligation, including any claims arising under title VII of the Civil Rights Act of 1964 and 1991, the Civil Rights Act of 1866, and the Age Discrimination in Employment Act, the Americans With Disabilities Act, the Worker Adjustment and Retraining Notification Act, the Employee Retirement Income Security Act, [here the document specifies several state laws] and all claims for worker's compensation, wages, damages, monetary or equitable relief, vacation, other employee fringe benefits or attorneys' fees. You understand that any payment or benefits provided to you under the terms of the agreement do not constitute admission by the Bank that it has violated any such law or legal obligation.

When you sign this, you seem to be signing away every right won by American workers since the Civil War. In addition, you are giving up any rights you may have under a contract, whether that contract exists as a specific document or is implied by court decisions. (See discussion of the Stealth Contract, in Chapter 6.)

You have agreed that you will not disclose or cause to be disclosed in any way, any information or documents relating to the operations of the Bank, the business or accounts of its customers, the terms of this agreement **or the fact that such agreement exists,** except for the purpose of enforcing it. You have also agreed that you will cooperate fully with the Bank in connection with any existing or future litigation against the Bank, whether administrative, civil, or criminal in nature, in which and to the extent the Bank deems your cooperation necessary. You will be remunerated for necessary, reasonable and documented out-of-pocket expenses in connection with such assistance.

Your lips are sealed. Let's say you're talking with another bank about a job. The interviewer asks a fairly innocent question about how you worked with customers in your previous job. According to this agreement, you must not only play mum but also play dumb. You can't answer the question, and you are not even permitted (by the letter of the pact) to say, "Sorry; I've signed an agreement not to talk about that aspect of my work . . . ."

Actually, that's just as well. Consider the effect on somebody who is thinking of hiring you if you were to deflect questions by saying you'd signed a restrictive nondisclosure agreement. The prospective employer wonders (with justification) if you are so tied up by your agreement that your effectiveness will be compromised. After all, they want to buy your experience along with your ability.

You agree that for a period of two years following the termination of your employment with [the company], you will not call upon, solicit or otherwise contact any of the following: (1) any customer of the Bank existing at the time of your termination of employment or existing during the period of six months prior thereto; (2) any person or business entity called upon, solicited or otherwise contacted by you during the one-year period prior to termination of your employment with the Bank; or (3) any person or business entity whom any **other** employee of the Bank has called upon, solicited or otherwise contacted during the three-month period prior to the termination of your employment with the Bank. You and the Bank agree that this agreement does not limit or abrogate your rights to be employed in, acquire an interest in or be otherwise connected with any person or business entity which is engaged in the same or similar business as the Bank or is in competition with the Bank.

Consider the sweeping nature of these restrictions. You're asked to refrain from contacting persons or businesses that did NOT become customers of the bank. Moreover, you're required to stay away from all those who have been contacted by anyone else in the company. If you know the names of all those who have been approached—or even spoken to—by all the people in the bank, you are indeed a prodigy—the equal of The Amazing Kreskin—and the bank ought to retain you at any cost.

All reasonable people know that such all-encompassing provisions are difficult, if not impossible, to observe. The idea, of course, is to have you on record, so that you can be taken to court for noncompliance.

You agree that for a period of two years following the termination of your employment you shall not, directly or indirectly, in any manner or capacity, induce any persons who at the time of the termination of your employment are employees of [the company] to discontinue his or her employment with the Bank or to become employed or otherwise affiliated with any business or entity by or for whom you are employed.

Construed broadly, this language might bar you from having a casual conversation with a former colleague and making a disparaging comment about the employer.

You will have up to forty-five (45) days from the date you receive this letter within which to consider its terms and the information contained in the attachment to this letter. During this period, you should consult with an attorney and other professional persons unrelated to the Bank, regarding the terms of this agreement.

The above paragraph is cover for the company, somewhat like the Miranda warning ("Read him his rights!") that watchers of TV cop shows are familiar with.

Your signature below indicates that you have carefully read this agreement and that you are entering into this agreement freely, knowingly, voluntarily and with a full understanding of its terms. Further, the terms of this agreement shall not become effective or enforceable until seven (7) days following the date of its execution, during which time you may revoke the agreement by notifying the undersigned in writing.

This letter sets forth the entire agreement between you and the Bank. The agreement may not be changed or altered, except by a writing signed by the Bank and you.

This agreement shall be interpreted for all purposes consistent with the laws of [relevant states]. If any clause of this agreement should ever be determined unenforceable, it is agreed that this will not affect the enforceability of any other clause or the remainder of this agreement.

Your signature below signifies that you have agreed to each and every provision in this letter.

Often, if one part of a contract is nullified, the whole contract is voided. Here, the company tries to forestall that possibility—a very real possibility because of the far-reaching nature of some of the provisions.

An Overly Broad Noncompete

In 1992, Univision wanted to keep its ex-president, Joaquin Blaya, from joining the rival Telemundo Group as president and CEO. *Television Digest* (August 3, 1992) reported that a New York State Supreme Court judge ruled that the noncompete clause in Blaya's agreement with Univision was too broad. It barred Blaya (and his colleague, José Cancela) from the entire Spanish-language TV business in the United States.

Calm, Cool Consideration

If you've been fired, you feel vulnerable. A company offer of more money can look tempting. But the price you pay can be too high.

You want to be free to find the best job you can find, or make the best connection you can make. That probably means talking to customers or ex-customers, employees or ex-employees—whoever may know or remember you. In fact, it would be surprising if your job search did *not* entail such conversations.

If the company that has just terminated you suggests that you sign a stringent noncompete agreement in return for a sweetened severance deal, ask yourself the following questions:

- Will this agreement keep me from pursuing *any* job possibilities?
- Assuming I agree, how much harder will it be for me to land a job?
- Am I tempted to sign and then just ignore some of the restrictions?

- Can I deal with a lawsuit for violation of contract?
- If a potential employer learns that I am bound by a noncompete, will that employer still hire me?
- Six months down the road, will I feel it was worth it to swap my freedom of action for some extra bucks?

No matter how tempting the offer, objective consideration of questions like these may push you in the direction of keeping all your options open. If you already have a good new possibility in mind—and if it does not involve the noncompete provision—then you may well want to sign, because you're giving up little or nothing.

Failing that happy prospect, be *very* careful about accepting limitations on your freedom.

Refine and Define

It's getting more and more difficult to avoid some form of limitation on competition and disclosure of information. The company enforces these provisions through the money not yet paid to you (either deferred compensation or severance). Get as much of that money as you can, as soon as you can.

Refine and define the provisions that describe the purported offenses that would put you in violation of the contract. They should be clear-cut, not vague or subject to interpretation. And they should be major: taking a job with a competitor, *not* doing a brief consulting job with a firm on the periphery of the industry; handing another company the secret formula for the fabulous soft drink, *not* inadvertently telling somebody the date of a forthcoming retirement party.

14

Perks and Special Provisions

S ome contracts cover a multitude of subjects. Other contracts stick to the big-ticket essentials: compensation, termination, golden parachutes.

Retirement provisions used to take a more central place in employment negotiations than they do now. Most corporations have broad-scale retirement plans in place. Key executives can, and do, bargain for favorable deals after retirement. But, as we have seen, these tend to involve extension and culmination of the compensation/incentive plans—bonuses and stock. The retirement arrangements grow naturally out of the other provisions of the agreement.

In particular cases, a company may provide specially crafted retirement deals, which are seen as benefiting the firm as well as the employee.

Lubricating the Glide into Retirement

In 1995, the Williams Companies worked out a deal with 60-year-old Chairman Joseph H. Williams. Williams relinquished his post to President Keith E. Bailey, 51. The company gave Williams $2 million as a "retirement differential"—compensation for his giving up salary and benefits through early retirement.

The firm described the arrangement as a "seamless" succession.

Most perks, if they are not included in the basic employment agreement, are described in separate documents—typically, letters and memos. As we have pointed out elsewhere, if you make sure such side documents are written accurately and completely, they can take on contractual force.

Your negotiating tactics will be the same whether you wrap perks and special provisions into one big document or keep them separate. But there are issues to be considered in deciding whether you want certain things included in the agreement at all.

Should Perks Be Written into the Contract?

Most senior management jobs carry status perks that enable the executive to live and work in a more comfortable style than subordinates—first-class air-travel, company cars, club memberships, chauffeured limos, yachts, overseas trips, and so on.

Although the practice is fading, we still see perks like these written into some contracts:

> *Company Automobile:* The Executive shall be provided with a company automobile under arrangements at least equivalent to those currently in effect with respect to other Company Senior Executives.

> *Country Club Membership:* The Company will reimburse the Executive for [his or her] initial membership fee, monthly dues, and greens fees (during the Period of Employment) for one country club membership to be approved by the Company. Upon conclusion of the Period of Employment, the Executive's right to such membership shall terminate with all rights thereunder reverting to the Company; if requested to do so, the Executive shall execute such assignments as necessary to accomplish this result.

Some employers suggest such provisions as a negotiating ploy. The manager, pleased by the unrequested proffer of these perks, may relax her or his pursuit of some more important aim.

Occasionally, managers will insist on exotic perks. An officer of one company (not GM) had the following in his contract:

> [The company will] Provide you with a chauffeur-driven Cadillac automobile or equivalent . . . .

In negotiating an employment agreement, you should concentrate on the important things. If marginal items find their way into the contract as a matter of course, fine. But to push hard for perks like cars and memberships is to divert energy that would be better used in another channel. Joining a country club may be important, and the company should pay for it. That can be worked out separately, as can the issues of what class you fly in (if that is indeed important to you) or whether you have to drive your own car.

Adversaries in a tough negotiation sometimes flare up at each other over the most trivial items, not because they think the items are important, but because they are suddenly venting the bottled-up tension fueled by the more momentous aspects of the session. Why risk flare-ups, resentment, or ridicule by padding out the document with needless provisions?

Here's an example of a needless provision in an actual job contract:

> *Vacations:* During each year of the term of this Agreement, Executive may take vacations at the standard number of days set by the Company's policy, or such longer period as the Board may authorize, during which time Executive's compensation shall be paid in full and he shall continue to participate in all other rights and benefits.

Here's another example of superfluity:

> *Expenses:* The Company will reimburse the Executive for all reasonable and necessary expenses incurred by him for or on behalf of or for the benefit of the Company, in the performance of his duties . . . .

Why write petty cash into a contract?

Once upon a time, some companies offered executives heaping bowls of perks as nontaxable compensation. The IRS caught on to this play. An employment agreement that contains big helpings of perks—particularly trivial or ego-stroking perks—can be a magnet for tax review. And it can draw the piercing scrutiny of stockholders.

That's not to say perks are unimportant. However, some executives demand all the perks in sight—and they do it for the wrong reason. In 1923, someone asked the great mountain climber George Leigh Mallory why he wanted to scale Mount Everest, which had never been climbed at that time. Mallory replied, "Because it is there." (The following year, Mallory died trying to climb Everest.) Some executives demand perks "because they are there"—and because someone else has them—rather than because they themselves really want them.

Think of the perks you really want. If a stretch limo doesn't appeal to you, don't fight for it just because somebody else has it. Instead, decide what perks you can use—those that will even be good for you. Some companies set up a cafeteria menu of perks. The executive can choose from the menu up to a designated dollar total: health club, $2,000; greens fees, $6,000; Lexus lease, $12,000; and so on. If your company doesn't have an official perks menu, try to select your preferred perks on an unofficial basis: "As for the country club dues, I don't play golf. But I do try to keep in shape. Let's substitute a tennis club, which costs less. As for a place to entertain clients and prospects, since everybody else is taking them to the country clubs, I'd like a membership in a good eating club . . . ."

Security and Substance Perks

The New York Times, on August 20, 1995, reported on a survey of 400 large companies, conducted by Hewitt Associates in Lincolnshire, Illinois. The survey showed that a number of once-popular executive perks are in decline: club memberships, company cars, first-class travel and airline VIP clubs, and chauffeur service, among others.

Other perks have become more popular: a home security system, and personal liability insurance.

Financial Counseling

Financial counseling has become quite popular. Here is a fairly typical excerpt from a contract:

> FINANCIAL AND TAX ADVICE
> During (i) the Period of Employment, (ii) the 12-month period following the termination of the Period of Employment as a result of Death or Disability, and (iii) the three-year period following the voluntary termination by Employee with Good Reason or the involuntary termination by Employer without Cause . . . Employer shall provide Employee (or, if Employee shall have died, his estate) at Employer's expense, third-party professional financial and tax advisory services, primarily oriented to planning in light of Employee's entitlement to compensation and employee benefits and appropriate in light of the financial circumstances of Employee (or his estate).

Being Outplaced in Your Parachute

Officers of Wellpoint Health Networks, Inc., get a golden parachute that includes outplacement services to the tune of up to one month's salary. The company picks the outplacer.

The extension of financial advice beyond the period of employment is important. This is exactly the time when you (or your family) may find this a life-saving perk indeed.

You can make a good case for financial counseling as a benefit: "The company will get at least as much out of this perk as I will. What with the tax laws and the financial markets, handling money wisely can take up a lot of time and energy. I want to devote everything I've got to the company, not my own finances. With a financial consultant available, I can do just that . . . ."

Be sure to choose your own independent financial adviser. Some employers have been known to resent some financial advisers whose bills the companies pay, because the advisers give the employee advice a company doesn't like. That's the caliber of independence you want in your adviser.

Up-Front Bonuses; Housing and Relocation

Executives who take new jobs get up-front bonuses for a number of reasons. One is to "make them whole" for what they've lost in deferred compensation and pension rights. We have already covered that topic, with current examples, in our discussion of compensation.

A second reason is a straightforward premium to lure the employee to the new company. The contract may lump this in with salary:

> 1. Employer shall pay Employee a salary of Four Hundred Thousand ($400,000) Dollars per year during each year of this Agreement, one twenty-fourth of said sum being payable on the 15th and last day of each and every month. Such salary may be adjusted from time to time by Employer.

> 2. A one-time cash payment of Two Hundred Fifty Thousand ($250,000) shall be made October 1, 1996.

The up-front bonus may be a straight cash payment, an award of stock, a special option deal, a deferred cash payment, or some combination of these. In negotiating a one-shot bonus, you may want to defer some of it. However, you must insist that the bonus, whatever its form, be *fully vested:* You get the whole thing even if you walk away from the job.

A common reason for a one-time bonus is relocation cost. Here is some characteristic language:

> Employer shall reimburse the Executive for reasonable expenses incurred in relocation, including, but not confined to: all costs of the physical move; en route travel expenses, including hotel and meals; temporary living expenses for Executive and family, including meals, for up to fifteen (15) weeks; three (3) househunting

trips for Executive and family; weekly commuting expenses until Executive has moved; closing costs and commissions involved in selling Executive's former residence and purchasing a residence in the area of Company headquarters; an additional amount to cover federal, state, and local taxes incurred as a result of the relocation; and any other reasonable relocation expenses.

Some companies provide low-interest or interest-free loans so that relocating managers can buy homes. Such loans can be used as golden handcuffs. For example, a drug company offers loans to senior executives. The company charges interest and holds a lien on the loan. However, each year a percentage of the loan is forgiven, unless the employee is fired for cause or quits.

The cost-of-living differential can be a problem in relocation. Here is an example of a provision designed to alleviate the problem:

. . . Company will review changes in the cost-of-living index for the _____ area, during the year ending June 30, 1996, as measured by the U.S. Bureau of Labor Statistics (or a reasonably comparable index), and will augment Executive's annual salary retroactive to July 1, 1996, by an amount at least equal to the increase in such cost-of-living index. The Company will undertake a similar review in July 1997, 1998, and 1999, with respect to a possible further increase in Annual Salary for each of those years.

Payment of Legal Fees

If there is any possibility that an executive may be involved in litigation connected with the job, it may be well to put a provision into the contract to ensure that the company will pay legal fees. A contractual provision covering legal fees for criminal or civil actions arising out of the executive's duties is common sense from the company's point of view. It avoids unseemly squabbling about who pays the lawyers if and when the occasion arises.

In negotiating such a deal, make sure you get clear language that says the company picks up the tab for legal expenses.

In that connection, it's worth noting that legal services is increasing in popularity as a perk. *The Wall Street Journal* (March 14, 1995) reported that "more employers are offering legal-service plans to employees, and the number of subscribers has nearly doubled since 1983, to 7.6 million, says the National Resource Center for Consumers of Legal Services, a clearing house for information on legal plans based in Gloucester, Va."

The *Journal* story emphasizes that, in these plans, "employees often end up paying the premiums themselves, a fact that isn't always effectively communicated."

On Trial for "Abuse of Perks"

James F. Smith, CEO of Orange & Rockland Utilities, Inc., of Rockland County, New York, was fired from his job, kicked off the board of directors, and (at age 59) indicted on more than twenty counts of grand larceny and falsifying business records. Smith was accused of diverting company funds to his personal use over fourteen years. For example, one alleged abuse had Smith charging the utility for meals that he bought for his friends.

Smith pleaded not guilty, asserting that he was only enjoying his "proper perquisites." He said, "If I'm guilty, [then] this is also true of a lot of businesspeople in America."

Smith chose trial before a judge, without a jury. (One observer said the people in the area so hated the utility that Smith would not have a chance before a jury.) Smith's lawyer, Jay Fischer, had sought expert witnesses on executive perks. He said that Smith's alleged crimes were really misjudgments as to what actually constituted legitimate perks.

The judge agreed, acquitting Smith on all counts and criticizing the prosecutor for bringing the charges. Smith's troubles didn't end there. The company was suing him for around $5 million.

There are pros and cons to employee legal plans. The point for those negotiating contracts is that job-connected legal expenses should be borne by the company.

Lifestyle and Lifesaving Perks: Child Care

Some people work out various kinds of lifestyle perks for themselves, for example, the assurance of time off during the skiing, hunting, or fishing season.

Others have more serious reasons to negotiate variations in schedule. You may want to work out a deal for flextime to help take care of a parent or other family member. Or, you may want to work at home for a considerable part of the time. Or, you might wish the company to pay for elder-care. An employer may say, "Don't worry about that. We'll work it out." It's best not to count on that vague promise. Insert an unambiguous provision in the agreement.

The scarcity of child care is not only a social problem, but a growing business problem. A provision covering child care can be a very important section of an agreement. You should try to make it flexible enough to fit your needs.

It may be that the best way to take care of personal responsibilities is to work at home. Again, don't leave that point vague and unresolved. The time will come when you need—urgently—to be at home during the workday, but the company "just can't spare you." Avoid an agonizing situation by inserting this provision:

> Executive may, at [his or her] sole discretion, work from [his or her] residence or a location of [his or her] choice. The Company will reimburse Executive for home office use, including, but not confined to, an appropriate computer/modem installation . . . .

Extras That Really Matter

Keep your contract clear of extraneous issues, ego-perks, and unwanted benefits. Decide on the perks that really mean something to you, will enhance your enjoyment of life, and will make you more effective on the job.

Then obtain clear contractual agreement on these issues.

You Win When You Get It in Writing

People want challenging and satisfying jobs, but they don't want to sell their soul to the employer. They want to be free to give the job their best, thereby benefiting employee and employer alike.

The employment contract, as it comes into more general use, is serving as a flexible instrument that can be made to apply to a wide variety of employer needs and employee needs.

Think about your contract—the one you want, the one you may already have. It can have enormous value if you run into problems. It has even greater value as the guideline along which your career develops, and as a blueprint for a productive and satisfying relationship between you and your employer.

Management ownership, spurred by stock plans, will continue. How much managers get paid (in cash, stock grants, or options) will be increasingly determined by yardsticks designed to measure overall company performance.

More and more managers will be negotiating contracts. The key provisions of these contracts will involve compensation, termination, severance, noncompete provisions, and **Perks and Parachutes.**

Plan well. Negotiate hard. When you have won a good employment agreement, you can concentrate on doing your all-out best for yourself and for the company.

Appendix 1

The Agee–Morrison Knudsen Contract

The eyebrows of the corporate world went up in 1988 when Morrison Knudsen announced the name of its new chairman and CEO: William J. Agee. The deal was spearheaded by Peter Ueberroth, a Knudsen board member and chairman of the Executive Compensation and Nominating Committee. William Agee had become a joint star of the business pages and the tabloids while he was at the helm of Bendix. He had led Bendix into a kind of "Charge of the Light Brigade" campaign to take over Martin Marietta. Martin Marietta turned on its would-be devourer ferociously. With Martin Marietta then threatening to take over Bendix, Bendix was forced into a shotgun marriage with Allied Corporation (now AlliedSignal Inc.).

Meanwhile, the lurid stories about Agee's romantic involvement with a senior Bendix executive, the up-and-coming Mary Cunningham, gave additional spice to the story. As *The Wall Street Journal* (March 31, 1995) pointed out, Agee and Cunningham were linked romantically "even though they were both married to other people. (They denied the rumors. They subsequently married, saying they had become involved much later.)"

Morrison Knudsen seemed an odd place for William Agee to surface in 1988. *Time* (April 3, 1995) commented that, in its glory days, "the Morrison Knudsen company helped create the very fabric of America by building such megastructures as the Hoover Dam, the San Francisco–Oakland Bay Bridge and the Trans-Alaska pipeline." Evidently, the old-line construction firm was looking for a leader of star quality to guide it to greater glory in the 21st century.

Instead, the company deteriorated into a shambles. In 1995, Morrison Knudsen, reporting titanic losses, forced its CEO out. There was wailing and gnashing of teeth. Agee was criticized for many things. One of the most prominent raps against him was that he abandoned the company's Boise, Idaho, headquarters and ran things by remote control from a "linkside villa" in California. *Forbes* columnist Neil Weinberg (February 27, 1995) wrote scathingly about "Agee's ego-driven moves into faddish infrastructure and railcar projects—plus accounting gimmickry like capitalizing costs that more prudent managers would expense. . . . Another danger sign: the high life led by Agee and wife Mary Cunningham Agee far from MK headquarters at their expensive Pebble Beach, Calif., home."

In the light of all this, it may be of particular interest to look over the employment contract that Morrison Knudsen granted to William Agee in 1991. Note particularly the stipulation that Agee "shall have the right to perform his duties out of any of his personal residences . . . ."

WILLIAM J. AGEE
EMPLOYMENT AGREEMENT

This agreement is made this 2nd day of April, 1991, between MORRISON KNUDSEN CORPORATION, a Delaware corporation ("MKC" or the "company") and WILLIAM J. AGEE ("Executive")

A. Executive is employed as Chairman of MKC, has rendered valuable services to MKC and has acquired an extensive background in and knowledge of MKC's business.

B. MKC desires to continue the services of Executive, and Executive desires to continue to serve MKC as Chairman.

In consideration of the foregoing recitals and the agreements set forth herein, MKC and Executive agree as follows:

1. TERM

MKC shall employ Executive and Executive accepts such employment for a term beginning on the date of this Agreement and ending December 31, 1995, upon the terms and conditions set forth herein, unless earlier terminated in accordance with the provisions herein.

Notwithstanding the foregoing, if this Agreement shall not have been terminated in accordance with the provisions herein on or before December 31, 1995, the remaining term of the Agreement shall be extended such that at each and every moment of time thereafter, the remaining term shall be one year unless (a) the Agreement is terminated earlier in accordance with the provisions herein or (b) on or after January 1, 1995, the Board of Directors notifies Executive in writing of its determination to have the date of this Agreement expire one year from the date of such notification.

This, then, was a self-renewing agreement, with at least a year's worth of life left in it at all times—unless somebody pulled the plug.

2. DEFINITIONS

For purposes of this Agreement, the following terms shall have the meanings set forth in this paragraph 2:

a. "Base Compensation" shall mean an amount per annum equal to the sum of (i) the annual base salary rate in effect for Executive immediately preceding termination of employment (excluding any reduction in base salary made in breach of this Agreement), (ii) an amount equal to the product of (A) and (B), where (A) equals the cumulative bonus paid to Executive over the three most recently completed calendar years prior to termination (including any bonus amounts deferred by Executive under any MKC deferred compensation plan or arrangement) divided by the cumulative base salary paid to Executive over the same three-year period (including any base salary deferred by Executive under any MKC deferred compensation plan or arrangement), and where (B) equals the amount set forth in 2. a. (i) above, (iii) continued participation in all basic and supplemental life, accident, disability, and other Company-sponsored insurance benefits provided to Executive immediately preceding termination (or, if continued participation in one or more of these benefits is not possible, benefits substantially similar to those which Executive would have been entitled to if he had continued as an employee of the Company at the same compensation level in effect immediately prior to termination), and (iv) continuance of vesting and benefit accrual under any Company-sponsored basic and supplemental retirement programs in effect for Executive immediately prior to termination (or, if continued participation in such programs is not possible, benefits substantially similar to those which Executive would have been entitled to if he had continued as an employee of the Company at the same compensation level immediately prior to termination).

This definition of Base Compensation is a termination-oriented passage, designed to come into play when and if there are questions about what Mr. Agee gets as severance. Note that even a high-level operator like William Agee makes sure that these benefits are secured to him. Note too the language assuring that, if a program is changed or dropped, the employee will receive something equivalent. This useful language is worth some hard bargaining to get included in any agreement.

b. "Board" means the Board of Directors of the Company.

c. "Cause" shall mean (i) willful refusal by Executive to follow a lawful written demand of the Board, (ii) Executive's willful and continued failure to perform his duties under this Agreement (except due to Executive's incapacity due to physical or mental illness) after a written demand is delivered to Executive by the Board specifically identifying the manner in which the Board believes that Executive has failed to perform his duties, (iii) Executive's willful engagement in conduct materially injurious to the Company, or (iv) Executive's conviction for any felony involving moral turpitude. For purposes of clauses (i), (ii), and (iii) of this definition, no act, or failure to act on Executive's part shall be deemed "willful" unless done, or omitted to be done, by Executive not in good faith and without reasonable belief that Executive's act, or failure to act, was in the best interests of the Company.

The definition of "Cause" can be critical. If the agreement does not build limits around the employer's freedom to terminate the contract for cause, the employee is at a severe disadvantage. Here, "Cause" is modified by the shrewd deployment of words like "willful," "continued," and "materially." The employee is further protected when "willful" is spelled out. This employee is permitted to plead good faith.

d. "Constructive Termination" shall mean Executive's voluntary termination of employment within ninety (90) days following the occurrence of one or more of the following events, unless such event is approved in writing by Executive in advance of such event:

(i) A failure by the Company to abide by any part of this Agreement that is not remedied within ten (10) business days of notification by Executive of such failure, including any violation of Executive's rights as described in Section 3 of this Agreement unless such rights are replaced by alternative rights of approximately equal value;

(ii) A reduction in Executive's title or responsibilities below Chairman;

(iii) Relocation of Executive's primary place of business more than fifty (50) miles from its location as of the date of this Agreement.

In (i), the "alternative rights of equal value" are not further spelled out, providing potential grounds for legal skirmishing. Here too, we see the important safeguards as to title, duties, and location, designed (among other things) to keep the employer from driving the employee out through harassment.

e. "Disability" shall be deemed to have occurred if Executive makes application for disability benefits under any Company-sponsored long-term disability program covering Executive and qualifies for such benefits.

One important question running throughout any contract is "Who decides?" In this case, the employee evidently decides if he has suffered a "disability."

f. "Retirement" shall mean Executive's termination of service with the Company in accordance with the provisions of the Company's Retirement Plan in effect for Executive.

g. "Retirement Plan" shall mean the Morrison Knudsen Corporation Retirement Plan, as amended from time to time.

3. EXECUTIVE'S RIGHTS REGARDING BASE SALARY, BONUS AND OTHER BENEFITS WHILE EMPLOYED BY THE COMPANY

The minimum annual base salary payable to Executive upon commencement of this Agreement shall be $750,000. The Executive Compensation Committee of the Board of Directors (the "Compensation Committee") will review Executive's base salary at least annually to determine the amount of any increase. Upon any such increase in Executive's base salary, such increased rate shall thereafter constitute Executive's minimum annual base salary for all purposes of this Agreement, except that the Company may reduce Executive's annual base salary during any year by not more than 10% below the base salary in effect at the beginning of the year as part of any general salary reduction which applies to all officers of the Company.

In lieu of participation in the Company's Executive Incentive Plan or other Company-sponsored annual bonus program, Executive shall be eligible for a target annual cash bonus of 50% of the base salary earned during the fiscal year, with the actual bonus determined by the Compensation Committee based on an assessment of MKC's financial performance and Executive's strategic accomplishments during the fiscal year. In no way should the target bonus amount be construed as limiting the actual bonus amount that may be paid to Executive for his performance in any fiscal year.

> *This clause harks back to the days when the compensation of top executives was determined by the board of directors on such broad criteria as "strategic accomplishments." Nowadays, the bonus pay of senior executives is much more likely to be tied to measurable criteria, notably stock prices.*

Executive shall participate in the Morrison Knudsen Key Executive Long-Term Incentive Plan at the Sharing Percentage contained in the Participation Agreement dated April 2, 1991.

Executive also shall be able to participate in all perquisites and health and welfare benefits generally available to other executive officers of the Company. In addition, Executive shall be provided with supplemental benefits at no cost to Executive which result in the following levels of coverage, inclusive of any coverage provided by basic Company-sponsored benefits:

(a) Pre-Retirement life insurance equal to three times Executive's annual base salary;

(b) Post-Retirement life insurance equal to one times Executive's annual base salary as of the date of Executive's Retirement;

(c) A target Retirement benefit at age 65 equal to 45% of Executive's Final Average Compensation as defined in the Company's Retirement Plan. Such benefit will accrue at the rate of 2% per year for calendar years 1989 through 1993, 6% per year for calendar years 1994 through 1998, and 1% per year for calendar years 1999 through 2003.

(d) Disability coverage from all Company-sponsored and government sources equal to 60% of base salary plus target bonus, less applicable offsets under the terms of the program(s).

Executive also shall have the right to perform his duties out of any of his personal residences, provided that such right does not result in behavior or actions injurious to the Company.

Today's technology makes working at home increasingly feasible and attractive to executives. Provisions covering this point will find their way into many employment agreements.

4. EXECUTIVE'S RIGHTS UPON TERMINATION

In the event that Executive's employment at MKC is terminated for any reason other than (a) death, (b) Disability, (c) Cause, (d) voluntary resignation by Executive not constituting Constructive Termination, or (e) the expiration of the term of this Agreement, MKC will pay to Executive Base Compensation for a period of two years. In addition, MKC will fully vest all invested stock options and restricted stock awards previously granted by MKC to Executive and fully vest and immediately pay to Executive any accrued award earned by Executive under the Morrison Knudsen Key Executive Long-Term Incentive Plan or any other Company-sponsored long-term cash incentive plan in which Executive is a participant.

Base Compensation payments shall be made when payments would otherwise have been made to Executive if he were still employed by MKC, except in such cases where a different payment schedule is provided for in other Company-sponsored plans or programs.

In the event Executive's employment at MKC is terminated for death, Disability, Cause, voluntary resignation not constituting Constructive Termination, or upon expiration of the term of this Agreement, Executive shall not be entitled to any benefits under this Agreement. This statement, however, shall not preclude Executive from any payments or benefits available to Executive from participation in other Company-sponsored plans or programs.

5. DESIGNATION OF BENEFICIARIES

If Executive should die while receiving Base Compensation payments pursuant to Paragraph 4, the remaining Base Compensation payments which would have been paid to Executive if he had lived shall be paid as designated by Executive on the attached Beneficiary Designation Form. Such payments shall be made at the same time and in the same manner as if Executive was alive to receive the payments, except in such cases where a different payment schedule is provided, or in other Company-sponsored plans or programs.

The filing of a new Beneficiary Designation Form will cancel all designations previously filed. Any finalized divorce or marriage (other than a common-law marriage) of Executive subsequent to the date of filing of a beneficiary designation shall revoke such designation, unless:

(a) In the case of divorce, the previous spouse was not designated as beneficiary, and

(b) In the case of marriage, Executive's new spouse had previously been designated as beneficiary.

The spouse of a married Executive shall join in any designation of a beneficiary other than the spouse.

If Executive fails to designate a beneficiary as provided for above, or if the beneficiary designation is revoked by marriage, divorce or otherwise without execution of a new designation, then the Compensation Committee of the Board of Directors of the Company shall direct the distribution of any benefits under this Agreement to Executive's estate.

> *Agee's contract devotes far more space than most to questions revolving around the benefits going to his spouse in various circumstances, including divorce. It seems somewhat out of the ordinary for members of the Board to be assigned to direct distribution of benefits if the Executive fails to designate a spouse, or if the designation is "revoked by marriage, divorce," and so on. The fact that Agee's wife is the high-profile manager Mary Cunningham adds interest to our consideration of this clause.*

6. DUTIES OF EXECUTIVE

Executive is presently employed by MKC as its Chairman. Executive agrees to devote substantially all of his time and energy to the performance of the duties of that position so long as his employment in that position shall be continued by MKC. Notwithstanding the above, Executive shall be permitted to serve as a Director or Trustee of other organizations, provided such service does not prevent Executive from performing his duties under this Agreement.

> *Most signers of contracts should consider having the "duties" of the position spelled out more than this.*

7. MITIGATION AND OFFSET

Executive shall not be required to mitigate the amount of any payment provided for in this Agreement by seeking employment or otherwise, nor to offset the amount of any payment provided for in this Agreement by amounts earned as a result of Executive's employment or self-employment during the period he is entitled to such payment.

> *Many severance deals reduce or discontinue pay and benefits if the recipient gets other work (which is why it's better to get a lump sum). An arrangement like Agee's makes sure he gets paid, no matter what.*

8. TAX "GROSS-UP" PROVISION

If any payments due Executive under this Agreement result in Executive's liability for an excise tax ("parachute tax") under Section 49 of the Internal Revenue Code of 1986, as amended (the "Code"), the Company will pay to Executive, after deducting any Federal, state or local income tax imposed on the payment, an amount sufficient to fully satisfy the "parachute tax" liability. Such payment shall be made to Executive no later than 30 days prior to the due date of the "parachute tax."

9. SUCCESSORS

The rights and duties of a party hereunder shall not be assignable by that party; provided, however, that this Agreement shall be binding upon and inure to the benefit of any successor of MKC, and any such successor shall be deemed substituted for MKC under the terms of this Agreement. The term successor as used herein shall include any person, firm, corporation or other business entity which at any time, by merger, purchase or otherwise, acquires all or substantially all of the assets or business of MKC.

> *It's important to make sure that the contract continues in force after the company merges or is taken over.*

10. ENTIRE AGREEMENT

With respect to the matters specified herein, this Agreement contains the entire agreement between the parties and supersedes all prior oral and written agreements, understandings and commitments between the parties. This Agreement shall not affect the provisions of any other compensation, retirement or other benefit programs of MKC to which Executive is a party or of which he is a beneficiary. No amendments to this Agreement may be made except through a written document signed by both parties.

11. VALIDITY

In the event that any provision of this Agreement is held to be invalid, void or unenforceable, the same shall not affect, in any respect whatsoever, the validity of any other provision of the Agreement.

12. PARAGRAPHS AND OTHER HEADINGS

Paragraphs and other headings contained in this Agreement are for reference purposes only and shall not affect in any way the meaning or interpretation of this Agreement.

13. NOTICE

Any notice or demand required or permitted to be given under this Agreement shall be made in writing and shall be deemed effective upon the personal delivery thereof if delivered or, if mailed, 48 hours after having been deposited in the United States mail, postage prepaid, and addressed in the case of MKC to its then principal place of business, presently Morrison-Knudsen Plaza, Boise, Idaho 83707, and in the case of Executive to

Morrison Knudsen Corp
Morrison Knudsen Plaza
P.O. Box 73
Boise, ID 83729

Either party may change the address to which such notices are to be addressed by giving the other party notice in the manner herein set forth.

> *"The dog must have eaten it" or "They lost it in the mail" is not a valid excuse for not responding.*

14. ATTORNEYS' FEES

In any action at law or in equity to enforce any of the provisions or rights under this Agreement, the unsuccessful party to such litigation, as determined by the Court in a final judgment or decree, shall pay the successful party or parties all costs, expenses and reasonable attorneys' fees incurred therein by such party or parties (including without limitation such costs, expenses and fees on any appeals), and if such successful party or parties shall recover judgment in any such action or proceeding, such costs, expenses and attorneys' fees shall be included as part of such judgment.

Notwithstanding the foregoing provision, in no event shall the successful party or parties be entitled to recover any amount from the unsuccessful party for costs, expenses and attorneys' fees that exceed the unsuccessful party's costs, expenses and attorneys' fees in connection with the action or proceeding.

> *For most, this looks like a risky provision. It's tough enough to bat-*
> *tle in court against a big corporation, with lawyers on retainer.*
> *Things get a lot tougher if you lose—and then have to pay them*
> *for their costs (albeit the liability is limited by the second of the*
> *two paragraphs).*

15. WITHHOLDING TAXES

To the extent required by law, the Company shall withhold from any payments under this agreement any applicable federal, state or local taxes.

16. APPLICABLE LAW

To the full extent controllable by stipulation of the parties, this Agreement shall be interpreted under Idaho law.

IN WITNESS THEREOF, Morrison Knudsen Corporation has caused this Agreement to be executed by its duly authorized representatives and Executive has affixed his signature, as of the date first above written.

[The agreement is signed by William J. Agee and by Peter V. Ueberroth, Chairman, Executive Compensation and Nominating Committee.]

Appendix 2

The Eisner–Disney Contract

Let's start with Michael Eisner. Although his contract with Disney contains numbers that may be beyond the reach of most of us—at least for now—it contains the basic elements. We are thankful for having Mr. Eisner's contract available from public sources. The head of the company that rose to greatness on the shoulders of Mickey Mouse and Donald Duck serves here as our "laboratory animal."

EMPLOYMENT AGREEMENT
DATED AS OF JANUARY 10, 1989
BETWEEN
THE WALT DISNEY COMPANY
AND
MICHAEL D. EISNER

Michael D. Eisner (**"Executive"**) and The Walt Disney Company, a Delaware Corporation (**"Company"**) hereby agree as follows:

1. Term

The term of this Agreement shall commence as of January 10, 1989 and shall terminate on September 30, 1998.

2. Duties

Executive shall be employed by Company as its Chairman and Chief Executive Officer. Executive shall report directly and solely to the Company's Board of Directors (**"Board"**).

Executive shall devote his full time and best efforts to the Company. Company agrees to nominate Executive for election to the Board as a member of the management slate at each annual meeting of stockholders during his employment hereunder at which Executive's director class comes up for election. Executive agrees to serve on the Board if elected.

3. Salary

Executive shall receive an annual base salary of $750,000. The Board, in its discretion, may increase the base salary upon relevant circumstances.

4. Bonus

(a) Executive shall, as provided in, and subject to, paragraph (e) below, receive an incentive bonus for Company's fiscal years ending September 30, 1989 and September 30, 1990, in an amount equal to 2% of that portion of the net income of Company for each such fiscal year in excess of the amount determined by multiplying stockholders' equity for each such fiscal year by .09. For purposes of all calculations of stockholders' equity under this Agreement, stockholders' equity for any fiscal year shall be the average of the four quarterly stockholders' equity figures reported by the Company for that fiscal year.

(b) Executive shall, as provided in, and subject to, paragraph (e) below, receive an incentive bonus for each fiscal year of Company which shall end after September 30, 1990 and on or before the termination of this Agreement and for such additional periods as are provided in paragraph (e) below, in an amount equal to 2% of that portion of the net income of Company for each such fiscal year in excess of the amount determined by multiplying stockholders' equity for each such fiscal year by .11.

(c) In the event that there shall be a combination of the Company with another company or a capital restructuring of the Company, or any other occurrence similar to any of the foregoing, and as a result thereof the amount or value of the bonuses payable pursuant to either or both of the bonus formulas set forth in paragraphs (a) and (b) above would be, or could reasonably be expected to be, significantly affected thereby, appropriate(s) will, at the request of either party, be negotiated to establish a substitute formula or formulas, or if the parties cannot agree as to whether or not an occurrence which would give rise to the right of either party to request adjustment(s) pursuant to the foregoing has occurred, the parties shall submit such matter to arbitration by a qualified individual investment banker with at least ten years' experience in corporate finance with a major investment banking firm. Neither said firm or said individual shall have had dealings with either party during the preceding five years. Upon failure to agree upon the selection of the arbitrator, each party shall submit a panel of five qualified arbitrators, the other party may strike three from the other's list, and the arbitrator shall be selected by lot from the remaining four names. The arbitrator shall have the authority only to determine (i) whether the matter is arbitrable under the conditions of this subparagraph (c) and (ii) the substitute formula or formulas that will yield an equitable and comparable result in accordance with the foregoing.

(d) Each incentive bonus shall be payable (i) 30 days following the date Company's audited consolidated statement of income for the applicable fiscal year becomes available or (ii) on the January 2 following the end of that fiscal year, whichever is later (the **"Bonus Payment Date"**).

(e) Executive shall be entitled to receive the bonus provided for in paragraph (a) or paragraph (b) above, as the case may be, for each fiscal year during which he is employed hereunder and, in addition, for the next twenty-four months after termination of his employment, except that said post-termination bonus coverage (i) shall only extend for twelve months after termination if Executive takes employment (other than as an independent producer) with another major entertainment company within twelve months of termination and (ii) shall not apply if Executive has been discharged for good cause. The bonus formula set forth in paragraph (a) above shall be applicable to any part or all of any period prior to September 30, 1990 in respect of which a post-termination bonus is payable, and the formula set forth in paragraph (b) above shall be applicable to any part or all of any period after September 30, 1990 in respect of which a post-termination bonus is payable.

5. Bonus Payments

(a) Bonuses for the fiscal years ending September 30, 1989 and September 30, 1990 shall be payable in cash.

(b) Bonuses for fiscal years ending after September 30, 1990 shall be payable in cash or a combination of cash and Restricted Stock (as hereinafter defined) as follows: that portion of the bonus for each such fiscal year which does not exceed the Cash Limit (as hereinafter defined) shall be paid in cash. To the extent that the amount of the bonus calculated in accordance with Section 4(b) hereof shall exceed the Cash Limit, the remaining unpaid portion of such bonus shall (except as otherwise provided in Section 12(a) (ii) hereof) be payable in Restricted Stock. For purposes of the foregoing, the term **"Cash Limit"** shall mean, with respect to any fiscal year of Company, the amount of the bonus which would be paid to Executive pursuant to Section 4(b) hereof if the net income of Company for such year were equal to the product of stockholders' equity for such year multiplied by .175.

(c) For purposes of this Agreement the term **"Restricted Stock"** shall mean shares of Company common stock which are issued to Executive pursuant to Company's 1987 Stock Incentive Plan (the **"Plan"**) in accordance with, and subject to, the following terms, restrictions, and conditions:

(i) All shares of Restricted Stock shall be subject to forfeiture (i.e., all right, title, and interest of Executive in such shares shall cease and such shares shall be returned to Company with no compensation of any nature being paid therefore to Executive), if Executive's employment with Company is terminated for good cause (as defined in Section 10(a) (iii)) hereof prior to the earlier of (x) the expiration of the three-year period commencing on the Bonus Payment Date upon which such shares were required to be delivered to Executive pursuant to Section 4(d) hereof (it being understood that if such shares are for any reason delivered to Executive on a date other than the Bonus Payment Date, such Bonus Payment Date shall nevertheless constitute the date on which such three-year period shall commence) or (y) September 30, 1998 (the **"Restricted Period"**). Any shares of Restricted Stock issued to Executive after September 30, 1998 shall be deemed to have been issued subject to restrictions which shall have expired, and, accordingly, will be free of all restrictions hereunder.

(ii) During the Restricted Period, Executive will have voting rights and will receive dividends and other distributions with respect to shares of Restricted Stock issued to him but will not be permitted to sell, pledge, assign, convey, transfer, or otherwise alienate or hypothecate such shares.

(iii) All restrictions on the shares of Restricted Stock issued to Executive hereunder will immediately lapse in the event of the death of Executive or disability of Executive resulting in a termination of employment by Company pursuant to Section 10(a) (ii) hereof.

(iv) All restrictions on the stock will lapse immediately in the event Company enters into an agreement pursuant to which either the Company or all or substantially all of its assets are to be sold or combined with another entity (regardless of whether or not such sale or combination is subject to the satisfaction of conditions precedent or subsequent) and, as a consequence thereof, the market for public trading of Company common stock would be, or could reasonably be expected to be, eliminated or materially impaired.

(v) Executive shall enter into an escrow agreement providing that the certificate(s) representing Restricted Stock issued to him will remain in the physical custody of Company (or an escrow holder selected by Company) until all restrictions are removed or expire.

(vi) Each certificate representing Restricted Stock issued to Executive will bear a legend making appropriate reference to the terms, conditions, and restrictions imposed. Any attempt to dispose of Restricted Stock in contravention of such terms, conditions, and restrictions, irrespective of whether the certificate contains such a legend, shall be ineffective and any disposition purported to be effected thereby shall be void.

(vii) Any shares or other securities received by Executive as a stock dividend on, or as a result of stock splits, combinations, exchanges of shares, reorganizations, mergers, consolidations or otherwise with respect to shares of Restricted Stock shall have the same terms, conditions, and restrictions and bear the same legend as Restricted Stock.

(d) In determining the number of shares of Restricted Stock to be issued in respect of any bonus, the Restricted Stock will be valued on the basis of the average closing price of Company common stock during the period starting on the third business day and ending on the twelfth business day following the release for publication by Company of its annual summary statement of sales and earnings for the applicable fiscal year (as such release is defined by Rule 16-b-3 (e) (1) (ii) promulgated by the Securities and Exchange Commission pursuant to the Securities Exchange Act of 1934, as amended).

(e) Company shall in due course after the execution of this Agreement (and in no event later than the date Restricted Stock is first required to be issued to Executive hereunder) adopt rules pursuant to the Plan regarding restricted stock which shall reflect the foregoing provisions and such other provisions as are in the reasonable opinion of Company's counsel customary with respect to restricted stock. In the event that the Plan should for any reason become unavailable for the issuance of Restricted Stock, Company shall cause the shares of Restricted Stock required to be issued to Executive hereunder to be issued pursuant to another plan of Company on substantially the same terms and conditions as such Restricted Stock would have been issued under the plan.

6. Stock Options

(a) Executive shall be granted options pursuant to the Plan to purchase (i) 1,500,000 shares of Company common stock having an exercise price equal to the per-share fair market value (determined in accordance with the applicable provisions of the Plan) of Company common stock on January 11, 1989 (the **"A Options"**) and (ii) 500,000 shares of Company common stock having an exercise price equal to the per-share fair market value of the Company common stock having an exercise price equal to the per-share fair market value of the Company common stock on such date plus ten dollars ($10) (the **"B Options"**). Seventy-five percent of both the A Options and the B Options will vest in increments as nearly equal as possible on September 30 of each year starting September 30, 1990, and continuing through September 30, 1995. The remaining twenty-five percent of both the A Options and the B Options will vest in increments as nearly equal as possible on September 30th of each year starting on September 30, 1996 and continuing through September 30, 1998. Such options shall be subject to, and governed by, the terms and provisions of the Plan except to the extent of modifications of such options which are permitted by the Plan and which are expressly provided for herein.

(b) Executive agrees to enter into a stock option agreement with Company containing the terms and provisions of such options together with such other terms and conditions as counsel for the Company may reasonably require to assure compliance with applicable state or federal law and stock exchange requirements in connection with the issuance of Company stock upon exercise of options to be granted as provided herein, or as may be required to comply with the Plan.

(c) If Company has not already done so, Company shall register Executive's shares pursuant to the appropriate form of registration statement under the Securities Act of 1933 and shall maintain such registration statement's effectiveness at all required times.

(d) Company shall, to the extent permitted by law, make loans to Executive in reasonable amounts on reasonable terms and conditions during his employment by Company to facilitate the exercise of the options granted to him as described above.

7. Benefits

Executive shall be entitled to receive all benefits generally made available to executives of Company. In addition, Company shall maintain during the term hereof a $3,000,000 split dollar life insurance policy on his life unless a physical examination (which he agrees to take) shows that he is uninsurable.

8. Reimbursement for Expenses

Executive shall be expected to incur various business expenses customarily incurred by persons holding like positions, including but not limited to traveling, entertainment and similar expenses, all of which are to be incurred by Executive for the benefit of Company. Subject to Company's policy regarding the reimbursement and non-reimbursement of such expenses (which does not necessarily provide for reimbursement of all such expenses), Company shall reimburse Executive for such expenses from time to time, at Executive's request, and Executive shall account to Company for such expenses.

9. Protection of Company's Interests

(a) During the term of this Agreement Executive shall not directly or indirectly engage in competition with, or not own any interest in any business which competes with, any business of Company or any of its subsidiaries; provided, however, that the provisions of this Section 9 shall not prohibit his ownership of not more than 5% of voting stock of any publicly held corporation.

(b) Except for actions taken in the course of his employment hereunder, at no time shall Executive divulge, furnish or make accessible to any person any information of a confidential or proprietary nature obtained by him while in the employ of Company. Upon termination of his employment by Company, Executive shall return to the Company all such information which exists in writing or other physical form and all copies thereof in his possession or under his control.

(c) Company, its successors and assigns, shall, in addition to Executive's services, be entitled to receive and own all of the results and proceeds of said services (including, without limitation, literary material and other intellectual property) produced or created during the term of Executive's employment hereunder. Executive will, at the request of Company, execute such assignments, certificates or other instruments as Company may from time to time deem necessary or desirable to evidence, establish, maintain, protect, enforce or defend its right or title to any such material.

(d) Executive recognizes that the services to be rendered by him hereunder are of a character giving them peculiar value, the loss of which cannot be adequately compensated for in damages, and in the event of a breach of this Agreement by Executive, Company shall be entitled to equitable relief by way of injunction or by any other legal or equitable remedies.

10. Termination by Company

(a) Company shall have the right to terminate this Agreement under the following circumstances:

(i) Upon the death of Executive

(ii) Upon notice from Company to Executive in the event of an illness or other disability which has incapacitated him from performing his duties for six consecutive months as determined in good faith by the Board.

(iii) For good cause upon notice from Company. Termination by Company of Executive's employment for "good cause" as used in this Agreement shall be limited to gross negligence or malfeasance by Executive in the performance of his duties under this agreement or the voluntary resignation by Executive as an employee of the Company without the prior written consent of the Company.

(b) If this Agreement is terminated pursuant to Section 10(a) above, Executive's rights and Company's obligations hereunder shall forthwith terminate except as expressly provided in this Agreement.

(c) If this Agreement is terminated pursuant to Section 10(a) (i) or (ii) hereof, Executive or his estate shall be entitled to receive 100% of his base salary for the balance of the term of this Agreement, together with the bonus provided for in Section 4(e) hereof. Company may purchase insurance to cover all or any part of its obligations set forth in the preceding sentence, and Executive agrees to take a physical examination to facilitate the obtaining of such insurance. If the physical examination shows that Executive is uninsurable, such death and disability benefits shall not be provided (except for the bonus), and Executive shall receive only normal Company levels of death and disability benefits.

(d) Whenever compensation is payable to Executive hereunder during a time when he is partially or totally disabled and such disability (except for the provisions hereof) would entitle him to disability income or to salary continuation payments from Company according to the terms of any plan now or hereafter provided by Company or according to any Company policy in effect at the time of such disability, the compensation payable to him hereunder shall be inclusive of any such disability income or salary continuation and shall not be in addition thereto. If disability income is payable directly to Executive under an insurance policy paid for by Company, the amounts paid to him by said insurance company shall be considered to be part of the payments to be made by Company to him pursuant to this Section 10, and shall not be in addition thereto.

11. Termination by Executive

Executive shall have the right to terminate his employment under this agreement upon 30 days' notice to Company given within 60 days following the occurrence of any of the following events:

(i) Executive is not elected or retained as Chairman and Chief Executive Officer and a director of Company.

(ii) Company acts to materially reduce Executive's duties and responsibilities hereunder. Executive's duties and responsibilities shall not be deemed materially reduced for purposes hereof solely by virtue of the fact that Company is (or substantially all of its assets are) sold to, or is combined with, another entity provided that (a) Executive shall continue to have the same duties and responsibilities with respect to Company's entertainment and recreation, filmed entertainment, and consumers products business and (b) Executive shall report directly to the chief executive officer and board of directors of the entity (or individual) that acquires Company or its assets.

(iii) Company acts to change the geographic location of the performance of Executive's duties from Los Angeles California Metropolitan area.

12. Consequences of Breach by Company

(a) If this Agreement is terminated pursuant to Section 11 hereof, or if Company shall terminate Executive's employment under this Agreement in any other way that is a breach of this Agreement by Company, the following shall apply:

(i) Executive shall receive a cash payment equal to the present value (based on a discount rate of 9%) of Executive's base salary hereunder for the remainder of the term, payable within 30 days of the date of such termination.

(ii) Executive shall be entitled to bonus payments as provided in Sections 4 and 5 above (it being understood, however, that all such bonus payments, if made pursuant to this clause, shall be paid in cash regardless of whether or not such payments exceed the Cash Limit).

(iii) All stock options and Restricted Stock granted by Company to Executive under the Plan or granted by Company to Executive prior to the date hereof shall accelerate and become immediately exercisable.

(b) The parties believe that because of the limitations of Section 11 (ii) the above payments do not constitute "Excess Parachute Payments" under Section 280G of the Internal Revenue Code of 1954, as amended (the "Code"). Notwithstanding such belief, if any benefit under the preceding paragraph is determined to be an "Excess Parachute Payment" the Company shall pay Executive an additional amount ("Tax Payment") such that (x) the excess of all Excess Parachute Payments (including payments under this sentence) over the sum of excise tax thereon under section 4999 of the Code and income tax thereon under Subtitle A of the Code and under applicable state law is equal to (y) the excess of all Excess Parachute Payments (excluding payments under this sentence) over income tax thereon under Subtitle A of the Code and under applicable state law, provided that the Company shall not be obligated to make a Tax Payment in excess of the value of 6.6667 Compensation Years. For the purposes hereof, the value of a "Compensation Year," including stock options and bonus entitlements, is defined as equal to two times the base salary set forth in Section 3.

13. Remedies

Company recognizes that because of Executive's special talents, stature and opportunities in the entertainment industry, and because of the creative nature of and compensation practices of said industry and the material impact that individual projects can have on an entertainment company's results of operations, in the event of termination by Company hereunder (except under Section

10(a)), or in the event of termination by Executive under Section 11, before the end of the agreed term, Company acknowledges and agrees that the provisions of this Agreement regarding further payments of base salary, bonuses and the exercisability of stock options constitute fair and reasonable provisions for the consequences of such termination, do not constitute a penalty, and such payments and benefits shall not be limited or reduced by amounts Executive might earn or be able to earn from any other employment or ventures during the remainder of the agreed term of this Agreement.

14. Binding Agreement

This agreement shall be binding upon and inure to the benefit of Executive, his heirs, distributees and assigns and company, its successor and assigns. Executive may not, without the express written permission of the Company, assign or pledge any rights or obligations hereunder to any person, firm or corporation.

15. Amendment; Waiver

This instrument contains the entire agreement of the parties with respect to the employment of Executive by Company and supersedes the Amended and Restated Employment Agreement dated as of September 22, 1984 between Company and Executive (it being understood, however, that this agreement shall not affect any stock options granted to Executive prior to the date hereof). No amendment or modification of this Agreement shall be valid unless evidenced by a written instrument executed by the parties hereto. No waiver by either party of any breach by the other party of any provision or condition of this Agreement shall be deemed a waiver of any similar or dissimilar provision or condition at the same or any prior or subsequent time.

16. Governing Law

(a) This Agreement shall be governed by and construed in accordance with the laws of the State of California.

(b) The parties are aware that Executive's obligation to provide services to Company hereunder for the full term of this Agreement (approximately nine years and eight months) may be limited by California Labor Code, Section 2855, which provides, in relevant part, that a contract of employment may not be

enforced against an employee beyond seven years from the commencement of service under such contract, and the parties have
considered the possible applicability of such statutory limitation
in negotiating the terms of this Agreement. The parties agree
that this Agreement (together with certain additional documents
and agreements specifically referred to herein) shall constitute
the sole and conclusive basis for establishing Executive's compensation for all services provided by him hereunder, regardless of
whether such services are provided before or after seven years
from the date hereof, notwithstanding the further provision of
California Labor Code, Section 2855, to the effect that a contract of employment may be referred to as affording a "presump-
tive measure of compensation" for services provided after seven
years from the commencement of services under such contract.
Executive hereby confirms his intent to provide services to the
Company under this Agreement for the full term hereof.

17. Notices

All notices which a party is required or may desire to give to
the other party under or in connection with this Agreement shall
be given in writing by addressing the same to the other party as
follows:

If to Executive to:

Michael D. Eisner
283 Bel Air Road
Los Angeles, California 90024

If to Company, to:

The Walt Disney Company
500 South Buena Vista Street
Burbank, California 91521
Attn: General Counsel

or at such other place as may be designated in writing by like notice. Any notice shall be deemed to have been given within 48
hours after being addressed as required herein and deposited,
first-class postage prepaid, in the United States mail.

Nothing is unimportant in a contract. For example, the routine specs as to how notice is to be given have become crucial in cases where the company claims it notified the executive of its intent to terminate the contract and the executive denies having received notice.

IN WITNESS THEREOF, the parties have executed this agreement this 6th day of March, 1989, effective as of the day and year first above written.

[Signatures]

Appendix 3

The Layman–Blount Contract

Michael Eisner's contract has an unusually long term: ten years. But that's nothing compared to the term of the pact we're about to examine.

At the start of 1994, Blount, Inc. signed an employment agreement with Senior Vice President/CFO Harold E. Layman. The term extends until two years before Layman's 65th birthday. Layman was 47 when he signed the contract!

Another interesting feature was definitely in Layman's favor. He has the right to quit any time, for any reason, with 30 days' notice. The company is, as we will see, pretty well locked in.

The contract does not specify Layman's compensation. This goes along with a trend toward making compensation (including bonuses, options, and so on) a separate issue, formalized through separate documents. Compensation may change from year to year; other elements of the employment agreement are more permanent. Incidentally, during Layman's first full year under the following contract, he received $200,000 in salary, a $180,000 bonus, and 50,000 stock options.

EMPLOYMENT AGREEMENT
between
Harold E. Layman and Blount, Inc.
Effective as of January 1, 1994

THIS AGREEMENT, made and entered into as of the 1st day of January, 1994, by and between Blount, Inc., a Delaware corporation ("Company"), and Harold E. Layman ("Executive")

WITNESSETH:

The parties, for and in consideration of the mutual and reciprocal covenants and agreements contained in this document, do contract and agree as follows:

1.0 Purpose and Employment: The purpose of this Agreement is to define the relationship between the Company, as an employer, and Executive, as an Employee. By the execution of this Agreement, the Company employs Executive and Executive accepts employment by the Company.

2.0 Compensation and Benefits: Based on the Executive's performance, the compensation in effect on the effective date of this agreement and as adjusted from time to time by the President and Chief Executive Officer and approved by the Compensation and Management Development Committee of the Board of Directors of the Company, and the Executive's position within the Company, the Executive shall be entitled to and the Company agrees to provide any and all basic benefits which are generally provided by the Company to its similarly situated employees. Further, the Executive shall be entitled to and the Company agrees to provide any and all working facilities, perquisites and incentives which are in effect on the date of this agreement and as may be adjusted or eliminated from time to time at management's discretion.

3.0 Duties: Executive shall serve the Company in a full-time salaried position designated by the Company. The position is to be defined using a written job description and be subject to the Hay Compensation Position Evaluation System or other systematic evaluation systems that the Company may employ.

4.0 Extent of Services: Executive shall devote full time to the conduct of the business of Blount, Inc., its divisions or affiliates. The Executive may not engage in any other business that requires his time or services, other than those associated with Blount or its affiliates, unless prior permission has been granted by the President of Blount, Inc.; provided, that the Executive may serve as a director of unaffiliated corporations if such service involves no conflict of interest, is within reasonable time commitments and permission to do so is obtained from the President of Blount, Inc.

5.0 Term: The term of Agreement shall be for a period beginning on the effective date of this agreement and ending two years prior to the date of the Executive's 65th birthday.

This Agreement is a contract of employment at will. This means that employment will continue only so long as both Company and Executive want it to do so. Subject to the minimum notice requirement set forth below, Executive is free to quit at any time at his discretion and Company is, subject to the severance payment provisions of Paragraph 7.0, free to terminate Executive's employment at any time at its discretion. The Agreement may be terminated by the Executive or the Company upon 30 days' written notice. If the Agreement is terminated for reasons other than normal retirement, death, total disability, Cause (Paragraph 9.0(d)), or voluntary termination, the Executive shall be paid as described in Severance Payment (Paragraph 7.0).

6.0 Conflicts of Interest: In matters that present the potential for conflicts of interest, the Executive is subject to the policies set forth in the Blount, Inc., corporate Policies & Procedures Manual and Blount Principles of Business Conduct.

7.0 Severance Payment: Except as provided in Paragraph 8.0 below, in the event that the Executive's employment is terminated by the Company for reasons other than normal retirement, death, total disability, Cause (as defined in Paragraph 9.0(d)), or voluntary termination (as set forth under Paragraph 9.0, titled "Exclusions"), the Company will pay to the Executive payments equal to two (2) times the participant's base salary during the preceding 12 months. The payments will be made in twenty-four (24) equal monthly payments following the termination date and will be forfeited if the Executive accepts employment with a competitor or its affiliated entities during the severance payment period. After the participant reaches age 55, any severance payments due under this agreement will be offset by any consulting fees paid by Blount after termination plus retirement income due from the Blount pension plan as well as any retirement benefit supplemental to the Blount pension benefit. In the event of a Change of Control as defined in paragraph 10.0, the Executive may at his option decide to leave the Company and be paid severance pay pursuant to this paragraph as though the Executive were terminated by the Company.

8.0 Forced Separation: If the Company reduces the Executive's base salary more than 25%, without making commensurate reductions in the salaries of a majority of the officers of Blount, Inc., the Executive may at his option decide to leave the Company and be paid severance pay pursuant to Paragraph 7.0 as though the Executive were terminated by the Company.

9.0 Exclusions: In the event the Executive's termination is for any of the following reasons, the provisions of this contract will not apply:

(a) Retirement

(b) Death

(c) Total disability

(d) Cause. "Cause" for termination by the Company shall include, but shall not be limited to, the following conduct of the Executive:

(1) Any act that is materially contrary to the best interests of the Company or its affiliated entities including, but not limited to, fraud, conviction of a felony, gross malfeasance, insubordination, failure to perform to satisfactory levels, material breach of any of the terms contained in this Agreement or refusal to comply with the reasonable policies, standards and regulations established by the Company.

(2) Willful and continued failure by the Executive to devote his full business time and best efforts to the business affairs of the Company.

(e) Voluntary termination by Executive not due to a change of control or forced separation.

10.0 Change of Control: A "Change of Control" means any of the following events:

(a) the sale by the Company of substantially all of its assets to a single purchaser or a group of associated or affiliated purchasers.

(b) the sale, exchange or other disposition, in one transaction to an entity or entities not affiliated with the Company, of more than fifty percent (50%) of the outstanding common stock of the Company other than a sale, exchange, or disposition of the common stock of the Company resulting from a public or private offering of common stock or other security convertible into common stock of the Company which offering is sponsored or initiated by the Company and approved by the Board.

Any stock purchase or acquisition under an ESOP or other employee plan whereby employees of the company, except W.M. Blount, acquire a majority of the stock is excluded from this "change of control" provision.

(c) the merger or consolidation of the Company in a transaction in which the stockholders of the Company receive less than fifty percent (50%) of the outstanding voting stock of the new or continuing entity.

11.0 Non-solicitation: During the period beginning on the date of this Agreement's execution and ending two (2) years following termination of the Executive's employment with the Company, Executive shall not hire or solicit any employees of the Company or any person that controls, is controlled by, or is under common control with any other person of the Company, to work for any other Person then in competition with the Company or any of its Affiliates, or, directly or indirectly, solicit or attempt in any manner to persuade or influence any present, future or prospective customer or client of the Company or any of its Affiliates to divert his or its purchases of products or services from the Company or any of its Affiliates to any person then in competition with the Company or any of its Affiliates. Executive agrees and acknowledges that he possesses valuable information with respect to customers and clients of the Company as a result of his employment and that violation of this provision would cause irreparable harm to the Company. Executive hereby specifically acknowledges the adequacy of the compensation to be paid by Company hereunder and of the other benefits provided by Company for all of the covenants undertaken by Executive under this Agreement. Executive shall be entitled to take such vacation and other leaves of absence as determined pursuant to the Company's vacation and leave policies as set forth in its employee benefits handbook, as amended from time to time.

12.0 Confidentiality: The Executive shall not disclose or furnish information about the Company's business to any third party except:

(a) As specifically authorized by Blount, Inc. or as reasonably necessary to carry out the duties performed by Executive hereunder;

or

(b) That demanded by a subpoena duly served.

13.0 Rights of Company Upon Breach: If Executive breaches or threatens to commit a breach of any of the provisions of this Agreement, the Company shall have the following rights and remedies, each of which rights and remedies shall be independent of the others and severally enforceable, and each of which is an addition to, and not in Lieu of, any other rights and remedies available to the Company at Law or in equity (including the right to recover damages):

(a) the right and remedy to have this Agreement specifically enforced by any court of competent jurisdiction, it being agreed that any breach or threatened breach of this Agreement would cause irreparable harm to the Company and that money damages would not provide an adequate remedy to the Company;

(b) the right and remedy to require Executive to account for and pay over to the Company all compensation, profits or other benefits derived or received by Executive or lost to the Company as a result of any actions constituting a breach of this Agreement;

(c) the right to terminate Executive's employment for cause under Paragraph 9.0 (d) of this Agreement.

14.0 Applicable Law: This Agreement shall be construed under and governed by the laws of the State of Alabama, and any action to enforce this Agreement or which otherwise arises under this Agreement shall be brought in Montgomery, Alabama.

15.0 Severability: In case any one or more of the provisions of this Agreement shall be found to be invalid, illegal or unenforceable in any respect, the validity, legality and enforceability of the remaining provisions contained herein shall not in any way be affected or impaired thereby.

16.0 Entire Agreement: This Agreement represents the entire agreement between the parties and may be amended, modified or superseded only by a written agreement signed by both of the parties.

[Signed by Harold E. Layman and John M. Panettiere, President and CEO of Blount, Inc.]

Appendix 4

The Feeney–
AMAX/Alumax Contract

AGREEMENT

AGREEMENT, dated November 15, 1993, by and between AMAX Inc., a New York Corporation ("AMAX"), Alumax Inc., a Delaware corporation ("Alumax"), and Helen M. Feeney ("Employee").

WHEREAS, there exists an employment arrangement between AMAX and Employee (the "Employment Arrangement");

WHEREAS, AMAX and Cyprus Minerals Company ("Cyprus") have entered into an Agreement and Plan of Reorganization and Merger, dated as of May 24, 1993 (the "Merger Agreement"), providing for the Merger (as defined in the Merger Agreement) of AMAX with and into Cyprus;

WHEREAS, immediately prior to the Effective Time (as defined in the Merger Agreement) of the Merger, AMAX will distribute to its shareholders all of the outstanding shares of common stock of Alumax;

WHEREAS, subject to the completion of the Merger, Alumax and Employee intend to enter into an employment arrangement effective upon completion of the Merger; and

WHEREAS, subject to the completion of the Merger and subject to Employee's entering into an employment arrangement with Alumax, AMAX and Employee have agreed to terminate the Employment Arrangement upon the terms and conditions provided herein;

NOW, THEREFORE, in consideration of the mutual covenants contained herein, and other good and valuable consideration, the parties agree as follows, all subject to the completion of the Merger and the effectiveness of the employment arrangement between Employee and Alumax;

1. Certain Payments By AMAX

(a) **Stock Options.** Employee agrees to cancel all of Employee's outstanding AMAX Options for which Employee will receive a cash payment pursuant to Section 6.10 (a) of the Merger Agreement.

(b) **Incentive Awards.** AMAX will pay Employee $41,530 in full payment of Employee's awards determined in accordance with Section 5.1 (b) of the AMAX Inc. Annual Incentive Compensation Plan for Executives (the "Incentive Compensation Plan") and $155,879 in full payment of Employee's awards under the AMAX Inc. Performance Share Plan.

(c) **Excess Benefits Plan.** AMAX will pay Employee $4,378 pursuant to Sections 2.05 (a) and 4.03 (d) of the AMAX Inc. Excess Benefit Plan.

(d) **Services After Merger.** AMAX will pay Employee (i) such Employee's current salary for any period after the completion of the Merger in which Employee performs services on a substantially full-time basis for AMAX or its successor by merger and (ii) upon termination of the performance of any such services any amount payable to Employee pursuant to Section 5.2 (a) of the Incentive Compensation Plan and Section 4 (a) (ii) of the AMAX Inc. Corporate Separation Policy for Corporate Officers.

2. Alumax Stock Options

(a) **Grant**

Immediately following the date that the employment arrangement between Alumax and Employee commences (the "Commencement Date") and the end of the 120-Day Period (as defined in Section 5), Alumax shall grant to Employee non-qualified stock options (the "Options") to acquire shares of common stock, par value of $.01 per share, of Alumax ("Common Stock"), in an aggregate amount equal to 44,110 shares multiplied by a fraction, the numerator of which is 15, and the denominator of which is the 120-Day Average Price (as defined in Section 5). Alumax and Employee agree that the number of shares of Common Stock subject to the Options or any other options granted or to be granted by Alumax to Employee under the Alumax Inc. 1993 Long Term Incentive Plan during any period of five consecutive years following the Commencement Date shall not exceed 300,000 shares.

(b) **Exercise Price**

The exercise price of each of the Options (the "Exercise Price") shall be equal to the 120-Day Average Price.

(c) **Vesting**

The Options shall vest at the rate of 20% per year on each of the first five anniversary dates of the Commencement Date; *provided, however,* that (i) Options that have not previously vested shall vest immediately, and all restrictions and risks of forfeiture shall lapse, upon (A) the death or Disability (as defined in Section 5) of Employee, (B) Employee's retirement on or after age 65, (C) termination of Employee's employment by Alumax without Cause (as defined in Section 5), or (D) a Change in Control (as defined in Section 5), and (ii) Options that have not previously vested shall not vest, and shall be immediately forfeited by Employee, upon (X) Employee's retirement before age 65, or (Y) termination of Employee's employment by Alumax with Cause or by Employee other than with Good Reason.

(d) **Term**

Vested Options may be exercised only within the first ten (10) years after the date of grant.

(e) **Exercise**

Except as described below, an Option that is vested may be exercised only by (i) written notice of intent to exercise the Option and (ii) payment or deemed payment of the Exercise Price to Alumax (contemporaneously with delivery of such notice) in cash or Common Stock of equivalent Fair Market Value. In its sole discretion the Committee may permit the Exercise Price to be paid in the form of Awards issued under Alumax's compensation plans, or other property (including notes or other contractual obligations of the Employee) to make payment on a deferred basis, such as through "cashless exercise" arrangements, to the extent permitted by applicable law. Common Stock utilized in full or partial payment of the Exercise Price shall be valued at its

Fair Market Value (as defined in Section 5) on the date of exercise. In the event of a Change in Control, the Employee shall be entitled to elect, during the 60-day period immediately following such Change in Control, in lieu of acquiring the shares of Common Stock covered by the Options, to receive, and Alumax shall be obligated to pay, the Change in Control Settlement Value (as defined in Section 8 (c) of the Alumax Inc. 1993 Long Term Incentive Plan) with respect to shares of Common Stock up to the number of shares covered by the Options, which amount shall be paid in cash.

(f) **Registration**

Employee shall sell shares of Common Stock acquired upon the exercise of Options only pursuant to an effective registration statement covering such sale or to an exemption from registration under the Securities Act of 1933, as amended.

(g) **Non-Transferability**

The Options may not be sold, pledged, assigned, hypothecated, transferred or disposed of in any manner other than by will or by the laws of descent and distribution. An Option may be exercised, during the lifetime of Employee, only by Employee's guardian or legal representative.

3.   Alumax Stock Units

(a) **Grant**

Immediately following the Commencement Date and the end of the 120-Day Period, Alumax shall grant to Employee units of compensation (the "Units") each of which shall represent the right to receive compensation paid in the form of one share of Common Stock and the aggregate number of which shall equal $189,370 divided by the 120-Day Average Price.

(b) **Vesting**

The Units shall vest at the rate of 20% per year on each of the first five anniversary dates of the Commencement Date; *provided, however*, that (i) Units that have not previously vested shall vest immediately, and all restrictions and risks of forfeiture shall lapse, upon (A) the death or Disability of Employee, (B) Employee's retirement on or after age 65, (C) termination of Employee's employment by Alumax without Cause or by Employee with Good Reason, or (D) a Change in Control, and (ii) Units that have not previously vested shall not vest, and shall be immediately forfeited by Employee, upon (X) Employee's retirement before age 65, or (Y) termination of Employee's employment by Alumax with Cause or by Employee other than with Good Reason.

(c) **Deferral of Payment**

By the end of each calendar year immediately preceding the calendar year in which any portion of the Units are scheduled to vest in accordance with Section 3 (b) above, Employee shall file with Alumax a written election form in which Employee shall elect the date or dates on which the shares of Common Stock represented by such Units shall be paid out to Employee; *provided, however,* that all vested shares of Common Stock shall be paid out to Employee no later than any Change in Control. Any dividends paid on vested shares of Common Stock between the date of vesting and the date of payment shall be paid out to Employee when such shares of Common Stock are paid out to Employee.

(d) **Change in Control**

In the event of a Change in Control (as defined in Section 5), the Employee shall be entitled to elect, during the 60-day period immediately following such Change in Control, to surrender shares of Common Stock received pursuant to this Agreement to Alumax and receive, in full settlement thereof, and Alumax shall be obligated to pay in cash, the Change in Control Stock Value (as defined in Section 8(b) of the Alumax Inc. 1993 Long Term Incentive Plan) with respect to the number of shares surrendered.

4. **Effect of Change in Common Stock**

In the event that outstanding shares of Common Stock shall be changed into or exchanged for a different number or kind of shares of Alumax or of another corporation (whether by reason of merger, consolidation, recapitalization, reclassification, stock dividend, split-up, combination of shares, or otherwise), or in the event of any extraordinary cash dividend, spin-off, distribution of assets (including stock of another corporation), or any other action not in the ordinary course of business that has a material effect on the equity represented by outstanding shares of Common Stock, appropriate adjustments, if any, as determined by the Board of Directors of Alumax or, at Employee's election, Lipper & Company, L.P. (or some other investment banking firm mutually acceptable to Alumax and Employee) shall be made in the number, kind, or exercise price of the Options and Shares.

5. Definitions

For purposes of this Agreement, the following capitalized terms shall have the meanings set forth below:

"Beneficial Owner," with respect to any securities, shall mean any person who, directly or indirectly, has or shares the right to vote or dispose of such securities or otherwise has "beneficial ownership" of such securities (within the meaning of Rule 13d-3 and Rule 13d-5 (as such Rules are in effect on the date of this Agreement) under the Securities Act of 1934, as amended (the "Exchange Act")), including pursuant to any agreement, arrangement or understanding (whether or not in writing); *provided, however,* that (i) a person shall not be deemed the Beneficial Owner of any security as a result of any agreement, arrangement or understanding to vote such security (x) arising solely from a revocable proxy or consent solicited pursuant to, and in accordance with, the applicable provisions of the Exchange Act and the rules and regulations thereunder or (y) made in connection with, or otherwise to participate in, a proxy or consent solicitation made, or to be made, pursuant to, and in accordance with, the applicable provisions of the Exchange Act and the rules and regulations thereunder, in either case described in clause (x) or clause (y) above whether or not such agreement, arrangement or understanding is also then reportable by such person on Schedule 13D under the Exchange Act (or any comparable or successor report), and (ii) a person engaged in business as an underwriter of securities shall not be deemed to be the Beneficial Owner of any securities acquired through such person's participation in good faith in a firm commitment underwriting until the expiration of forty days after the date of such acquisition.

"Cause" shall mean (i) the willful engaging by Employee in conduct which is not authorized by the Board of Directors of Alumax or within the normal course of Employee's business decisions and is known by Employee to be materially detrimental to the best interests of Alumax or any of its subsidiaries, (ii) the willful engaging by Employee in conduct which Employee knows is, or has substantial reason to believe to be, illegal to the extent of a felony violation, or the equivalent seriousness under laws other than those of the United States, and which has effects on Alumax or Employee materially injurious to Alumax,

Here is another reminder that business today is global. "Cause" includes serious crimes committed in other countries as well as the United States.

(iii) the engaging by Employee in any willful and conscious act of serious dishonesty, in each case which the Board of Directors of Alumax reasonably determines affects adversely, or could in the future affect adversely, the value, reliability or performance of Employee to Alumax in a material manner, (iv) the willful and continued failure by Employee to perform substantially Employee's duties, which absence has not been certified in writing as due to physical or mental illness in accordance with the procedures set forth in this Section 5 (under "Disability"), after a written demand for substantial performance has been delivered to Employee by the Board of Directors specifically identifying the manner in which Employee has failed to substantially perform Employee's duties, or (v) the sustained and unexcused absence of Employee from the performance of Employee's duties to Alumax for a period of 180 days or more within a period of 365 consecutive days, regardless of the reason for such absence, unless Employee demonstrates that such absence is due to Disability. Any act, or failure to act, based on authority given, pursuant to a resolution duly adopted by the Board of Directors of Alumax or based upon the advice of counsel for Alumax shall be conclusively presumed to be done, or omitted to be done, in good faith and in the best interests of Alumax, and shall not be deemed to constitute Cause under subdivisions (ii) or (iii) of this definition.

This language protects the employee against being made the scapegoat for someone on a higher level.

Notwithstanding the foregoing, there shall not be deemed to be a voluntary termination by Alumax with Cause unless and until there shall have been delivered to Employee a copy of a resolution duly adopted by the affirmative vote of not less than three-quarters of the entire membership of the Board of Directors of Alumax at a meeting of such Board held after reasonable notice to Employee and at which Employee has an opportunity, together with Employee's counsel, to be heard before such Board, finding that, in the good-faith opinion of such Board, Employee was guilty of the conduct set forth and specifying the particulars thereof in detail.

The board of directors must turn itself into a court and conduct a full-fledged trial before firing the employee for cause under the language of this section.

"Change in Control" shall mean the satisfaction of one or more of the following conditions:

(i)   any person is or becomes the Beneficial Owner, directly or indirectly, of securities of Alumax representing 20 percent or more of the combined voting power of Alumax's then-outstanding securities (a "20% Beneficial Owner"); *provided, however,* that (a) the term "20% Beneficial Owner" shall not include any Beneficial Owner who has crossed such 20 percent threshold solely as a result of an acquisition of securities directly from Alumax, or solely as a result of an acquisition by Alumax of Alumax securities, until such time thereafter as such person acquires additional voting securities other than directly from Alumax and, after giving effect to such acquisition, such person would constitute a 20% Beneficial Owner; and (b) with respect to any person eligible to file a Schedule 13G pursuant to Rule 13d-I (b) (1) under the Exchange Act with respect to Alumax securities (an "Institutional Investor"), there shall be excluded from the number of securities deemed to be beneficially owned by such person a number of securities representing not more than 10 percent of the combined voting power of Alumax's then-outstanding securities;

(ii)   during any period of two consecutive years beginning after the commencement of the Period of Employment, individuals who at the beginning of such period constitute the Board of Directors of Alumax together with those individuals who first become Directors during such period (other than by reason of an agreement with Alumax in settlement of a proxy contest for the election of directors) and whose election or nomination for election to the Board was approved by a vote of at least two-thirds

($\frac{2}{3}$) of the Directors then still in office who either were Directors at the beginning of the period or whose election or nomination for election was previously so approved (the "Continuing Directors"), cease for any reason to constitute a majority of the Board of Directors of Alumax;

(iii) the stockholders of Alumax approve a merger, consolidation, recapitalization or reorganization of Alumax, or a reverse stock split of any class of voting securities of Alumax, or the consummation of any such transaction if stockholder approval is not obtained, other than any such transaction which would result in at least 75% of the total voting power represented by the voting securities of Alumax or the surviving entity outstanding immediately after such transaction being beneficially owned by persons who together owned at least 75% of the combined voting power of the voting securities of Alumax outstanding immediately prior to such transaction, with the relative voting power of each such continuing holder compared to the voting power of each other continuing holder not substantially altered as a result of the transaction; *provided that*, for purposes of this paragraph (iii), such continuity of ownership (and preservation of relative voting power) shall be deemed to be satisfied if the failure to meet such 75% threshold (or to preserve such relative voting power) is due solely to the acquisition of voting securities by an employee benefit plan of Alumax or such surviving entity or of any subsidiary of Alumax or any such surviving entity;

(iv) the stockholders of Alumax approve a plan of complete liquidation or dissolution of Alumax or an agreement for the sale or disposition of all or substantially all the assets of Alumax; or

(v) any other event which the Board of Directors (not taking into account any vote of Employee) determines shall constitute a Change in Control for purposes of this Agreement;

provided, however, that a Change in Control shall not be deemed to have occurred if any of the following conditions (each, an "exception") is satisfied:

(1) Unless a majority of the Continuing Directors of Alumax determines that for purposes of any or all of the provisions of this Agreement the exception set forth in this paragraph (1) shall not apply, none of the

foregoing conditions would have been satisfied but for one or more of the following persons acquiring or otherwise becoming the Beneficial Owner of securities of Alumax; (A) any person who has entered into a binding agreement with Alumax, which agreement has been approved by two-thirds (⅔) of the Continuing Directors, limiting the acquisition of additional voting securities by such person, the solicitation of proxies by such person or proposals by such person concerning a business combination with Alumax (a "Standstill Agreement"); (B) any employee benefit plan, or trustee of other fiduciary thereof, maintained by Alumax or any subsidiary of Alumax; (C) any subsidiary of Alumax; or (D) Alumax.

(2) Unless a majority of the Continuing Directors of Alumax determines that for purposes of any or all of the provisions of this Agreement the exception set forth in this paragraph (2) shall not apply, none of the foregoing conditions would have been satisfied but for the acquisition by Alumax of another entity (whether by merger or consolidation, the acquisition of stock or assets, or otherwise) in exchange, in whole or in part, for securities of Alumax, provided that, immediately following such acquisition, the Continuing Directors constitute a majority of the Board of Directors of Alumax, or a majority of the board of directors of any other surviving entity, and, in either case, no agreement, arrangement or understanding exists at that time which would cause such Continuing Directors to cease thereafter to constitute a majority of the Board of Directors or of such other board of directors.

(3) A majority of the Continuing Directors determines that a Change of Control shall not be deemed to have occurred. Notwithstanding the foregoing, unless a majority of the Continuing Directors determines otherwise, no Change in Control shall be deemed to

have occurred with respect to Employee if the Change in Control results from actions or events in which Employee is a participant in a capacity other than solely as an officer, employee or director of Alumax.

If you hold considerable stock, and you join forces with those engaged in a takeover, your parachute may not open.

"Committee" shall mean the Human Resources and Compensation Committee of Alumax's Board of Directors.

"Disability" shall mean the absence of Employee from Employee's duties with Alumax on a full-time basis for one hundred eighty (180) days within any period of three hundred and sixty-five (365) consecutive days as a result of Employee's incapacity due to physical or mental illness as certified in writing by a physician selected by Employee and reasonably acceptable to Alumax (it being understood that such physician shall be deemed reasonably acceptable to Alumax if, within a period of fifteen (15) days after Employee notifies Alumax of the name of such physician, Alumax does not object to the use of such physician), unless within thirty (30) days after written notice to Employee by Alumax, in accordance with the provisions of Section 12, that Employee's employment is being terminated by reason of such absence, Employee shall have returned to the full performance of Employee's duties and shall have presented to Alumax a written certificate of Employee's good health prepared by a physician selected by Employee and reasonably acceptable to Alumax.

"Fair Market Value" of a share of Common Stock shall mean the closing sale price of the Common Stock reported on the Composite Tape for securities listed on the New York Stock Exchange in *The Wall Street Journal* on the trading day immediately preceding the relevant valuation date (it being agreed that, if such a closing price for the Common Stock is not so reported on such date, the closing price on such day shall, for purposes of this paragraph, be deemed to be the market price per share of the Common Stock on such date as determined in good faith by the Board of Directors of Alumax).

Voluntary termination by Employee with **"Good Reason"** shall mean a voluntary termination by Employee resulting from Alumax (i) reducing Employee's base annual salary as in effect immediately prior to such reduction, (ii) effecting a change in the position of the Employee which does not represent a promotion from Employee's position provided for herein, (iii) assigning Employee duties or responsibilities which are materially inconsistent with such position, (iv) removing Employee from or failing to reappoint or reelect Employee to such position, except in connection with a termination as a result of death, Disability, voluntary termination by Employee, retirement by Employee or Cause, or (v) otherwise materially breaching its obligations under this Agreement, in each case after notice in writing from Employee to Alumax and a period of 30 days after such notice during which Alumax fails to correct such conduct.

"120-Day Average Price" of a share of Common Stock shall mean the average of the closing sale prices of the Common Stock reported on the Composite Tape for securities listed on the New York Stock Exchange in *The Wall Street Journal* for the first 120 trading days that the Common Stock is fully listed on the New York Stock Exchange; *provided, however,* that if before the end of such 120-day period (a) any person shall have acquired, or publicly disclosed an intention or proposal to acquire (whether by tender offer, exchange offer, or otherwise), Beneficial Ownership of securities of Alumax that would result in such person being a 20% Beneficial Owner, (b) any person shall have proposed, or publicly announced an intention to propose, a merger, consolidation or similar transaction involving Alumax or any of its subsidiaries (other than mergers, reorganizations, consolidations or dissolutions involving existing subsidiaries of employer), (c) Alumax shall have publicly proposed, or publicly announced an intention to propose, the disposition, by sale, lease, exchange or otherwise, of assets of Alumax or its subsidiaries representing 30% or more of the consolidated assets of Alumax and its subsidiaries or (d) the Board of Directors of Alumax determines, in its sole discretion, without regard to the vote of the Employee, that a third party has taken action involving a possible Change in Control of a material part of Alumax's business or assets and such action is affecting the public trading price of the Common Stock, the 120-day period shall be deemed to have ended prior to the date of the public announcement of any such acquisition, disclosure, proposal or the making of such determination.

"**120-Day Period**" shall mean the period of 120 days (or shorter period) used to determine the 120-Day Average Price.

There is more language here than in most contracts about the employee's stock holdings, especially in case of a merger or takeover. Among other things, language is designed to negate a possible stock windfall caused by a run-up on rumors of a takeover.

6. Termination of Employment Agreement

AMAX and Employee mutually terminate the Employment Arrangement and release each other from any and all claims and restrictions thereunder, except as otherwise provided in Section 1(d).

7. Excise Tax Gross-Up

In the event that any payments or grants referenced in this Agreement (the "Total Payments") become subject to the tax imposed by Section 4999 of the Internal Revenue Code of 1986, as amended (the "Code"), (or any similar tax that may hereafter be imposed) as a result of or in connection with the Merger (the "Excise Tax"), AMAX shall pay to Employee at the time specified below an additional amount (the "Gross-up Payment") (which shall include, without limitation, reimbursement for any penalties and interest that may accrue in respect of such Excise Tax) such that the net amount retained by Employee, after reduction for any Excise Tax (including any penalties or interest thereon) on the Total Payments and any federal, state and local income or employment tax and Excise Tax on the Gross-up Payment provided for by this Section 5, but before reduction for any federal, state or local income or employment tax on the Total Payments, shall be equal to the sum of (a) the Total Payments, and (b) an amount equal to the product of any deductions disallowed for federal, state or local income tax purposes because of the inclusion of the Gross-up Payment in Employee's adjusted gross income multiplied by the highest applicable marginal rate of federal, state or local income and employment taxation respectively, for the calendar year in which the Gross-up Payment is to be made.

*An exhaustive way of saying that the company will shield the em-
ployee from taxes on bonuses and stock.*

For purposes of determining the amount of the Gross-up
Payment, Employee shall be deemed (A) to pay federal income and
employment taxes at the highest marginal rate of federal income
and employment taxation for the Calendar year in which the
Gross-up Payment is to be made; (B) to pay any applicable state
and local income taxes at the highest marginal rate of taxation for
the calendar year in which the Gross-up Payment is to be made,
net of the tax reduction in federal income taxes which could be obtained from deduction of such state and local taxes if paid in such
year (determined without regard to limitations on deductions
based on the amount of Employee's adjusted gross income); and
(C) to have otherwise allowable deductions for federal, state and
local income tax purposes at least equal to those disallowed because of the inclusion of the Gross-up Payment in Employee's
adjusted gross income. In the event that the Excise Tax is subsequently determined to be less than the amount taken into account
hereunder at the time the Gross-up Payment is made, Employee
shall repay to AMAX at the time that the amount of such reduction in Excise Tax is finally determined (but, if previously paid to
the taxing authorities, not prior to the time the amount of such reduction is refunded to Employee or otherwise realized as a benefit
by Employee) the portion of the Gross-up Payment that would not
have been paid if such Excise Tax had been applied in initially
calculating the Gross-up Payment, plus interest on the amount
of such repayment at the rate provided in Section 1274 (b) (2) (B)
of the Code. In the event that the Excise Tax is determined to
exceed the amount taken into account hereunder at the time
the Gross-up Payment is made, AMAX shall make an additional
Gross-up Payment in respect of such excess (plus any interest and
penalties payable with respect to such excess) at the time that the
amount of such excess is finally determined.

The Gross-up Payment provided for above shall be paid on
the thirtieth day (or such earlier date as the Excise Tax becomes
due and payable to the taxing authorities) after it has been determined that the Total Payments (or any portion thereof) are subject to the Excise Tax.

AMAX shall have the right to control all proceedings with the Internal Revenue Service that may arise in connection with the determination and assessment of any Excise Tax and, at its sole option, AMAX may pursue or forgo any and all administrative appeals, proceedings, hearings and conferences with any taxing authority in respect of such Excise Tax (including any interest or penalties thereon); *provided, however*, that AMAX's control over any such proceedings shall be limited to issues with respect to which a Gross-up Payment would be payable hereunder and Employee shall be entitled to settle or contest any other issue raised by the Internal Revenue Service or any other taxing authority. Employee shall cooperate with AMAX in any proceedings relating to the determination and assessment of any Excise Tax and shall not take any position or action that would materially increase the amount of any Gross-up Payment hereunder.

8. Commencement of Employment Arrangement

Alumax and Employee agree that the employment arrangement between them shall commence upon completion of the Merger; *provided, however*, that Employee shall begin receiving Employee's annual salary from Alumax only after Employee no longer is entitled to receive salary payments from AMAX pursuant to Section 1(d).

9. Governing Law; Disputes; Arbitration

(a)   This Agreement is governed by and is to be construed and enforced in accordance with the laws of the State of New York. If under such law, any portion of this agreement is at any time deemed to be in conflict with any applicable statute, rule, regulation, ordinance or principle of law, such portion shall be deemed to be modified or altered to the extent necessary to conform thereto or, if that is not possible, to be omitted from this Agreement; and the invalidity of any such portion shall not affect the force, effect and validity of the remaining portion hereof.

(b)   All reasonable costs and expenses (including fees and disbursements of counsel) incurred by Employee in seeking to enforce rights pursuant to this Agreement shall be paid or reimbursed to Employee promptly by AMAX or Alumax (whichever of the two entities granted such rights), whether or not Employee is successful in asserting such rights, except that Employee shall repay to AMAX or Alumax, as the case may be, any such amounts to the extent that a court issues a final, unappealable order setting forth a determination that Employee's claim was frivolous or advanced by Employee in bad faith.

Some employers try to impose the costs of unsuccessful lawsuits on the employee, thus creating a powerful deterrent to legal action. Ms. Feeney's agreement goes pretty far in the opposite direction. If she sues the company on valid grounds, the company pays her legal costs no matter what. The next paragraph, however, cuts down significantly the size of the arena in which legal action might be taken.

(c) Any dispute or controversy arising under or in connection with this Agreement shall be settled exclusively by arbitration in New York, New York, in the case of a dispute between AMAX and Employee, or Atlanta, Georgia, in case of a dispute between Alumax and Employee, by three arbitrators in accordance with the rules of the American Arbitration Association in effect at the time of admission to arbitration. Judgment may be entered on the arbitrators' award in any court having jurisdiction.

(d) Any amounts that have become payable pursuant to the terms of this Agreement or any judgment by a court of law or a decision by arbitrators pursuant to this Section 5 but which are not timely paid shall bear interest at the prime rate in effect at the time such payment first becomes payable, as quoted by the Morgan Guaranty Trust Company of New York.

10. Notices

All notices under this Agreement shall be in writing and shall be deemed effective when received (in AMAX's case, by its Secretary, or Alumax's case, by its President) or seventy-two (72) hours after deposit thereof in the U.S. mails, postage prepaid, for delivery as registered or certified mail, addressed, in the case of Employee, to him [The contract reads "him" at this point, though the employee is female. This is boilerplate copy, and perhaps the gender was not changed. "Him or her" would seem to be a better choice.] at Employee's address specified below, and in the case of AMAX or Alumax, to its principal United States corporate headquarters, attention of the Secretary, or to such other address as

Employee, AMAX, or Alumax may by notice designate in writing at any time or from time to time to the other party. In lieu of notice by deposit in the U.S. mail, a party may give notice by prepaid cable, telegram, telex or telecopy and such notice shall be effective twenty-four (24) hours after it has been properly sent.

11. Withholding

All payments to be made to Employee under this Agreement will be subject to required withholding taxes and other deductions.

12. Successors; Binding Agreement

(a)   Any successor (as hereinafter defined) to AMAX or Alumax shall be bound by this Agreement. For purposes of this Agreement, "Successor" shall mean any person that succeeds to, or has the practical ability to control (either immediately or with the passage of time), AMAX's or Alumax's business directly, by merger or consolidation, or indirectly, by purchase of AMAX's or Alumax's voting securities, all or substantially all of its assets or otherwise.

(b)   For purposes of this Agreement, "AMAX" shall include any corporation or other entity which is the surviving or continuing entity in respect of any amalgamation, merger, consolidation, dissolution, asset acquisition or other form of business combination.

13. Miscellaneous

(a)   This Agreement constitutes the entire understanding between AMAX and Employee relating to employment of Employee by AMAX and supersedes and cancels all prior arrangements or agreements and understandings with respect to the subject matter of this Agreement and such other written agreements.

(b)   This Agreement may be amended but only by a subsequent written agreement of the parties.

(c)   Notwithstanding anything herein to the contrary, AMAX shall only be liable to Employee for any default on AMAX's obligations expressly provided in Sections 1 and 7; Alumax shall only be liable to Employee for any default on Alumax's obligations expressly provided herein; and neither AMAX nor Alumax shall be liable for any default on the other party's obligations.

This Agreement shall be binding upon and shall inure to the benefit of Employee, Employee's heirs, executors, administrators and beneficiaries, and shall be binding on and inure to the benefit of AMAX and Alumax and their successors and assigns.

IN WITNESS WHEREOF, the parties hereto have executed this agreement as of the year and day first above written.

> [Signed by representatives of AMAX and Alumax and Ms. Feeney]

Index